FIGHTING MEN OF WORLD WAR II
AXIS FORCES
UNIFORMS, EQUIPMENT AND WEAPONS

FIGHTING MEN
OF WORLD WAR II
AXIS FORCES

UNIFORMS, EQUIPMENT AND WEAPONS

David Miller

CHARTWELL
BOOKS, INC.

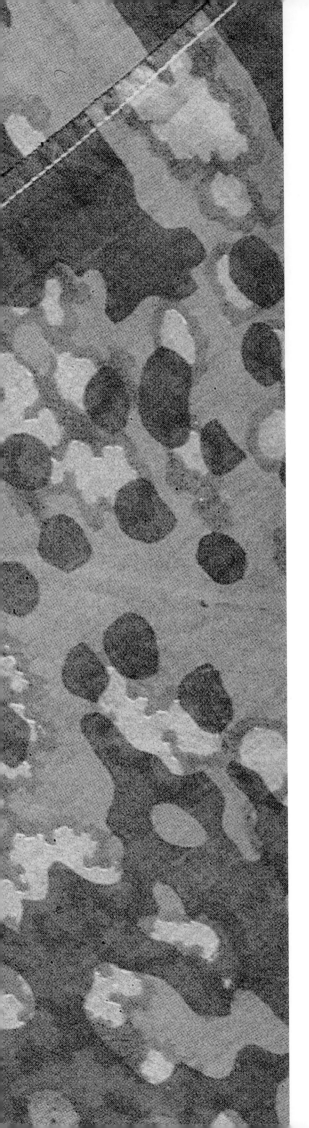

Copyright © 2010 Pepperbox Press Ltd.

This edition published in 2011 by
CHARTWELL BOOKS, INC.
A division of BOOK SALES, INC.
276 Fifth Avenue Suite 206
New York, New York 10001
USA

ISBN-13: 978-0-7858-2815-0

Printed in China

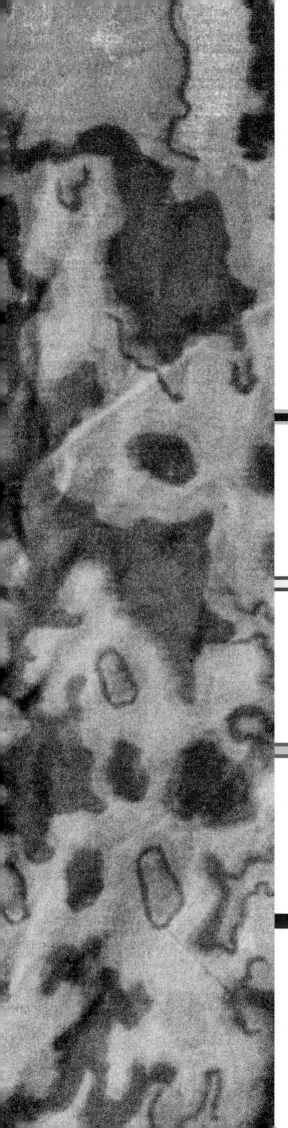

CONTENTS

INTRODUCTION

Many books have been published about World War II — the war that changed the face of the modern world. Aircraft, armor, warships, strategies, battles, theaters of war and elite units have all been covered repeatedly and exhaustively.

But who has thought to devote an entire volume to the average fighting man?

The starting point of our book is to ask the questions: what was it like to serve your country? Did your uniform keep you warm and dry in cold climates and cool in hot? Were your boots comfortable? Were your weapons and equipment adequate for the tasks demanded of you? What comforts could you expect: food, cigarettes, medical support and letters home? Would you win a medal? More importantly, would you survive? In short all issues that must have occupied the soldier's thoughts on a daily basis, quite apart from the ideals of why he was fighting.

In these pages we show how the average Axis fighting man fared. David Miller's painstakingly researched text first explains how the soldier fitted into his organization, then goes on to describe his equipment, weapons, uniforms and personal items.

Specially commissioned color photography, taken in museums and private collections around the world, show genuine wartime equipment and weapons in detail. These images are placed alongside selected archive photography showing the equipment in use in the field.

This highly illustrated book is for military enthusiasts, collectors and modellers everywhere.

GERMANY

The German Army that was rebuilt after defeat in World War I took account of many of the lessons of that war, and developed a concept of operations that emphasised mobility and speed of reaction, and which promoted independent initiative and aggressive action from the most junior leaders.

German infantrymen were on the whole tough and determined fighters. They were seemingly unstoppable in the early years of the war as they swept across Europe, the Soviet Union and even north Africa. But once they went on to the strategic defensive they also fought bitterly for every foot of ground, usually in the face of superior numbers, artillery, armor and airpower. There were never enough of them, though, and as the war progressed more and more came from occupied territories, from surplus manpower in the *Luftwaffe* and the *Kriegsmarine* (Navy), and finally from the old and young in the barely-trained *Volkssturm* (Home Guard).

GERMAN INFANTRY

As in virtually every other army, it was the German infantry that bore the brunt of their nation's fighting during World War II. In combination with the armored and mechanized units, the infantry fought its way across western Europe between 1939 and 1942, and it was the infantry that fought a dogged fighting withdrawal between 1943 and ultimate defeat in 1945. They were, course, supported by the armor, artillery, engineers and other combat arms, as well as by the *Luftwaffe* (air force) but the infantry was by far the biggest arm, which captured and held ground, and which was the last to concede it in the final days.

German infantrymen were hard-fighting, determined, and resolute opponents but, fortunately for the Allies, there were never enough of them.

As the war progressed, casualties and manpower shortages caused the army to increase the number of foreign troops enlisted from territories that had

above A German infantryman carrying an MG42 machine gun and wearing a tunic with the early-style dark green collar. His shoulder straps are field gray however. He has a green camouflaged net over his helmet, which provided both camouflage and protection from mosquitos.

been overrun, although only in a few cases did they prove to be up to reasonable standards of military efficiency and general trustworthiness. Within German resources, surplus manpower in the *Luftwaffe* and the *Kriegsmarine* (navy) were eventually formed into infantry forces, while the last resort was the *Volkssturm*, an assembly of barely trained civilians, who were either too young, too old or too unfit for conventional service in the army itself.

There were many divisions and regiments in the German Army whose predominant arm was infantry, but which had a variety different roles and titles. The most common fighting divisions were:

- *Infanterie Division*. A standard, infantry-heavy, combat division, marching on its feet and with virtually all its transportation by horse, except for the anti-tank units, which were fully mechanized.

- *Grenadier Division*. In late 1942 Hitler ordered that all infantry divisions be redesignated as *Grenadiers*, a traditional term, with every infantry private soldier, formerly *Schütze*, being retitled *Grenadier*. The new name did not imply any new organization, re-equipment or reroling, and was solely a public relations and morale-boosting exercise.

- *Gebirgsdivision*. Mountain divisions, formed by the army, were specially selected, trained and equipped for mountain warfare. They were essentially organized as infantry divisions, but with much special equipment; even so, they were often employed in the straight infantry role.

- *Jäger Division*. *Jäger* is the traditional German term for a hunter, a somewhat romantic figure, and, when used in the military context, it applied to a motorized formation, which was generally known to the Allies as a "light" division. A number of such divisions were later upgraded into *Panzer* (i.e., armored) divisions.

- *Infanteriedivision (Motorisiert)*. All elements of the division were mounted in wheeled vehicles. These were often smaller than a standard infantry division.

above This one is wearing a greatcoat with green collar and his shoulder straps show the white piping of the infantry arm. Around his waist is a leather belt carrying two sets of triple ammunition pouches for the Kar98 rifle. His helmet is the later type without the rolled rim.

- *Panzergrenadier Division*. A fully motorized infantry formation, but with a much higher proportion of self-propelled weapons than a motorized division, plus a tank or assault gun unit. It was designed to work with *Panzers*.

- *Volks/Volksgrenadierdivision*. *Volk* means "of the people" and was a term with particular resonance in Nazi propaganda. In reality, this was a fine-sounding title for some third-rate divisions formed by Himmler in 1944–45, essentially for the last-ditch defense of the Fatherland. Some were designated *Volk* and others *Volksgrenadier* but there were no significant differences between them.

There were other types, including *Sturm* (assault) divisions formed for a specific attack and zbV (special employment) divisions raised for specific tasks. Static formations included *Festung* (fortress), *Bodenständige* (area defense) and *Küstenverteidigungsdivision* (coastal defense divisons). *Sicherungsdivision* (security divisions) were formed for rear area security and anti-partisan duties.

left Infantrymen crossing the Oder in a light boat. Wearing sidecaps and without their full combat order they are not expecting trouble. The white piping *(waffenfarbe)* on the standing NCO indicates the infantry branch, while the lightning flash on his arm shows he is a signaller.

below An array of collar patches and other badges. The colored strip inside the "bar" symbol indicates arm of service (see "Uniforms" section later). Most patches shown are on a dark background, apart from the red ones (field officers) and the dark green (mechanized unit). The rectangular patches on the right were sometimes slid over the shoulder straps to indicate the unit or subunit the wearer belonged to.

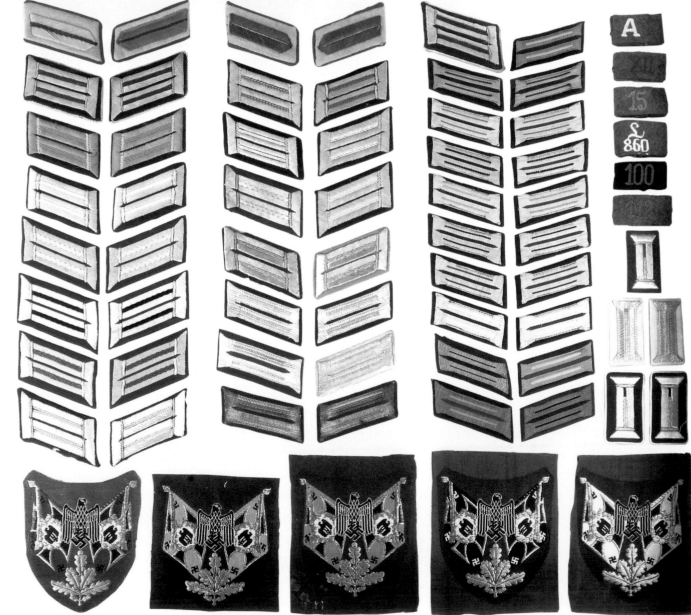

OTHER FORCES

Members of Hitler's inner circle were able to use their influence to raise and equip special units within their own sphere of influence. *Reichsmarschal* Göring was able to raise the *Fallschirmjäger* (paratroops) as part of the Luftwaffe, whereas in most other nations they were part of the army. In addition, in 1943–44 surplus *Luftwaffe* personnel were hastily formed into infantry divisions, always with dire results. The *Kriegsmarine* (navy) also raised several infantry divisions in 1944–45, also with poor results. Finally, Himmler raised the *Waffen-SS*, which was in essence a parallel army, organized and equipped in line with the normal army *(das Heer)*, but which was answerable to him as *Reichsführer* SS. Some of the early *Waffen-SS* units were organized and employed as conventional marching infantry but were quickly converted to the more exciting and dramatic *Panzergrenadier* mounted in armored personnel carriers.

above Waffen-SS soldiers in trucks moving through a ruined village. The men have camouflaged smocks and helmet covers. Throughout the war Germany was never able to provide as much motorized transport for its forces as did the United States, Britain and Canada.

RANKS

The German Army's system of ranks was rather more flexible than in other armies, where precise ranks were allocated to specific posts. The Germans used *Stellengruppen* (position groups) which gave a range of ranks to fill a post. Thus, the post of infantry squad commander, for example, could be filled by an NCO in the "G" (*Gruppenführer*) range which comprised *Unterfeldwebel*, *Unteroffizier* and *Obergefreiter*, while the "Z" group of officers covered both *Leutnant* and *Oberleutnant*.

Secondly, it was always within the gift of the unit commander to deploy his men as he saw fit, bearing in mind the unit's current mission, the numbers of men available, their personal qualities, and his own past experiences. Thirdly, as the war progressed the numbers of men being sent to the front-line units dropped significantly and commanders had to leave gaps as they saw fit.

The *Waffen-SS* used their own rank system which is described later.

OFFICERS

The first and most obvious grouping was into officers and other ranks, with officer ranks running in eleven steps from *Leutnant* (lieutenant) to *Generalfeldmarschall* (field-marshal) and other ranks in nine steps from *Schütze* (enlisted man) to *Stabsfeldwebel* (staff-sergeant).

Officers could also be described as belonging to one of three groups:

• *Kompanieoffiziere* (company-grade officers). This was the lowest group, comprising lieutenant, senior lieutenant and captain. These were also sometimes known as *Hauptleute*.

• The next group, *Stabsoffiziere*, covered majors, lieutenant-colonels and colonels. The term translates literally into English as "staff" officers, but in this context does not mean officers employed in

left Chevrons worn on the tunic sleeve by a Senior Lance Corporal.

headquarters staff appointments, but rather those described in the US Army as "field-grade" officers.

• The third and highest group were *Generäle* (generals), which covered all ranks from major-general to field marshal.

Where officers were concerned, there were several significant differences from US and British practice. First, while the German Army sometimes set up formations designated as brigades, there was no rank of brigadier-general (US) or brigadier (British). Secondly, the German Army had an additional rank of *Generaloberst* (colonel-general) which was immediately below *Generalfeldmarschall* (field marshal) and equivalent to the US and British rank of general (often known in those armies as a "full" general). Thirdly, there was a rank between *Generaloberst* and *Generalleutnant* in which generals were in employments relevant to their arm-of-service and thus retained that arm as a suffix, for example, *General der Infanterie*, *General der Artillerie*, *General der Nachtrichtentruppen* (generals of infantry, artillery, signal troops) and so on.

NON-COMMISSIONED OFFICERS

The *Portepee*, or sword-knot, was a centuries-old device consisting of a leather strap attached to the sword guard, through which the man placed his hand and then tightened it around his wrist using a slide, thus ensuring that he could not unintentionally drop the sword. Over the centuries it became a symbolic and decorative item, and

above A weary Lieutenant consults a map in his trench. His shoulder strap has the stylized gothic lettering "GD" on his shoulder strap, indicating he is a member of the *Grossdeutschland* division.

above Soldiers from the *Berliner* division being awared the Iron Cross. The Sergeant-Major nearest the camera has old-style shoulder straps with a pointed tip.

Shoulder boards (soldiers and NCOs)

Private	Lance Corporal	Senior L/Cpl	Staff L/Cpl	Corporal	Sergeant	Senior Sgt	Sgt Major	Staff Sgt

Shoulder boards (Officers)

2nd Lieutenant	Lieutenant	Captain	Major	Lt Colonel	Colonel

Collar patches

Private to Staff L/Cpl

Corporal to Staff Sgt

Officers

Sleeve Patches (NCOs only)

Private 1st class	L/Cpl	Senior L/Cpl	Staff L/Cpl

Army rank badges, all shown with white infantry piping. Other branches would have other colors around the edge of the shoulder boards. Sleeve patches and shoulder boards were originally on a dark gray-green background but as the war progressed they became the same field gray as the tunic. Originally shoulder boards had the regiment number or unit designation but this practice was largely discontinued after 1940.

Ranks		Stellen-gruppe	Typical Appointments		Remarks
German	English		German	English	
Generalfeld-marschall	Field marshal	A	Ober-befehlshaber	Commander-in-Chief	Introduced April 1936
Generaloberst	Colonel General				
General	General	F	Kommandierender General	Commanding General	
Generalleutnant	Lieutenant-general	D	Divisions-kommandeur	Divisional commander	
Generalmajor	Major-general	I	Infanteriebrigade-kommandeur	Brigade commander	
Oberst	Colonel	R	Regiments-kommandeur	Regimental Commander	
Oberstleutnant	Lieutenant-colonel-	B	Bataillons kommandeur	Battalion commander	
Major	Major				
Hauptmann	Captain	K	Kompanieführer	Company commander	
Oberleutnant	First Lieutenant	Z	Zugführer	Platoon commander	Maximum two platoon commanders in a company were officers
Leutnant	Second Lieutenant				
Stabsfeldwebel	Staff/Senior	O	Oberfeldwebel	Senior NCO	This group also known as Unteroffiziere mit Portepee
Oberfeldwebel	Sergeant				
Feldwebel	Sergeant				
Unterfeldwebel	Junior sergeant	G	Gruppenführer	Junior NCO	This group also known as Unteroffiziere
Unteroffizier	Corporal				
Obergefreiter	Senior Lance Corporal		ohne Portepee		
Gefreiter	Lance-corporal	M	Mannschaft	Enlisted Man	Schütze changed to Grenadier, November 1942
Oberschütze/ Obergrenadier	Private first-class				
Schütze/Grenadier	Private/Grenadier				

consisted in the German Army of a decorative cord or strap, with a fancy tassel and crown. All officers carried a sword and *Portepee*, but senior NCOs (*Feldwebel* upwards to *Stabsfeldwebel*) also carried them, and thus came to be described as *Unteroffiziere mit Portepee* (NCOs with sword-knot), which approximates to the British Army term "senior NCOs." The remaining NCOs, *Obergefreiter* to *Unterfeldwebel*, were then known as *Unteroffiziere ohne Portepee* (NCOs without sword-knot).

A particular appointment, and one of great importance in every German infantryman's life, was that of *der Spiess*, a term which literally translates as "the spear", but which was the name given to the senior NCO in a company or equivalent-sized unit. His duties were very similar to those of a company first-sergeant in the US Army or a company sergeant-major in the British and Dominion armies. They involved discipline, personnel matters and general administration in barracks, but in the field he was responsible for virtually all administrative work, in order to leave the *Kompaniechef* free to exercise his command functions.

SOLDIERS

Soldiers were known as *Mannschaft*, which translates literally as "people" and here the Germans gave full rein to their fascination with descriptive titles. A private soldier in the infantry was designated *Schütze* until November 1942 when he was redesignated *Grenadier*, a title dating back to Frederick the Great. But infantry privates could also be designated *Fusilier* in a regiment bearing that honor title, or *Jäger* in a light infantry or mountain unit. Private soldiers in specialist corps also bore titles relevant to that corps: *Funker* for signalers, *Fahrer* for drivers of horse-drawn vehicles, *Kraftfahrer* for drivers of mechanized vehicles, and so on.

SHOULDER BOARDS

An array of army shoulder boards of different ranks. Notice the variation in size, shape and background color, even where they are supposed to be made in the same dark grey or field grey. German uniform colors were never very "uniform", especially as material shortages worsened.

You can see shoulder boards for private solders with the cloth background, then those for NCOs with the same background but with fabric braid sewn on.

Junior officer ranks had straight silver piping covering the shoulder board, while senior officers had interwoven braid. Arm of service was indicated by the colored piping or *Waffenfarbe*

around the edge of the shoulder board (and sometimes collar). Colors here include: white (infantry), red (artillery), meadow green (Panzer Grenadier) yellow (communications), blue (medical) and black (pioneer).

Many of these have symbols, letters and numbers to denote the individual unit the wearer belonged to.

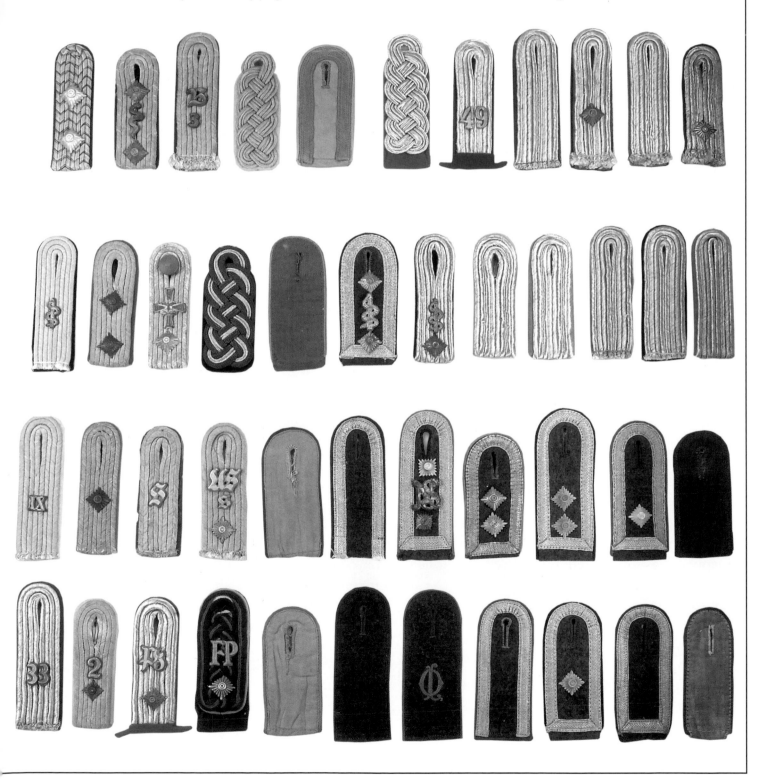

THE INFANTRY REGIMENT

The organization of the infantry changed throughout the war, initially as a result of operations in the first few years, then later when manpower and materials became scarcer.

In practice, formations differed considerably from the official structure, owing to a mixture of shortages, casualties and local circumstances. And as with many armies, individual units could sometimes 'acquire' extra equipment to which they were not entitled.

COMMAND

The infantry regiment *(Infanterieregiment)* was commanded by a colonel *(Oberst)* with a personal staff of two officers – *adjutant* (Adjutant) and assistant adjutant, the latter, for reasons of tradition, bearing the title of *Ordonnanzoffizier*. These were supported by the regimental headquarters *(Regimentsstab)* consisting of drivers, grooms, despatch riders and clerks.

Sub-units under direct regimental command comprised: communications platoon *(Nachrichtenzug)*, cavalry/reconnaissance platoon *(Infanteriereiterzug)*, and an engineer/pioneer platoon *(Infanteriepionierzug)*. Logistic support was provided by an Infantry Column, Light *(leichte Infanteriekolonne)*, together with specialists scattered among the fighting units, while regimental transport was organized into three echelons. Finally, there was a regimental band.

The fighting strength of the regiment was concentrated in three infantry battalions. In every infantry

above Grenades were usually carried like this, stuffed into the belt. This man has rifle ammunition pouches and is carrying a belt for the section machine gun.

regiment throughout the army the battalions were numbered in an identical sequence, as were the three rifle companies and the machine gun company within each of those battalions, and these were then followed by the regimentally-controlled infantry gun and machine gun companies.

	Infantry Battalions		Regimental Units	
Battalion	Rifle Companies	Machine gun Company	Infantry Gun Company	Mortar company
I	1,2,3	4	–	–
II	5,6,7	8	–	–
III	9,10,11	12	–	–
–	–	–	13	14

above Mortars were popular with infantry commanders as being effective fire support weapons that were under their own control.

In the final two years of the war, some regimental commanders brought the regimental support elements under centralized control, which they then designated 15 Company. This was directly equivalent to the headquarters company in Allied armies.

An infantry regiment in early 1941 should have had the men and equipment as shown in the table.

Men		3,152
Personal weapons:	rifles	2,115
	machine pistols	204
	pistols	870
Machineguns:	light	112
	heavy	36
Crew-served support weapons:	anti-tank guns	49
	Lt mortars (51mm)	27
	mortars (81mm)	18
	infantry guns	8

The *Nachrichtenzug* (Communications Platoon) consisted of one officer, six NCOs and 25 men, all infantrymen who had attended special courses as opposed to signal corps personnel. Equipment included four manpack radios, telephone, cable and two field switchboards.

REITERZUG (CAVALRY PLATOON)

The *Wehrmacht* continued to employ cavalry units throughout the war, as described later. As well as these separate units, each infantry regiment had it's own cavalry platoon for reconnaissance and security duties.

The strength of this varied throughout the war. The 1941 version had 53 men and 53 horses. Their weapons were rifles, machine pistols and a light machine gun for every 12-man team.

THE INFANTRY REGIMENT

The organisation of the infantry changed throughout the war, initially as a result of operations in the first few years, then later when manpower and materials became scarcer.

In practice, formations differed considerably from the official structure, owing to a mixture of shortages, casualties and local circumstances. And as with many armies, individual units could sometimes 'acquire' extra equipment to which they were not entitled.

THE INFANTRY BATTALION

The infantry battalion was the fundamental building block of the German fighting force, but detailed organization, equipment and manpower strengths could vary between theaters and according to the stage of the war. The description which follows is of one version of the 1941 battalion; it was the basis of all subsequent reorganizations and may be taken as typical and illustrative of the organizational principles.

The battalion comprised some 845 all ranks who were split between: battalion headquarters; three rifle companies; machinegun company; signal detachment; and logistic support.

BATTALION HQ

In combat, the battalion commander usually moved with a small command group. His adjutant would manage the main headquarters, which included signals, the commanders of support weapons subunits, liaison officers for artillery and other attached support, clerical and support staff and the battalion aid post.

COMMUNICATIONS

Field radio was never available in sufficient quantities, and in 1941 the infantry battalion was only supposed to have three manpack radios for links from battalion HQ forward to companies. The signals component also made extensive use of field telephones and lamps, and many messages had to be carried by hand, either on foot, one horseback or on motorcycle.

below German commanders at all levels were expected to lead from the front. This Sgt Major wears early war high quality uniform and totes a P.08 Luger.

TRANSPORT

Battalion transport consisted predominantly of horse-drawn wagons, with a very small number of trucks. This transport was divided into three *Tross* (trains), each commanded by a senior NCO, the senior of whom was answerable to the commanding officer. These three elements comprised the *Gefechtstross* (battle transport) for immediate support, the *Verpflegungstross* (rations and forage transport) and the *Gepäcktross* (baggage transport), comprised of light trucks, held slightly further back.

above Unlike most armies, German soldiers wore their bravery medals on their combat tunics. This man has an Iron Cross 2nd Class and carries an MP40 machine gun with the longer magazine pouches on his belt.

MACHINE GUN COMPANY

Designated the Machine Gun Company of the Infantry Battalion, this sub-unit was equipped with twelve machine guns and six mortars, and might better have been known as the Support or Heavy Weapons Company. It was 201 men strong and under the direct control of the battalion commander. It had a small headquarters group, three machine gun platoons and a medium mortar platoon.

Each machine gun platoon had two squads, both of which were armed with two heavy machine guns, for a total of twelve weapons for the company. In the German system, the machine guns themselves were identical with those carried by the infantry sections, but were designated *schwer* (heavy) because they could be fitted to tripod mounts and anti-aircraft mounts.

The Medium Mortar Platoon had a small HQ section, mainly because the 81mm mortar teams were normally dispersed in direct support of rifle companies. There were three squads, each led by an NCO, consisting of two teams each with an NCO in charge and six men. There were six mortars in total, usually transported in a two-wheeled horse-drawn cart.

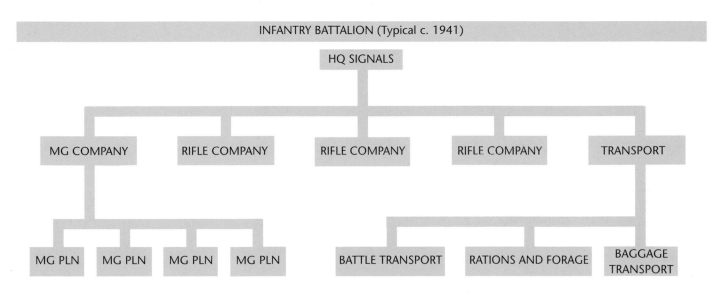

INFANTRY BATTALION (Typical c. 1941)

HQ SIGNALS

MG COMPANY — RIFLE COMPANY — RIFLE COMPANY — RIFLE COMPANY — TRANSPORT

MG PLN — MG PLN — MG PLN — MG PLN

BATTLE TRANSPORT — RATIONS AND FORAGE — BAGGAGE TRANSPORT

THE RIFLE COMPANY

Each infantry battalion had three rifle companies commanded by a captain, each containing three rifle platoons, an anti-tank squad and a transport squad. Company HQ Company headquarters was a small group comprising of the Commander, the *Speiss* (sergeant major) a few men providing clerical and signals support and one or two message couriers. Company HQ also had direct command of the Anti-Tank squad. In 1941 this consisted of a commander and three two-man detachments, each armed with a single anti-tank rifle.

above This group is operating in the snow and ice, caught in the open with no cover. Some have cold weather clothing and white camouflage paint on their helmets. Note the use of the sledge for carrying supplies and ammunition.

left A machine gun team loads a 200-round belt into their MG34. They have early-war helmets with the separate turned rim and painted in a smooth finish. This paint scheme created unwanted shine and was soon replaced by rougher, non-reflective finishes.

THE RIFLE PLATOON

The rifle platoon (*Schützenzug*) comprised a small HQ, with four rifle squads and a light mortar squad. The rifle squad (*Schützengruppe*) was the smallest complete sub-unit in the infantry. In the Polish campaign the squad was thirteen strong but this proved difficult to control and was reduced to ten men for all subsequent campaigns. However,

above An infantryman makes himself as comfortable as he can in his hastily-dug foxhole. He is wearing a splinter-camouflage cover over his helmet and has an entrenching tool, water bottle, gas mask case, various mess tins, food tins and other equipment scattered around him.

as the war progressed, full-strength squads became a rarity. Each platoon also had a Light Mortar Squad of three men who carried a single, man-portable 50mm mortar.

Man	Weapon	Duties
Squad commander	9mm *Machinepistole* 38 or 40	Squad leader
Number 1	7.92mm *Maschinengewehr* 34 (MG34) LMG, plus 9mm *Pistole* 08	Fired the LMG
Number 2	9mm *Pistole* 08 ammunition, spare barrels	Assisted No 1; carried
Number 3	Rifle – 7.92mm *Gewehr* 98	Ammunition supply for MG34
Number 4	Rifle – 7.92mm *Gewehr* 98 leader	Senior rifleman/deputy squad
Numbers 5–9	Rifle – 7.92mm *Gewehr* 98	

COMMUNICATIONS

COMMAND

The German Army set very particular store on the personal behavior and fluence of the commander at all levels. His first priority was that he had to be physically located where he could most effectively command the current operation, combining closeness to the enemy with protection from enemy fire. This also required that the location of his headquarters be known to all concerned, which in purely physical terms was done by placing a metal identifying flag outside the HQ. Almost to the end of the war, one of the principal criteria was that he should have access to the wire network, since that was his main means of communication, rather than by radio.

The staff at each level had its prescribed tasks and composition, and one of the well-understood principles was that the commander should not be troubled with administrative matters, nor with detail or trivia. At the most forward level, the *Spiess* (company sergeant-major) commanded the *Gefechtstross*, leaving his company commander free from concerns over administrative matters. The same principle was applied at battalion and regimental level, where the supply and administration staff was stationed with one of the trains.

At divisional level and above orders were usually issued in documentary form, but at regiment and below they were issued orally, although whatever the means there was always an emphasis on keeping a written record.

COMMUNICATIONS

To achieve all this it was vital to have an efficient communications system, which was considered by commanders at all levels to be the key to the successful and timely application of force. But, the technology of the time was not advanced, production facilities were limited and other elements in the army, such as the *Panzers*, *Panzergrenadiers* and *Artillerie*, were always given greater priority, as was the *Waffen-SS*. Thus, the infantry divisions and

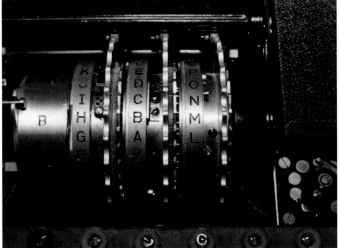

above High level communications were protected by the Enigma coding machine. The one shown here is a "three-rotor" type – other models used four.

regiments found themselves at the end of the line, forcing them to make do with some very slow and antiquated means of communication.

METHODS

The best method of communication for the type of mobile warfare envisaged in the late 1930s was radio, but there were never sufficient sets and those that were available were very heavy. As a result,

above Signallers from an SS Police unit on the eastern front. These units were often used on anti-partisan actions and had a reputation for extreme brutality and ruthlessness.

right Signallers with their cumbersome and fragile field radio. Note the despatch riders in the background ready to take messages on to their intended recipients.

the lowest level where radios were to be found was company headquarters. Wire was laid in large quantities and efforts were made to lay a central "spine" or "trunk" during an advance into which the various headquarters and units could connect, thus saving a considerable amount of time and resources. If the advance was very rapid, however, it was seldom possible for the wire/cable laying teams to keep up, but they came into their own when the various headquarters and units were either at a short halt in an advance or in a static defensive position.

Lamp and flag signalling were available, but could only be used in one-to-one links and depended upon both ends being able to see each other; i.e., line-of-sight. In the final resort, much depended on messages being carried by couriers (*Melder*), either on horseback, motorcycle, bicycle or foot.

RADIO

The best method of communication in mobile warfare was radio, but there were never sufficient sets and those that were available were very heavy. As a result, the lowest level where radios were to be found was company headquarters.

German military radios were considered, even by the Allies, to be very well made and of advanced design, although, as in all contemporary armies, they were heavy and even the so-called "man-portable" (*tragbare*) sets were a severe load for the operators carrying them. Some radios were installed in trucks with special bodies, which gave a much better working environment, while others were carried aboard specially-designed horse-drawn *Infanterie-Nachrichtenwagen* (infantry communications wagons) or even two-wheeled, hand-drawn carts.

Sets with the word *Tornister* (pack) in their title were designed to be carried on a man's back, although often the battery had to be carried by a second man, since the combined weight was simply too much. In general, German radios were heavier and more cumbersome than their US equivalents, but were, nevertheless, reasonably effective. The main problem was their small numbers and there were usually three-to-five per battalion, which were held in a pool and allocated by the commanding officer, as required.

WIRE AND TELEPHONES

Wire was laid in large quantities and efforts were made to lay a central "spine" or "trunk" during an advance into which the various headquarters and units could connect, thus saving a considerable amount of time and resources. If the advance was very rapid, however, it was seldom possible for the wire/cable laying teams to keep up, but they came into their own when the various headquarters and units were either at a short halt in an advance or in a static defensive position. Within infantry regiments cables and wires had to be laid and recovered manually. One method involved a two-wheeled cable trolley, with one man pulling, the second a short distance behind using a crookstick to push the wire into the hedgerow or verge, and the third tying back. To achieve speed, wires were

usually laid along the surface and only raised on poles or buried in a trench at places where they might be destroyed by passing traffic.

SWITCHBOARDS

There were several designs of field switchboards, which were used to route telephone calls within headquarters. The 10-line board provided for seven local subscribers and three trunk connections, which capacity could be doubled by connecting two together. Where more capacity was required, the FK16 (*Feldklappenschrank* = field telephone exchange) was used which had a 30-line capacity, and several units could be coupled together to increase capacity at larger headquarters. Both the 10-and 30-line switchboards normally operated using magneto signalling, but, with an adaptor, could be joined into civilian central-battery systems.

VISIBLE LIGHT SIGNALING

Blinkgerät (signalling lamps) were always carried within infantry regiments and battalions, their

primary purpose being to provide temporary substitutes for broken wire routes. There were two types, both of which were mounted on a tripod and powered by batttteries or manually-cranked generators. They consisted of a parabolic mirror, a light source and a Morse-key which depressed the mirror. Range depended on visibility, weather and physical obstacles, but the larger one had a choice of two light sources, electric bulb or oxyacetylene flame, with the latter giving much greater ranges

MESSENGERS

In the absence of any electronic means and in order to deliver written or bulky items, the main means of communication within regiments and battalions was using *Melder*; i.e., human couriers. There were no less than 48 of these on the establishment of an infantry battalion. Most of these were supplied with bicycles, eleven had horses, and the remainder were on foot.

MESSAGE GRENADES

A form of last-resort communications was provided by message-carrying mortar bombs, of which there were several types. The more powerful was the

Meldewurfgranate (message-throwing bomb) which was fired from a 50mm mortar. The projectile consisted of a red-painted light aluminum tube with a removable head and a fixed tail, which incorporated the charge. The head was removed to reveal a message pad and sharpened pencil, and the written message was then inserted, the head replaced and the projectile launched from the mortar. It had a range of between 660 and 1,100 yards and at about 300 feet from impact it started to generate a dense cloud of black smoke which continued after it hit the ground, thus enabling it to be located and collected. The Message Grenade for Light Pistol (*Nachrichtpatrone für Kampfpistole*) was similar in principle, but smaller, as it was fired from the signalling pistol carried in every platoon headquarters.

SUPPLIES AND TRANSPORT

Throughout the war, transport within infantry divisions was predominantly horse-drawn, far more so than in US and British units. Only the *Panzer* (armored) and *Panzergrenadier* (mechanized) divisions were fully motorized. Logistical transport was organized into units designated "columns" *(kolonne)*, whose lifting capability was indicated in their title by the prefix *leicht* (light) or *schwer* (heavy). Thus, a *Fahrkolonne* (horse-drawn column) could lift a load of 30 tonnes, while a *leichte Fahrkolonne* (light horse-drawn column) could lift 17 tonnes and a *schweres Kraftwagen Kolonne* (heavy motorized column) 60 tonnes. Similarly, a *leichte Kraftwagen Kolonne für Betriebstoff* (light motorized column for gasoline) lifted 5,500 gallons and a *schweres Kraftwagen Kolonne für Betriebstoff* (heavy motorized column for gasoline) 11,000 gallons.

The number of *kolonne* allocated to an infantry division varied with its mission and geographical situation, but was usually nine, which could be of varying types.

INFANTRY COLUMNS, LIGHT

Infantry regiments operated their own light columns, designated *leichte Infanteriekolonne*, which were intended primarily for carrying the regiment's first-line ammunition supply. The system was not, however, always consistent and, for example, while the artillery battalion in the infantry regiment had its own Artillery Column, Light *(leichte Artilleriekolonne)*, the anti-tank battalion did not and its ammunition was carried on company or battalion transport.

AMMUNITION

Logistics planners worked on a daily ammunition "quota" which was laid down for every weapon on the authorized table of establishment. The planning norm was that an army, which normally consisted of two corps, held three "quotas," of

below Another metal water flask, this time the smaller 5 litre type.

above Water supply is an important consideration for any front-line soldier. This metal flask held 10 litres of drinking water.

above The German fuel can, still known as a "Jerrican" today, was a sturdy and effective design, especially compared to the fragile "flimsies" in British service.

above A typical ammunition supply column on the eastern front. The German Army was never anywhere near a fully-mechanized force.

which two were carried within infantry divisions and the third by echelons under direct control by army staff, which stocks were either on wheels or in readily-accessible dumps. These daily "quotas" were figures derived by calculation modified by experience, and were intended solely for use by planners. They were not average daily expenditure rates; it is inconceivable, for example, that every rifleman in every infantry regiment would fire 90 rounds per day. Some of these daily quotas applicable to the infantry were:

For each rifle	90 rounds
For each light machinegun	2,500 rounds
For each heavy machinegun	4,500 rounds
For each 50mm mortar	120 bombs
For each 81mm mortar	30 bombs
For each infantry gun	180 shells
For each 37mm AA gun	1,500 rounds

RATIONS

Rations were also "scaled" but in this case the daily ration was the amount expected to be eaten by one man each day. The German soldier's ration was rather plainer and considerably more frugal than that for his American or British counterpart and amounted to:

Bread	26.5oz
Cold food for evening meal	4.2oz
Salt	0.5oz
Meat	7.1oz
Drink	0.9oz
Peas	6.3oz
Sugar	1.4 oz
TOTAL	46.7oz (2.9lb)

Each man carried one day's rations in his pack or bread-bag, there was one day's rations per man in each field kitchen, two days in the unit supply transport (*Verpflegungstross*) and a further one day per man in the divisional supply column. There was also a ration of two cigarettes and two cigars per man per day, with some 64,000 being held by the division.

above and above left A smaller insulated food container which could be carried on a man's back or in a small vehicle.

above and far left This metal box is thermally insulated to allow food for a group of men to remain warm as it is transported from the cookhouse. The open view shows the insulated interior and a separate sealable container.

HORSES

An impression has built-up since 1945 that the German Army of World War II was a fully mechanized force, whose tanks, self-propelled artillery, automobiles and trucks smashed their way across Europe in vast numbers, carrying all before them. In reality, however, these armored units represented only a small part of the army. By far the greater proportion of German strength was in the infantry divisions, where, as had been the case for centuries, the infantry marched on their feet and virtually all other tactical movement depended upon the horse.

A few figures will help put this in perspective:

• The German plan to invade southern England (Operation Sea Lion) in 1940 involved a force comprising 175,00 men and 34,000 motor vehicles. But it also included 57,500 horses, of which some 4,000 were to have been in the first wave and 7,000 in the second.

left Leather harness for use with a horse.

• The invasion of Yugoslavia and Greece involved fifteen divisions: eight infantry, three mountain, two motorized infantry and two armored. This came to a total of 380,000 men who were supported by 65,000 horses.

• The German forces that invaded the Soviet Union (Operation Barbarossa) involved three million men, 3,350 tanks, 600,000 vehicles, and between 600,000 and 700,000 horses.

Right through to the end of the war, the standard, front-line infantry regiment depended upon horses

above A horse-drawn supply cart struggles through the mud on the eastern front.

above Sturdy Russian ponies were one of the few reliable modes of transport when the bitter cold of the Russian winter gripped the front. This one is pulling a traditional peasant sledge or *pulk*.

for transporting its heavy weapons, resupplying ammunition, towing its kitchens, bring forward the rations, and the carriage of wounded, supplies and baggage. Thus, a 1941 infantry regiment, with three infantry battalions, had an establishment of 606 horses. Unlike trucks they did not need supplies of gasoline or huge workshops for repair and maintenance; on the other hand they could not be parked and left unattended until required but needed daily supplies of food and water, as well as some general care and attention.

The consequences of this dependence on the horse were great, as it limited the overall speed of advance – or, in the later days, of withdrawal – to that of an animal which, whatever its glamorous, traditional image as a cavalry charger, suffered from some major limitations. Further, this dependence on the horse had a major impact on the field army, since, because of the immense difference in speed-of-advance and cross-country movement, it was impossible to mix tanks and infantry at divisional level or below.

This meant that tanks had to be concentrated in *Panzer* divisions where the relatively few trucks available would move with them and the integration of tanks and infantry at brigade/regimental level, as was routine with the Allies, was never possible with the German Army. In a major advance the *Panzer* divisions with their fast-moving, truck-borne logistic support always outstripped the infantry divisions, sometimes leaving gaps through which an enemy could slip. Another problem was that the infantry divisions, gallantly pushing forward on foot in an effort to catch up with the Panzers, clogged up the roads and defiles such as bridges, thus impeding (and sometimes even preventing) *Panzer* division resupply convoys from getting through. All this greatly complicated matters at every level, be it strategic, operational or tactical.

UNIFORMS

All armies wear a standardized form of dress known as uniform, but, despite the intentions of those making the rules, it is usually only on formal parades that absolute conformity with the regulations and with each other, right down to the smallest detail, is ever achieved. The German infantry, despite its reputation for correctness, was no exception and it is very rare, except on the most formal occasions, to see a picture of a group of officers or soldiers in which all are dressed exactly alike.

The German infantry had three basic orders of dress: field service uniform (*Feldanzug*); parade dress (*Paradeanzug*); and walking-out uniform (*Ausgehenanzug*). There were other minor orders of dress which included: sports kit (*Sportanzug*); service uniform (*Dienstanzug*); and denim fatigue uniform (*Drillichanzug*), which was a hard-wearing denim two-piece outfit for routine training and

above Collar badges and breast eagle of a junior officer's tunic. The shoulder strap shows he is a lieutenant, while the numbers on it indicate his regiment.

right An infantry Lieutenant wearing an officers' quality M1936 tunic, complete with scalloped and pleated pockets and green-backed collar. His belt and holster are in black leather rather than the brown worn by most officers. He has his trousers untucked and outside his boots, while he has removed the stiffener from his service cap to give a slightly rakish, floppy shape.

above This helmet has the pre-1943 edge with the rolled-over rim. Early helmets had a smooth paint finish, but this one has a rougher matt finish to avoid reflections and shine.

fatigues. All of these were field-gray (*Feldgrau*) in color, except for the denim outfit, which was made of an off-white unbleached material.

As with all armies, these various uniforms included indications of the wearer's rank or status. These were:

OFFICERS.

- **Headdress.** Peaked cap with silver chinstraps; sidecap with silver piping.
- **Equipment** (belts, pouches, cross-straps, holster, etc) were of brown (as opposed to black) leather
- **Shoulder straps.** Basic rank was indicated by: straight-laid silver cords – second lieutenant to captain; interwoven silver cords– major to colonel; interwoven gold and silver cords – general officers.
- **Quality.** Parade uniforms and headgear were of noticeably better quality.

NON-COMMISSIONED OFFICERS.

- NCO status was indicated by silver lace border on shoulder straps and collar.
- Rank was indicated by combination of lace and stars.
- Otherwise clothing and equipment were identical with those for soldiers.

SOLDIERS.

- **Collar** with patch.
- **Shoulder strap.** Black with *Waffenfarbe* underlay.
- **Rank.** Worn on left sleeve:

WAFFENFARBE

All armies divide their troops into specialisations, such as infantry, engineers, artillery, logistics and so on, and give soldiers some sort of distinguishing mark on their uniform so that this can be recognized. Many armies indicate an individual's arm-of-service by means of cloth or enamel badges, but the German Army did so by means of colors, known as *Waffenfarbe*. There were many such colors, but those most likely to be seen in an infantry setting were:

above Soldiers in a relaxed pose with mess tins and rations. The figure on the left is wearing the white denim working tunic while the others are wearing the normal *Feldgrau* tunic. The NCO in the centre is wearing the belt while the soldier on the right isn't.

Arm of Service		Color *(Waffenfarbe)*
	English	German
Infantry	White	*Weiss*
Mountain troops	Light green	*Hellgrün*
Armored infantry	Meadow green	*Wiesengrün*
Artillery	Bright red	*Karmin*
Medical	Cornflower blue	*Kornblumenblau*
Transport	Light blue	*Hellblau*
Pioneer/engineer	Black	*Schwarz*
Communications	Lemon Yellow	*Zitronengelb*

These colors appeared on various items of clothing:

- **Peaked caps.** Piping on the crown and the top and bottom edges of the cap-band.
- **Sidecaps.** Inverted chevron on front of cap.
- **Collar patches.** Underlay and inserts in stripes.
- **Shoulder straps.** Underlay.

above centre Badges such as the breast eagle were produced in many styles throughout the war. The top one is typical of those made for camouflage smocks while the lower one is machine-embroidered 'bevo' quality with metallic thread.

left Panzer (armor) crews wore a black uniform with a short double-breasted tunic, short boots, gaiters and soft peaked cap. This man is from an SS armored unit and has a Model 1924 grenade stuffed into his belt.

right This figure is wearing the two-piece white denim overalls used as working dress for many personnel. In this case he is a mechanic about to work on a vehicle.

TUNICS

All ranks were issued with Service Tunics, the only differences between those for officers and other ranks being one of quality.

MODEL 1936 SERVICE TUNIC

The *Heeres Dienstanzug* M1936 was the basis for all future designs and was the usual German field-gray color made from a wool/rayon mix in a single-breasted, high-collar, four-pocket design. The turn-over collar was faced with a dark-green material and carried two collar-patches in silver braid. The National Emblem (eagle with swastika) was positioned above the right breast pocket. There were

right A junior officer of a mountain unit, complete with edelweiss badge on his right sleeve. His tunic has the green collar backing, while his shoulder straps are edged in the green piping of a mountain unit. His belt is in the officers' brown colour. The shoulder strap is for his gas mask canister, which is at the back.

above A group of comrades from a private photograph, typical of those taken by millions of soldiers in all armies. Notice how their tunics don't have scalloped pocket flaps, a sign of wartime economy measures. Even though they are not in an operational setting and wearing the handy and lightweight sidecap, the figure on the right still has a bayonet frog attached to his belt.

four removable metal hooks at waist level, two front, two back, to hold the belt in position and also help bear some of the weight of the personal equipment; there were holes to enable these to be positioned at three different heights to suit the wearer's build. The shoulder straps were of the same material as the collar and, like the belt hooks, could be removed for laundering. The sleeves were straight cut with no cuffs. This jacket was worn both in the field and in barracks. In the latter conditions the collar was buttoned and a neckband worn, but when in the field the band was removed and the top button undone. NCOs (*Unteroffiziere*) wore exactly the same jacket but with the addition of silver braid along the edges of the collar and rank badges on the shoulder straps. Trousers were of a similar material and shoes or boots were worn as appropriate.

The officers' tunic was of very similar design, but better quality, the most noticeable visual difference being that the sleeves were fitted with deep cuffs. One noticeable feature for all ranks was that all those entitled to do so wore the ribbons and badges of the many German awards, and in particular the Iron Cross, even in combat.

MODEL 1943 SERVICE TUNIC

As in so many fields, the vast increase in numbers in the armed forces, coupled with shortages in both materials and skilled workers, led to a drastic cutback in quality and quantity of clothing. This resulted in the Field Jacket Model 1943 (*Feldbkluse* M1943) which was of a greatly simplified design. The collar and shoulder straps were no longer lined with green material and pocket design was greatly simplified (no pleats and straight cut). Also, a much greater proportion of rayon to wool not only reduced costs on that account but also enabled a much cheaper dying process to be used. The resulting cost-reduction was apparent in the appearance of the jackets, which were very much less smart. At the same time a similarly reworked trouser design went into production, which used the same materials as the blouse, but which were kept up by a cloth belt rather than suspenders (braces).

below A member of the *Feldgendarmerie* (military police) with traffic sign and a metal gorget on his chest. His tunic is made from fairly coarse material with simple pockets and field-gray collar and shoulder straps. He has a document pouch attached to his belt and a torch/signalling lamp above his left breast pocket.

THE *AFRIKA KORPS*

When the German army deployed to north Africa they were equipped with tropical uniforms and equipment. Normally portrayed as a light sand colour, the uniforms as issued were more of a mid-brown which faded to sandy-yellow with use. In the early days soldiers were issued with wide-brimmed lightweight sunhelmets, but these were soon discarded in favor of the soft cotton tropical peaked cap.

Tropical versions of boots and equipment were also produced, in the main swapping leather for woven canvas or similar.

These lightweight uniforms and associated equipment were not just used in the western desert but were also worn in Italy, Greece and other Mediterranean theaters. Some of this equipment remained in service through the European campaigns until the end of the war.

top German motorized and armored units deployed to north Africa became known as the *Afrikakorps*, and were authorized to wear this woven cuff-band on the sleeves of their uniforms.

above A woven breast eagle in *Afrikakorps* colors. The badges had this blue-gray color on a brown background similar to that of the uniform.

left A formation of troops in tropical uniform. The brown color quickly faded to a sandy-yellow color in the sun, while many soldiers also deliberately bleached their uniforms after issue to give that 'desert veteran' look.

above An early pattern sunhelmet in the dark brown color, complete with leather chin strap and national shield on the side.

below Tropical pattern trousers showing the loose cut and drawstrings to pull in bottom of trousers.

above As with all uniforms, and especially German ones, there were many variations of color and manufacture from batch to batch. This is a dark brown tropical tunic made from denim material, complete with the gray-blue collar and breast badges.

above Tropical uniform also included shorts such as these shown here. They would be worn with short boots and rolled-down socks.

MODEL 1944 SERVICE TUNIC

The ever-worsening production situation led to a complete redesign of the field blouse, which, whether deliberately or by chance, was similar in design to the British "battledress" jacket. The skirt was deleted and replaced by a half-inch wide waistband, the number of pockets was reduced to two, and while the belt hooks were retained there was only one height available. Collar patches were also retained, but without any *Waffenfarbe*; the collar braiding for NCOs was discontinued and the National Emblem was a new cheaper design.

A new feature late in the war was the introduction of a denim outfit in a reed-green color, primarily for wear in summer conditions. Known as the Reed-Green Denim Field Service Uniform (*Schilfgrüner Drillich Felddienstanzug*) this was much more durable and easier to wash, and the buttons were held in position by brass split rings, enabling them to be removed before laundering. The removable neckband could be worn when the collar was closed and the sleeves ends could be buttoned. Rank badges were of a subdued design and NCO collar braiding was retained but in a dull-gray cotton rather than silver.

GREATCOATS

There were a large variety of designs of greatcoat (*Mantel*) but the most commonly worn was blue-gray in color with a dark green collar which was introduced in the late 1930s. The collar was normally worn closed by all except holders of the Knight's Cross, who were allowed to leave it open so that their neck-badge could be seen. The greatcoat stretched down to the wearer's calves and had

left: A late-war tunic with unpleated pockets, shortened tunic skirt and hastily-made from poor-quality material.

right: A Lieutenant from a pioneers unit wearing an officers' pattern greatcoat. Note the green-backed collar and deep turned-back cuffs. He is also wearing a black belt with shoulder strap in the 'Sam Browne' style initially popularized by the British.

MOTORCYCLISTS

the usual badges of rank on the shoulder, but no collar patches or national emblem. There were large turn-back cuffs. On parade it was usually worn with the Sam Browne belt by officers and the black leather belt and ammunition pouches by other ranks. As with other uniforms, a much simpler and cheaper design was introduced in 1943. This had a much larger collar, which could be turned up for protection against the weather but this was of the same gray material as the rest of the coat and not dark-green.

above This belt is made from brown leather, normally seen on officer's equipment. But the buckle is a standard 'Other Ranks' issue, with the Nazi eagle in the centre and "*Gott Mit Uns*" around the eagle.

left A well-made greatcoat with NCO lapels with white infantry *Waffenfarbe*. This one has the gray collar and epaulettes.

right A despatch rider wearing the waterproofed motorcyclist's greatcoat and with his goggles above his helmet. He also has the late-pattern short boots with fabric gaiters wrapped around the top of his boots and bottom of his trousers.

As explained elsewhere, the German infantry made large-scale use of motorcycle despatch riders. Such men were always exposed to the climate, but in bad weather, and especially in Russia in the winter and rainy seasons, their life was especially difficult. They were, therefore, issued with a special Motor-cyclists' Protective Greatcoat (*Schützmantel für Kraftradfahrer*). This was a loose-fitting garment which fitted over the normal uniform and made of a rubberized, waterproof material. It was double-breasted, had a wool-lined collar and included four large pockets. It was so designed that the coat tails could be buttoned around the wearer's legs, thus enabling him to continue to ride his motorbike safely. It was usually worn in combination with overboots and gloves/mittens.

REPORTING UNIFORM

There were many different forms of dress for particular ranks or occasions, but one was of particular importance to the soldiers in an infantry unit. Known as the Reporting Uniform (*Meldeanzug*) this was, in fact, more of an order of dress than a separate uniform in its own right, and was unique to *der Spiess*, the German equiv-alent of the US Army's Company First-Sergeant and the British Company Sergeant-Major. The jacket bore the twin rings around the sleeve that denoted this appointment, but the second and third buttons on the jacket were always undone in order to accommodate the *Meldebuch* (reporting book), a leather cover in which the *Spiess* carried the docu-ments peculiar to his trade.

above A set of goggles and the metal container they were supplied in. Goggles such as these were worn by motorcyclists and were also prized by vehicle drivers and gunners, especially where conditions were dusty or sandy.

left This diorama shows a motorcycle despatch rider wearing a greatcoat, gloves, helmet, goggles, short boot and gaiters. Note the large pack on the back of his motorcycle and the sub-machine gun slung around his chest.

Parade Dress

As in any army, German parade dress (*Paradeanzug*) was designed to impress both wearers and spectators alike. In the German Army, this dress consisted of a smart, well-cut tunic, with green, high-necked collar, green sleeve-cuffs and long trousers, or riding breeches for officers. Cloth piping in the appropriate *Waffenfarbe* was applied to these trimmings and also to the jacket. Rank was indicated by shoulder straps for officers and senior NCOs, and by chevrons on the left sleeve for junior NCOs.

For very formal parades officers wore a belt made of silver braid, with two green stripes and a circular buckle embossed with a Nazi eagle surround by laurel leaves. For less formal occasions a German form of the British Army's Sam Browne leather belt was worn, which was especially popular with Adolf Hitler and other Nazi leaders. The German pattern was brown in color, featured a "blind buckle" which was permanently in position, the belt being secured by means of the two studs to the wearer's left. In peacetime the belt was worn with the cross-strap (*Schulterieme*) over the right shoulder, or, less

above A selection of woven badges for various uses. The left column shows a range of breast eagles made to various standards by different manufacturers and at different times in the war. The later types at the bottom were much of simpler manufacture and were on triangular or rectangular patches. The central column shows a range of cuff-bands and collar patches, including those identifying members of the *Afrikakorps,* officers' training schools, and, at the bottom, members of the last-ditch *Volkssturm* home guard units. On the right are some more breast eagles and a selection of cap badges.

formally and when in combat, without the strap. If worn in combat, the brown leather made the wearer's officer status readily apparent to the enemy, so some dyed the belt and strap black, but by 1942 it had fallen out of use, at least on the battlefield.

Unlike many other armies, the parade uniform headdress was the steel helmet (*Stahlhelm*), together with leather cartridge pouches and high marching boots (*Schnürstiefel*), which were known outside Germany as "jackboots."

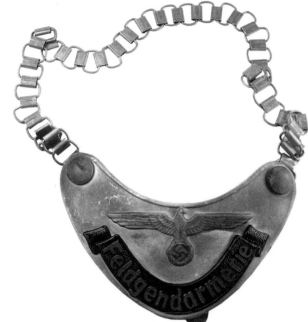

above A metal gorget on a chain was the badge of office of military policemen. The gorgets were usually worn well-polished and had "*Feldgendarmerie*" picked out in luminous paint, beneath the Nazi eagle. A key role of the *Feldgendarmerie* was to direct troops and traffic, especially at night. The luminous paint helped vehicle drivers locate the *Feldgendarmerie* in the dark.

above Daggers were an important element of the ceremonial uniform of many Nazi political and military organizations. This one is actually a *Sturmabteilung* or SA dagger, worn by members of this original Nazi party paramilitary organization, and is unusual in that it has an inscription showing it was a gift from Ernst Rohm, the SA leader. Rohm was eventually arrested and shot by the SS when he was seen as a threat to Hitler's position. Sensible SA members quickly ground off the Rohm inscription on their daggers, so this one is an unusual intact survivor.

above A close-up of the engraving on the dagger.

below A ceremonial dagger and scabbard, with the knotted cord or Portepee on the dagger's handle to differentiate the wearer's rank. This dagger is actually a *Luftwaffe* one.

above Another ceremonial dagger, this time with "*Alles fur Deutschland*" engraved on the blade.

HEADGEAR

STEEL HELMET (*STAHLHELM*)

The German *Stahlhelm* first entered service in 1916 and was developed as a result of experience in the early years of World War. The steel shell incorporated a pronounced peak at the front and a deep skirt (to protect the wearer's neck) at the rear. There were also two prominent hollow bosses which combined the function of ventilating holes and mounts for a face-mask (which was seldom, if ever, used).

This Model 1916 was replaced by the Model 1935 which was slightly smaller and lighter, with a less pronounced peak and skirt, and while the ventilation holes were retained, they had no protruding studs. By 1939 all frontline infantry units had this version, although the Model 1916 was being worn by second and third line units, including infantry, right up to the end of the war.

A later version, the Model 1943, was introduced to simplify manufacture and lacked the separately

above The *Stahlhelm* became the iconic symbol of the German soldier. The one seen here has the remains of the gray paint scheme along with the eagle decal.

applied rim of the earlier models.

All versions of the helmet were painted field-gray both inside and out, although the shades varied slightly between manufacturers. From 1934 onwards, it was decorated with two transfers – a

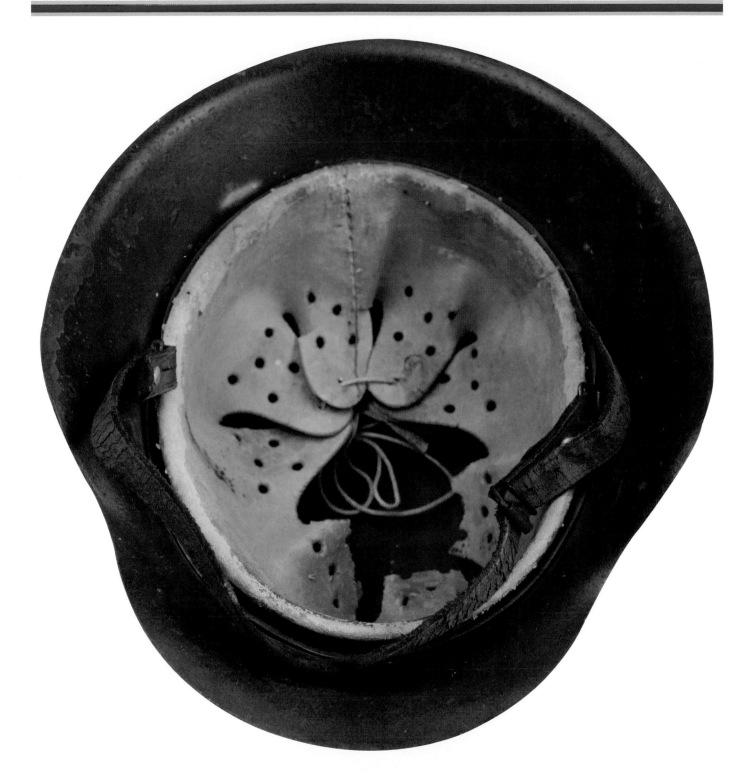

above An excellent view of the leather liner and chin strap. The liner could be adjusted using the tie string to suit the wearer, while the strap had an adjustable buckle.

right Early war helmets had a rolled rim. Late-war production (seen here) removed this as an economy measure and used a straightforward cut edge.

above Instead of the national shield on the side, this helmet bears SS insignia. It also has a black paint scheme which suggests it saw ceremonial use rather than combat.

right The interior of the SS helmet above. The wearer's name can be seen painted on the inside of the rim. Note also the rolled edge rim and how it compares to the helmet on the previous page.

Wehrmachtadler (military eagle) on the left and a tricolor shield in the national colors of red, white and black on the right, but these were discontinued during the war. Helmets for tropical service, such as in the Afrikakorps, were painted a sand-yellow, while on the Russian front they were overpainted white during the winter months. The Model 1935 helmet weighed between 30 and just over 40 ounces depending on size, of which there were five; the Model 1943 weighed slightly less. All were fitted with a leather liner, adjustable black chinstrap, and had cooling vents on either side.

above This helmet has the faint remains of a camouflage pattern painted on it. Such patterns were often applied at unit level.

Above: A helmet with 'chicken wire' netting and face screen The wearer could attach foliage or hessian strips to the wire as camouflage and to break up the outline of the helmet.

51

HELMET COVERS

As in other armies, the German infantry quickly found that it was necessary to break up the outline of the helmet by adding foliage, which had to be secured to the helmet by some means. The first was by ad hoc methods using leather straps, rubber bands cut from motor vehicle inner tubes, chicken wire or sacking. Purpose-made nets made of green string were also used, and many infantrymen made use of captured British nets, which were considered superior. Eventually a reversible cloth cover was issued, with temperate coloring on one side and winter warfare white on the other; this had built-in cloth straps on the camouflaged side only, into which foliage could be inserted.

left Some *Wehrmacht* soldiers cut up *Zeltbahn* to make splinter-camouflaged helmet covers.

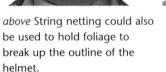

above SS units had a range of reversible camouflage helmet covers such as the one seen here.

above String netting could also be used to hold foliage to break up the outline of the helmet.

above Some soldiers put the strap from their breadbag around their helmet to give somewhere to mount foliage.

above Camouflaged helmet covers and fabric face veils help make this machine gun team more difficult to spot.

UNIFORM CAP

The Uniform cap *(Schirmmütze)* was worn by all ranks, including private soldiers, although there were some variations in embellishments, and officers' caps tended to be of a much superior quality. This cap had a field-gray top, a wide band of a blue-green material and a short black shiny peak with a raised ridge along the outside edge to give it strength. Set dead-center in the front was a capbadge, consisting of the circular National Cockade (three concentric rings of red (inner), silver and black (outer), surrounded by an oakleaf cluster in white metal. Above this was a stylized eagle with outstretched wings, its talons resting on a swastika. In all cases, the piping around the crown of the cap and along the top and bottom edges of the capband was in the relevant Waffenfarbe. The caps of soldiers *(Mannschaft)* and junior NCOs *(Unteroffiziere)* had black chinstraps secured by small black buttons, while the officers' cap had twin silver cords in place of the chinstrap and silver buttons. General officers' caps had gold cords with gilt buttons, and the piping was gold as opposed to *Waffenfarbe* color. General officers' badges were of silver up to January 1943, when they were changed to gold. These caps were often worn on operations, but almost invariably with the spring in the crown having been removed. This gave the crown – and, indeed, the whole cap – a softer, almost floppy, appearance, and left much to the wearer's initiative to achieve the shape he wanted.

top and above The green piping and silver strap on the field hat at top shows the wearer is a *Panzergrenadier* officer, while the red piping and no strap on the hat below indicates the wearer is an NCO from an artillery or self-propelled gun unit.

left An immaculate field cap belonging to an SS officer (note the death's head badge and curved wingtips on the eagle. This one has the spring stiffener inside the crown, unlike the two hats above.

OFFICERS' FIELD CAP OLD-STYLE

The Officers field cap appeared in two different designs. The Old Style (*Offizierfeldmütze älterer Art*) was very similar to the Schirmmütze but without a wire to keep the shape of the crown. The national emblem and oakleaf-cluster/ cockade was embroidered cloth, and the black peak had no stiffening ridge on the outer edge. As with the *Schirm-*mütze, however, the piping around the crown and along the top and bottom edges of the blue-green cap-band was in the owner's *Waffenfarbe*, except for general officers (gold) and chaplains (purple). This old-style cap was supposed to have been finally phased out on 1 April 1942, but was so much liked that it continued in use to May 1945.

OFFICERS' FIELD CAP NEW-DESIGN

The new Officers' field cap (*Offizierfeldmütze neuer Probe*) introduced in December 1938, was quite different, being essentially a better quality version of the soldiers' M38 Field Cap (the fore-and-aft or sidecap). It was made of better quality field-gray cloth and had silver piping along the upper edge.

above and left Two examples of the officers' field cap. The one above belonged to a signals officer.

FIELD CAP

The Field cap (*Feldmütze*) was of a design known to the British as a "sidecap" or "fore-and-aft." It was originally intended for use in very cold weather, with side flaps which could be let down to protect the ears and neck, with the narrower buttoned section under the chin. These flaps were very seldom used for the purpose for which they had been designed and were normally in the raised position, secured in place by hooks which engaged in a metal grommet. It was used as a field cap in circumstance not requiring a steel helmet, and could be easily folded and stowed away, when not required.

above and left Two field caps – the one above with the red trim of an artillery soldier.

MOUNTAIN CAP

This peaked cloth Mountain cap *(Bergmütze)*, which became almost universal throughout the German Army, had its origins in a cap worn by civilian mountaineers in Austria in the 18th century and which was adopted by ski-troops of the Imperial Austro-Hungarian Army in 1914 and in about 1916 by German mountain troops. It was made of a cotton material and had a stiffened peak to give some protection against the sun and glare from the snow; it also had sideflaps, as in the fore-and-aft, which could be lowered to protect the ears and buttoned under the chin. Adopted by the German mountain troops *(Gebirgsjäger)* in the 1930s it had an embroidered National Emblem and cockade on a single cloth backing and two silvered buttons. Having qualified for the *Gebirgsjaeger*, the officer or soldier was awarded a metal *Edelweiss* (see below). There was also a white cotton cover to be added during the winter months.

above A mountain soldier with a peaked *Bergmutze* or mountain cap. He also has goggles to protect his eyes from glare and snow reflections at high altitudes.

STANDARD FIELD CAP, MODEL 1943

A clothing regulation of June 1943 introduced a new Standard field cap *(Einheitsfeldmütze)*, which incorporated features of both the *Bergmütze* and the *Tropischemütze*. It had a larger peak than the mountain troops' cap, but retained the side-flaps and buttons; and the National Emblem and Cockade were combined into a single design sewn onto the crown above the two buttons. General officers had a gold piping around the crown and all other officers silver piping.

left The mountain cap proved to be so useful that it formed the basis of the Model 1943 standard issue field cap.

SUNHELMET

On first deployment to North Africa in 1941, *Afrikakorps* infantry were issued with the traditional European' sunhelmet *(Tropische Kopfbedeckung)*, of the type known to the British as the solar topi (or topee). In the German case, these were made of pith, had prominent ventilation holes in the crown, were khaki in color and bore two metal shields; on the right in national colors and on the left the German eagle. These were adopted, presumably on the advice of their Italian allies, reinforced by movies about the British in India, but once in the desert the Germans found, as, indeed, had the British some years earlier, that the helmets were of absolutely no value and they were quickly discarded.

above An early pattern sunhelmet in brown, complete with national eagle on the side.

above and left This sunhelmet is in a lighter, sand color.

TROPICAL CAP

As described above, the sunhelmet was impracticable and quickly discarded, to be replaced by a Tropical cap *(Tropischemütze)* which was generally similar to the *Bergmütze*, but lighter, being made of sand-colored cotton drill and with a somewhat larger peak, which was designed to keep out the tropical sun. Unlike the *Bergmütze* there were no flaps to be let down, but there was machined stitching along the line where the top of the flaps would have been. Not having flaps meant that there was no actual need for the two buttons at the front, but they were retained for decorative purposes. There was also a grommet either side for ventilation. The National Emblem and a National Cockade were separate and in the usual positions, but made of machine-woven thread on dull tan cloth backings.

above A tropical cap, complete with fold-down neck protection, worn in the main by *Luftwaffe* personnel of the *Ramcke* parachute brigade and Herman Goering Division in north Africa and Italy.

above The tropical cap soon replaced the sunhelmet and was made from lighter material than the field cap.

left A *Luftwaffe* side cap in lightweight tropical material and desert colors.

COLD-WEATHER HEADGEAR

Several forms of headgear were issued to alleviate the effects of the Russian winter. The most commonly seen was the toque *(Toque)*, which was a knitted, double-layer woollen tube, open at both ends. This was pulled over the head so that one end could be inserted into the collar, while the other end was pulled down to the chin leaving an open gap for the face, but with head, ears, neck and crown protected. It could be worn with almost any other type of headgear including the steel helmet.

There were a number of designs of fur-lined caps *(Pelzmützen)*, some of which were official issue, but others were undoubtedly made at home and despatched to the front by an anxious family. One official design was based on surplus crash liners from the discontinued *Panzer* beret. The original liner was made of thick black felt covered with oil cloth and this was now given an additional covering of gray cloth and a stiffened peak, but with an additional fur-lined flap which could either be let down to protect the neck, ears and throat, or tied up across the crown to keep it out of the way. Some of these caps had national insignia at the front, others did not. A close-fitting hood was also produced, which was reversible white or gray. This had a large skirt which covered the wearer's neck and shoulders and which was normally worn inside the jacket or other overgarment.

FUR CAPS

The terrible winter conditions of the Russian Front led to a wide variety of cold weather headgear, some of which were of the soldiers' own design and manufacture, or were sent to him by anxious relatives.

CAP BADGES

While the number of cap-badge designs did not begin to approach the many designs worn by the British and Dominion armies, the German Army still had a fair number.

The National Emblem *(das Hoheitszeichen)*. This comprised a stylized eagle with outspread wings and looking to its left. Its talons rested on a wreath enclosing the symbol of the NSDAP, the swastika *(das Hakenkreuz)*. This was always the topmost badge.

The Reich Cockade *(die Reichskokarde)* comprised three concentric circles: red (inner), silver and black (outer). In most forms of headgear, it was surrounded by a wreath of oak leaves which symbolized strength.

left In their first Russian winter German soldiers were largely left to improvise warm weather clothing and headgear from civilian furs and other materials.

right A fine set of metal eagle, metal cockade and wreath on the front of an officer's peaked field cap.

left A selection of cap badge eagles including Luftwaffe and army versions.

above Two versions of the woven cockade and wreath that was mounted at the front of the peaked cap.

Tradition badges *(Erinnerungsabzeichen)*. In a very small number of cases some units were allowed to wear additional capbadges to show links to former units of the Imperial Army. Such badges were small and worn between the National Emblem and the *Reich* Cockade. The only infantry unit with such an honor was *Infanterie Regiment 17*, which wore a *Totenkopf* (death's head) badge consisting of a skull atop crossed bones, indicating its links with the former Brunswick Infantry Regiment Nr. 92.

Mountain Troops. All officers and soldiers of the mountain troops *(Gebirgsjäger)* wore an *Edelweiss*, which was introduced in May 1939. This came in two forms:

Schirmmütze. On the peaked service cap, the Edelweiss was made of white metal, had gilt stamens but no stem and was worn on the crown beneath the National Emblem.

Bergmütze. A slightly larger *Edelweiss*, also of white metal, this time with an added stem, which was worn on the left side of the *Bergmütze* immediately above the wearer's left ear.

Jäger **Troops.** From August 1942 officers and soldiers in Jäger units wore a badge comprising a sprig of three oakleaves with an acorn. Like the *Edelweiss* this was worn on the *Feldmütze* above the wearer's left ear.

Ski-Jäger. From August 1944 soldiers of *ski-jäger* units, essentially *Ski-Jäger* Brigade Nr 1, wore a badge consisting of the *Jäger* badge as described above, but with an added single ski.

Chaplains. Army chaplains wore a small Gothic cross on their headgear.

Additional Units. Late in the war some formations and units were authorized to wear small badges on their *Einheitsfeldmüze* (left side) and the service cap *Schirmmütze*, which were located between National Emblem and *Reichskokarde*. These usually took the form a small metal button with the divisional sign in enamel.

DECORATIONS

The subject of decorations and medals is a huge one, with many volumes written on all aspects of the subject. All we can do here is show some of the more common decorations awarded to the German soldier, and especially those that might be seen on a combat uniform.

The Germans were more likely to wear the actual medal on their combat tunic than some of their opponents, who mainly reserved them for ceremonial wear. German "combat" awards such as the Assault badge or Tank Destroyer badge were nearly always worn in combat.

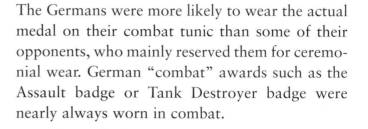

left The Iron Cross 2nd Class was awarded for acts of exceptional bravery. Some recipients wore the medal on their combat tunic; others wore the ribbon sewn to the second buttonhole of their tunic.

above This Iron Cross 2nd Class has never been awarded and is in the original packaging.

above : The Wound Medal was awarded to those wounded in action.

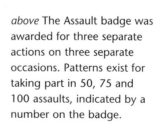

above The Assault badge was awarded for three separate actions on three separate occasions. Patterns exist for taking part in 50, 75 and 100 assaults, indicated by a number on the badge.

above and left The War Merit medal was awarded to both civilian and military personnel. This one has crossed rifles to indicate that the recipient has seen combat action.

right A superb example of the the "75" version of the Assault Badge.

above The Close Combat clasp was awarded in bronze, silver and gold for 15, 30 and 50 days of unsupported close combat respectively.

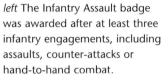

left The Infantry Assault badge was awarded after at least three infantry engagements, including assaults, counter-attacks or hand-to-hand combat.

above Arm shields were given to commemorate a campaign or series of actions. This one is the Krim shield, given to those who fought in the Crimea from 1941–42.

left An Italian-instigated medal, this was intended to honor the German–Italian alliance and was awarded to German soldiers who fought in the Afrikakorps.

above The Tank Destroyer decoration was worn high on the right sleeve and awarded to those who had destroyed a tank in close combat.

above The Eastern Front medal was given to those who fought through the Russian winter of 1941–42. The winter had been so severe that the soldiers nicknamed the medal the *Gefrierfleischorder* or "Frozen Meat Order".

right The official certificate given to a recipient of the Iron Cross.

BOOTS

top Snowshoes were an essential aid to mobility in mountainous and severe winter conditions.

above Short ankle boots became more common towards the end of the war and were worn with gaiters or puttees.

It is scarcely surprising that the line infantry placed great importance on their boots, which represented their basic means of transportation! Types included:

Marching boots (*Marsch-stiefel*). This was the basic marching boot, made of black leather, whose uppers reached to just below the knee. The soles were lined with metal studs laid out in a regulation pattern.

Ankle boots (*Schnür-schuhe*). These were short, lace-up, black leather boots whose top came to just above the ankle-bone.

Mountain boots (*Berg-schuhe*). These were of heavy construction and with double soles. The edges of the soles and heel were lined with iron cleats and the soles were covered with special studs, all designed to grip on rocks and ice. There were five pairs of holes for lacing-up and a further four pairs of hooks above that. A waterproof join was essential, so the trousers were tucked into the top edge of the boots and the join then usually covered with a puttee (see left).

Desert boots (*Tropische Schnürschuhe*). These were made of sand-colored canvas and reached to just below the knee. They were fitted with long laces, which passed through the normal eyes to the level of the ankle and were then criss-crossed up two rows of hooks. This was an excellent design, much admired by Germany's enemies, and which formed the basis for the very successful British jungle-boot.

Overboots. Various designs of overboot were used to combat the cold on the Russian front to prevent frostbite. These included one type made of plaited straw and several made of felt, either on its own or in combination with leather. All were very large and were intended to be worn in addition to the normal issue boots.

ANKLETS

above Here the baggy camouflage trousers come down to the ankle boots.

right The high leather "jackboot" became a symbol of the German fighting man.

The most popular boots were the long marching boots (*Marschstiefel*) in which the trouser ends were tucked into the top of the boot. As in so many other fields, by 1942 shortages within the Third Reich began to tell – this time of leather – forcing production to switch to ankle boots. There was then the problem of how to deal with the trouser ends and three answer were produced:

Anklets (*Stoff Gamaschen*). Also known in English as gaiters, these were a strip of canvas about 4 inches wide with reinforcing strips of leather. They were secured in place by leather or canvas straps which fitted into metal buckles.

Puttees (*Wickelgamaschen*). This was an item which originated with the British Army in India and consisted of a long strip of gray cloth measuring some 29 x 3 inches. One end tapered to a point to which was stitched a long cotton tape of the same color. The cloth was wound several times around the ankle to cover the top of the boot and the end of the trouser leg and then secured with the tape. *Gebirgsjäger* normally wore gray puttees, but there was also a type of white spat which fitted over the tops of the boots.

left The high leather boots had studs driven into the soles.

right Leather and canvas boots made for desert and tropical service. Many Afrikakorps soldiers discarded them in favor of shorts and ankle boots.

right Once the severity of the Russian winter was realized, these felt and leather overboots were made to fit over the normal boots of sentries in snow conditions.

CAMOUFLAGE

While the SS are well known for their use of camouflage clothing, the first standard German pattern was instituted by the army. Their "splinter" pattern was originally used on *Zeltbahn* camouflaged shelters, but enterprising units also made smocks and helmet covers from the same material.

The SS adopted camouflage more enthusiastically and introduced more than eight patterns throughout the war. Most garments were printed on both sides of the material with a green "summer/spring" version of the pattern on one side and a brown "fall/winter" style on the reverse.

The first SS pattern was known as "plane tree", which was followed by variations of "oak leaf" then "pea" or "dot" patterns. Later patterns were introduced but did not see much service.

above The splinter pattern had hard edges and an overprinted "falling rain" pattern.

left A *Wehrmacht* pioneer wearing a two-piece splinter camouflage outfit, with white winter camouflage on the inside.

right An SS camouflage smock in the spring/summer "plane tree" pattern. The fall pattern is on the reverse of the material.

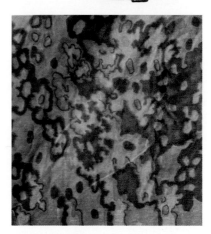

left This figure seems rather relieved to be surrendering! He is wearing a later version of the *Wehrmacht's* splinter camouflage but with much softer outlines to the color patches. This style was known as "marsh" or "water" pattern.

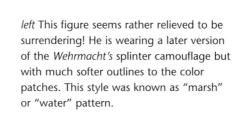

above SS patterns were copyrighted to make sure the Army couldn't use them. This is the fall version of the "plane tree" pattern.

right An SS field cap in faded "oak leaf" summer/spring pattern. The hat could be turned inside out to show the fall/pattern.

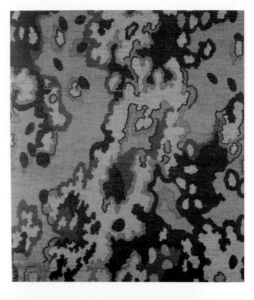

right A very faded example of the spring/summer variant of the SS "oak leaf" pattern.

left A smock in the summer variant of the SS "palm tree" pattern, with jagged lines outlining some of the green patches.

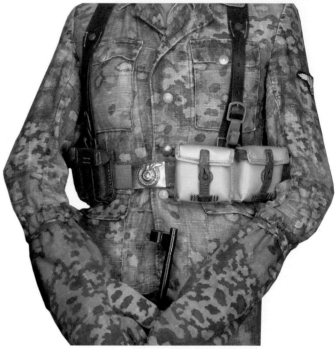

above A late-war tunic and mitten gloves in SS "oak leaf" pattern. Tunics such as these were intended to replace the earlier smocks.

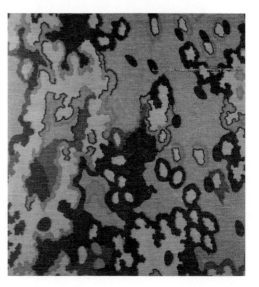

left A paratrooper in the *Luftwaffe* "splinter B" variant of the army pattern.

right The fall/winter variant of the SS "oak leaf" pattern.

above A helmet net which also functioned as a mosquito net and camouflaged face veil.

right An NCO from an artillery or assault gun unit wearing a padded winter jacket with fur-lined collar. He is wearing short boots with gaiters and has binoculars in the case around his neck. From his belt hangs a map case and a pistol holster.

left An SS soldier in "dot" or "pea" pattern camouflage. This was an attempt to produce an all-season pattern and there was only the one variant. He is also wearing a sidecap, rifle ammunition pouches on his belt and a gas cape across his chest. Note the entrenching tool on the right.

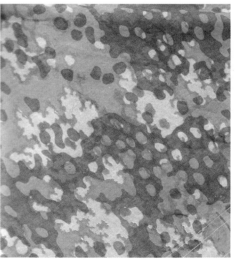

left A faded example of the SS "dot" pattern. While there was only one official pattern, the exact details of the print varied from batch to batch.

PERSONAL FIELD EQUIPMENT

above The infantryman's backpack was the *Tornistor*, a fabric and leather item with a cowhide cover flap and which was attached to the "Y" harness on the shoulder. The *Tornistor* opened up and was intended to hold spare boots, clean shirt and other items necessary for living in the field.

As with all armies, the German Army had a Field Service Order *(Feldanzug)*, which required its infantrymen to carry a considerable amount of weaponry, ammunition, equipment (such as entrenching tools), spare clothing, gas mask, field dressing, emergency food supply, water bottle and a minimum of personal items about his body. The individual items were standardized, and some, such as the ammunition pouches, could only be worn in one way, but there were inevitable minor variations, depending partly on local orders, partly on circumstances (e.g., very hot or cold weather), but also on what was currently on issue, with supplies of all items decreasing in both quantity and quality towards the end of the war. Finally, combat experience also taught lessons.

The general idea was that a man should be able to carry everything that he needed to survive and

left The front view of the Tornistor, showing the side that rested against the soldier's back. The hooks at the top which attached to the "Y" harness are clearly visible, as are the "D" rings on top of the pack to which the Zeltbahn shelter and blanket were strapped.

fight, the basic limiting factor being rations, for which the individual soldier only had space for two days supply. Most of the items were contained in the large pack *(Tornister)* which was normally carried on unit transport and with which, ideally,

the soldier was reunited each evening. In actual combat the soldier carried a reduced load, but one which always included a small haversack *(Brot-beutel)*, whose contents included the day's rations, and a water bottle.

left When in light fighting order the soldier would carry essential items, including a day's rations, in the a bag known as a *Brotbeutel* or "breadbag". Contents could include washing kit, field cap and other items. The bag was normally attached to the belt and hung down at the back.

right Another breadbag, this time made from a much greener fabric than the previous. As well as being attached to the belt, the bag could also be slung over the shoulder using a long woven fabric strap. The two strap loops at the back were used to attach a waterbottle and mess tins.

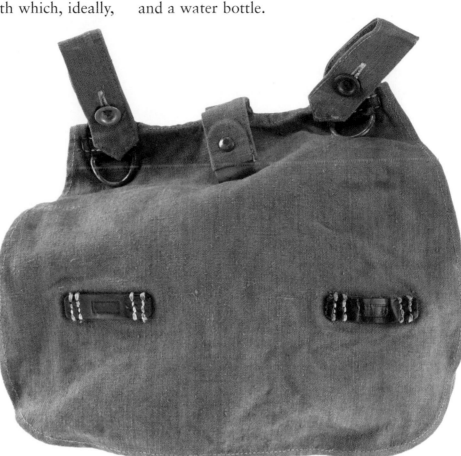

Inside Pack (Tornister)			On Outside of Pack		
Canvas clothing, suit	*Drillichanzug*	1	Boots	*Stiefel*	1
Sewing outfit	*Nähzeug*	1	Laces	*Schuhriemen*	2
Clothes brush	*Kleiderbürste*	1	Mess tin	*Kochgfeschirr*	1
Boot brush	*Wichsbürste*	1	Greatcoat	*Mantel*	1
Rifle-cleaning outfit	*Gewehr Reinigungsbeutel*	1	Bivouac sheet	*Zeltbahn*	1
In Pack Lid			**Haversack (Brotbeutel)**		
Shirts	*Hemden*	2	Washing/ shaving gear	*Wasch und Rasierzeug*	1
Drawers	*Unterhosen*	2	Field Service Cap	*Feldmütze*	1
Socks, pairs	*Socken*	2	Drinking cup	*Trinkbecher*	1
Foot bandages, pairs	*Fusslappen*	2	**On Belt**		
Scarves	*Halsbinden*	2	Bayonet	*Seitengewehr*	1
Iron ration	*Eiserne Portion*	1	Waterbottle	*Feldflasche*	1
Cartridges	*Patronen*	30	Gas mask	*Gasmaske*	1
Bivouac ancilliaries	*Zeltzubehör*	1	Entrenching tool	*Kurzer Spaten*	1

The German infantryman's belt and harness system allowed him to carry his basic equipment and ammunition in relative comfort. His tunic, trousers and boots were fine for operations in temperate climate but turned out to be inadequate for the severe Russian winter. This figure has a field grey uniform of early war quality and is kitted out in full marching order, complete with backpack, full belt gear and rolledgreatcoat and *Zeltbahn* (half-shelter).

The collar badges and braid trim show that this man is an NCO in an infantry unit.

The black leather "Y" harness was attached to the ammunition pouches or belt at the front and to the belt at the back.

Soldiers were issued with a rectangular gas cape made from impregnated paper or rubberized fabric. The cape was kept in this fabric pouch, held shut with two press buttons. The pouch could be worn (as here) across the chest, attached to the strap for the gas mask canister; or could be attached to the canister itself.

As an NCO or squad commander, this man carries an MP40 submachine gun on a leather sling around his neck.

His tunic is of mid-war production and is still of reasonable quality material and cut. Both the breast and skirt pockets are pleated while the collar is finished with dark green material. The tunic is in army *'feldgrau'*, a greenish-gray color which varied considerably depending on the uniform maker and individual production batch.

He has a single triple pouch which holds three magazines for his MP40. Most of pouches were made from canvas, but the one shown here is in black leather. The little pocket in front holds a loading tool.

NCOs and officers were issued with leather map cases such as the M1935 model, shown here hanging from the belt. The case has room for pens, pencils, chinagraph markers, compasses etc and opens out to reveal the map under a transparent waterproof cover.

A black leather belt forms the foundation of his field equipment, with harnesses and pouches all being attached to it. The belt buckle has the Nazi eagle and emblem with the motto *"Gott Mit Uns"* around it.

The M1935 helmet had a rolled edge to give a rounded rim. Before the war, helmets were given a smooth, shiny paint surface, but combat experience caused various matt colors and rough textures to be applied instead. Shown here is the Nazi symbol decal that was applied to the left side until 1943.

A shield in the national colors of black, white and red was applied to the right side of the steel helmet until the middle of 1940.

Hanging from loops on the belt is a canvas M1931 *Brotbeutel* or "bread bag". In it would be kept the day's rations, perhaps a cleaning kit, and other small personal items. The *Brotbeutel* originally came with a long shoulder strap which could be used to carry other packs or bags, or could even be strapped around the steel helmet to enable camouflage materials and foliage to be attached.

This man is carrying his equipment in marching order, and arrayed around the top of his large pack are a *Zeltbahn* and blanket. The camouflaged (army "splinter" pattern) *Zeltbahn*, or quarter-shelter, could be worn as a poncho or could be joined together with others to form a tent. Alongside it is a light gray blanket. Both are strapped on to the outside of the pack and can be removed without having to remove or open the pack.

A gas mask was kept in a cylindrical metal container, normally suspended over the shoulder on a separate strap. This container on this example is painted gray.

The M1939 large pack, or *Tornister*, was made from canvas with a cowhidecovered flap. Inside the soldier would carry washing and shaving kit, spare clothing, underwear, socks and shoes, weapons cleaning kit and other items. Many had an external strap on the lower edge of the cover flap, but this variant doesn't.

There were many variations of M1935 canteen. This one has a thick woolen cover and a leather strap holding a metal cup with wire handles. It is held by a small strap hanging from the belt.

The M1931 mess tin set has both a deep pot and a lid that could be used as a cooking pan. This one is painted in olive drab.

For most of the war the German soldier wore wide cut trousers tucked into high leather boots, as shown here. From 1943 onwards more and more soldiers had shorter boots with trousers tucked into short gaiters or puttees.

The most common army boot was the high marching boot, made of black leather and reaching up to just below the knee. The soles incorporated a pattern of metal studs.

ITEMS CARRIED BY THE INFANTRY SOLDIER

above A member of a machine gun team moves toward a trench. As well as his rifle and personal equipment he carries a case of ammunition and a box for a spare barrel on his back.

BELT

The basic carrying system consisted of a belt and Y-shaped yoke or harness, all made of blackened leather. The belt *(Koppel)*, which served as the anchor for the whole system, was made of plain black leather and was secured at the front by a brass buckle with a circular badge on the outer ring of which was inscribed the words *"Gott Mit Uns"* (God with us). Various items could be suspended from the belt. At the rear and resting on the wearer's left buttock was a leather carrier for a 22-inch long entrenching tool *(Tragbares Schanzzeug)* with a 5.7 x 17.3 inch blade. Up to about 1939–40 the bayonet (Seitengewehr) was suspended from the same carrier, but thereafter it was carried separately, in its own black leather frog which fitted between the tool carrier and ammunition pouch; i.e., on the

wearer's left hip. Also suspended from the belt were, on the wearer's right buttock, a small canvas haversack, known as the *Brotbeutel* (breadbag) which contained the wearer's immediate personal requirements: razor, washing equipment, eating utensils, and combat rations.

HARNESS

Most of the items in the harness were made of black leather and were connected to each other by means of brass hooks and rings, leather loops, or leather straps and brass buckles. The harness consisted of two shoulder straps, which were fastened in the front by D-rings to hooks on the ammunition pouches or holster, passed under the shoulder straps on the tunic and fastened at the rear to a circular metal ring located approximately between the shoulder blades. Also secured to this ring was a leather strap which was anchored to the belt. High on the shoulder straps were two D-rings to which were secured a yoke made of canvas straps.

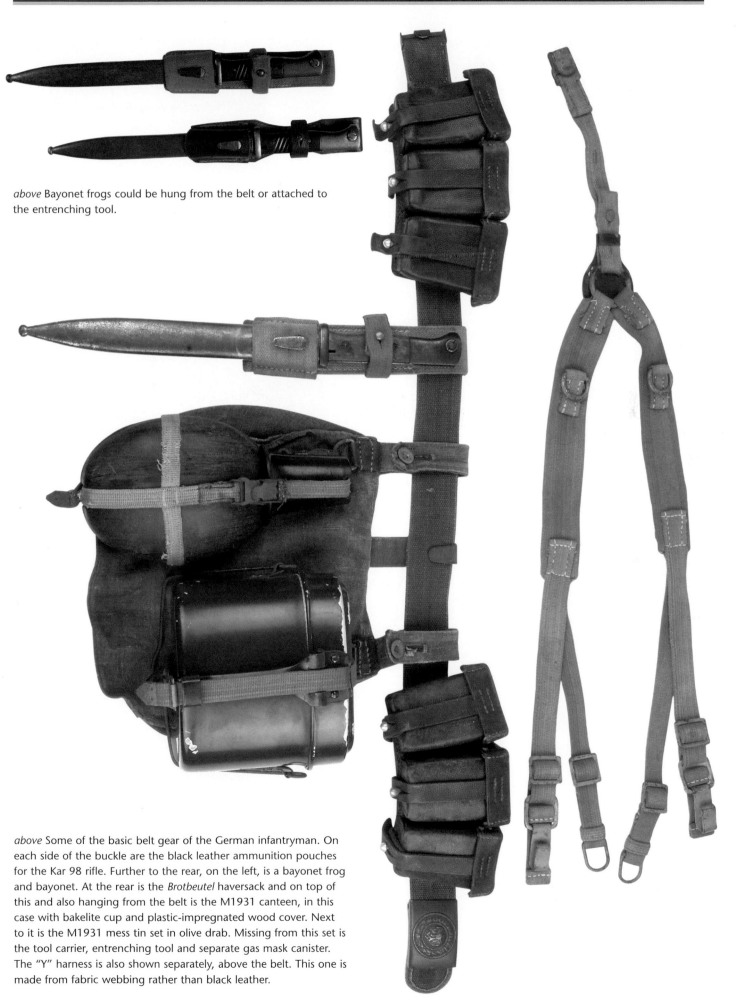

above Bayonet frogs could be hung from the belt or attached to the entrenching tool.

above Some of the basic belt gear of the German infantryman. On each side of the buckle are the black leather ammunition pouches for the Kar 98 rifle. Further to the rear, on the left, is a bayonet frog and bayonet. At the rear is the *Brotbeutel* haversack and on top of this and also hanging from the belt is the M1931 canteen, in this case with bakelite cup and plastic-impregnated wood cover. Next to it is the M1931 mess tin set in olive drab. Missing from this set is the tool carrier, entrenching tool and separate gas mask canister. The "Y" harness is also shown separately, above the belt. This one is made from fabric webbing rather than black leather.

At the front were the ammunition pouches, also of blackened leather, which varied in design according to the wearer's weapon, but all were attached to the belt by leather loops at their rear and connected to the yoke by metal clips. Riflemen carried six pouches in two groups of three, each of which carried two five-round ammunition clips, for a total of sixty rounds per man. Those armed with MP40 or MP44 machine pistols had longer pouches to accommodate the larger magazines; these were angled inwards to ease withdrawing a new magazine and the yoke shoulder strap was secured to the outer edge rather than to the center. Many of these longer pouches were made from heavy fabric rather than leather.

Men armed with a pistol had a holster on the left side of the belt and an ammunition pouch on the right.

In combat order, the wearer carried his *Zeltbahn* (see later) wrapped neatly and suspended from the yoke, together with the respirator in its cylindrical container.

right The gas mask was held in a cylindrical metal container, usually painted gray, but in this case yellow.

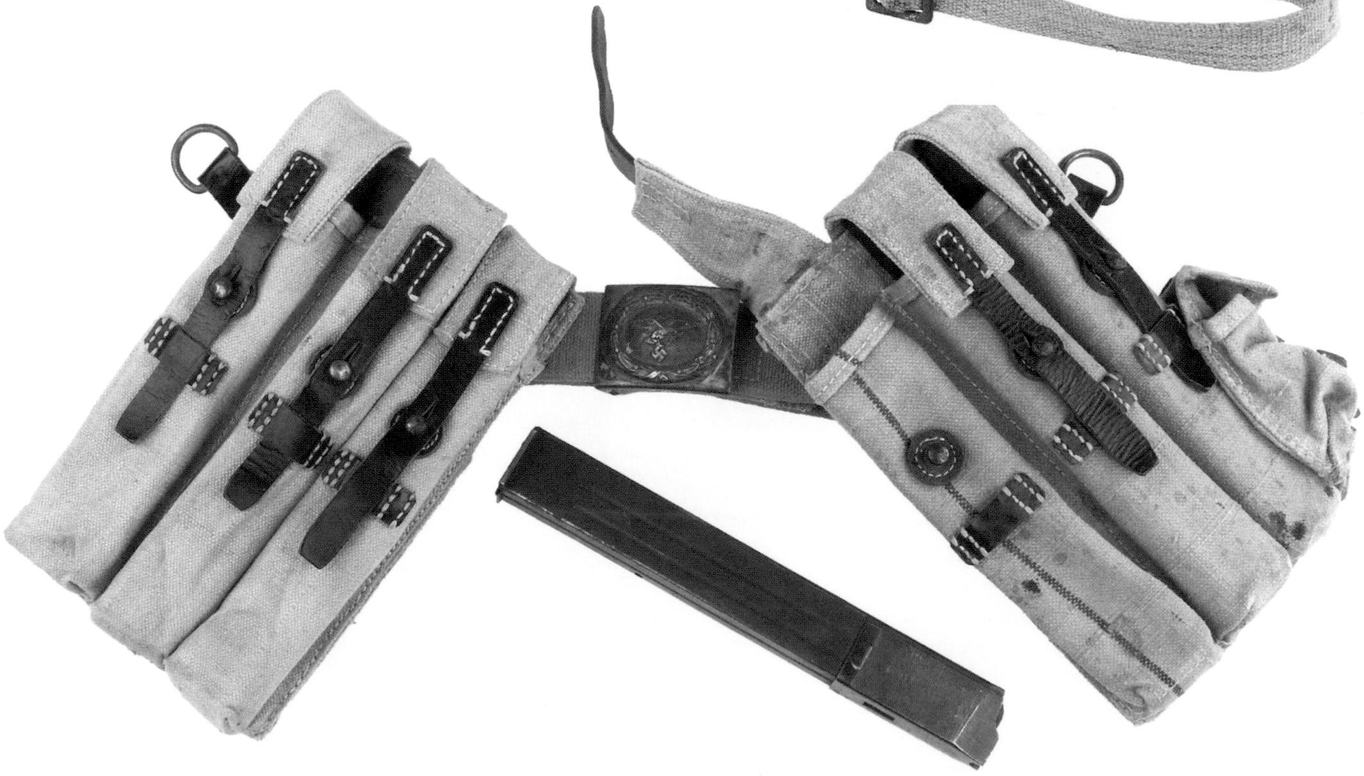

above Men equipped with the MP38 or MP40 sub-machine guns had these triple ammunition pouches sized for the long 32-round magazines. Initially these pouches were made from leather, but many later ones were made from fabric with leather fixings, as seen here.

In marching order the large pack was suspended from the D-rings at the top of the shoulder straps and the soldier then added his greatcoat, which was wrapped in the *Zeltbahn*, in a "horseshoe" around the top of the pack. Officers and most NCOs also carried a leather map case and binoculars, each of which had its own leather case.

right Two examples of the "Y" harness, one in the original black leather, the other in lighter woven fabric. The single rear strap was attached to the rear of the belt while the two shoulder straps were passed through the tunic shoulder straps then attached to hooks on the ammunition pouches on the front of the belt. In this way heavy loads were distributed evenly on the waist and shoulders. Initially introduced for tropical and hot climates, fabric harnesses were also used elsewhere towards the end of the war as materials ran out.

above NCOs and officers often carried a leather case which held a map, pencils, markers, and message paper.

WATER BOTTLE AND CANTEEN

Water was carried an aluminum water bottle with a woolen cover and drinking cup, which fitted over the top of the bottle. Cups varied in design and material, and both metal and bakelite were used. This combination could be either suspended directly from the belt or attached to the cover of the haversack.

The canteen (mess-tin) consisted of a deep container and shallow lid, which fitted together and were attached to each other by a leather strap. This could be suspended from the belt or from a metal A-frame which could be carried on the wearer's back.

above the M31 waterbottle normally had a felt cover, which was supposed to help insulate the contents from extremes of temperature. This one has the larger metal cup which has held on by the leather strap around the outside.

left and above Clearly visible on these two bottles is the metal screw top, complete with the holding strap to prevent it being lost in the dark!

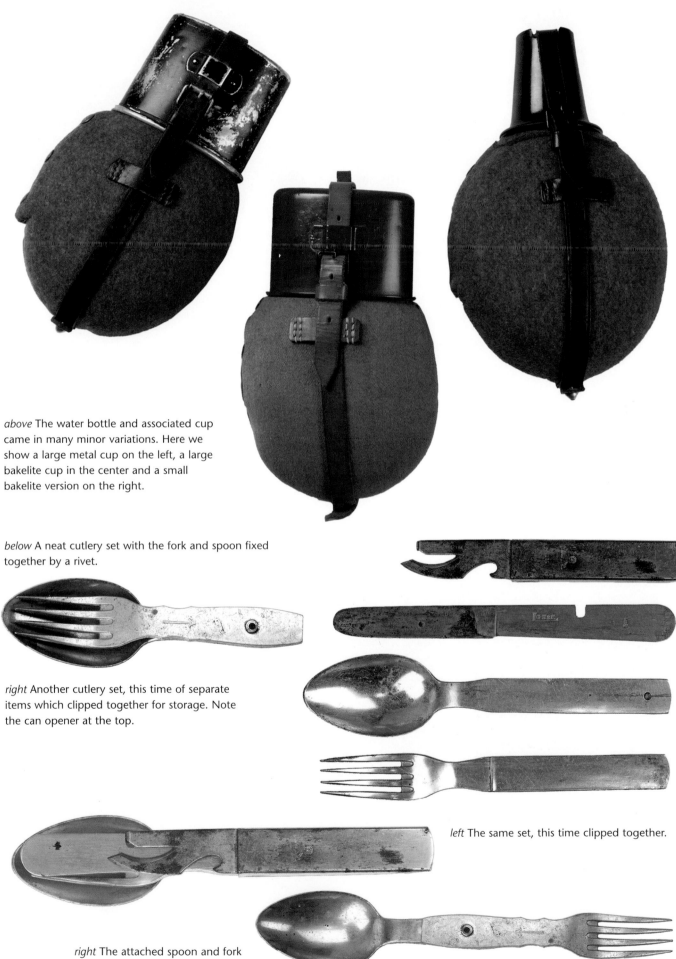

above The water bottle and associated cup came in many minor variations. Here we show a large metal cup on the left, a large bakelite cup in the center and a small bakelite version on the right.

below A neat cutlery set with the fork and spoon fixed together by a rivet.

right Another cutlery set, this time of separate items which clipped together for storage. Note the can opener at the top.

left The same set, this time clipped together.

right The attached spoon and fork opened out for use.

above Two sets of mess-tins in olive drab (some were painted gray). The lid doubles as a shallow pan, complete with fold-down handle.

left Most mess-tins ended up with chipped paint after some service, such as the one on the left. The one on the right is in almost pristine condition and doesn't appear to have seen much campaign service. Note the leather strap used to attach the mess-tins to the breadbag or sometimes to the back of the "Y" harness.

above SS troops setting up in a farmyard. The rifleman has Kar98 ammunition pouches, a gas cape on his chest and two grenades tucked into his belt.

GAS MASK

In all orders of dress the standard issue gas mask was carried in a cylindrical container with fluted sides, which was suspended from a canvas sling. A gas cape was also carried in its own canvas or rubberized pouch. The mask continued to be carried to the end of the war, but few units carried the cape after about 1941, when it was widely seen as irrelevant.

left The gas mask case was a cylindrical metal container, usually slung over the shoulder with its own strap.

left An opened canister, showing the gas mask packed inside.

Left and right The gas mask was a compact unit with a changeable filter at the front. German soldiers carried gas masks almost all the way through the war, even long after the chances of gas being a worthwhile Allied weapon had passed.

right The belt was a strong item made from black or sometimes brown leather. Most field equipment and ammunition pouches were hung from this, and it was supported by the "Y" shoulder harness.

FIELD DRESSING

All, regardless of rank, carried two field dressings (*Verbandpäkchen*). The dressing itself consisted of a medicated pad measuring 2.5 x 4 inches, attached near to the end of a cotton bandage (11 feet x 2.5 inches). This was inside a semi-waterproof paper wrapper which, in its turn, was encased in a khaki-colored drill outer cover. Each package measured 3 inches by 2 inches and both were carried in a special pocket on the inside of the right-hand skirt of the jacket.

above Bandages and field dressings were carried by all solders, no matter the rank. Unit standard procedures usually specified where they were to be carried, which allowed a wounded man's comrades to find his dressing quickly.

right The folding entrenching tool was an essential part of the frontline infantryman's kit. Folded, it hung from a strap on the belt kit.

left Improvisation is an essential skill for the field soldier, typified by this handy kit bag, converted from a standard military-issue shirt.

MAKING LIFE EASIER

Life in the field can be hard, even when not in combat. The German military made strenuous efforts to provide simple comforts to personnel, although as with most armies, the front line troops were never as well catered for as their rear area colleagues.

Overall, Germany was never able to devote as much resources to troop comfort as Britain and the United States, although German troops were usually much better off than Soviet soldiers in this respect.

above Mail from home was an important morale booster for every soldier. These are letters captured on the battlefield by Allied troops.

left: Most soldiers were issued with these Bakelite dishes intended to carry butter, fat or other foodstuffs in their ration packs.

left: A civilian radio receiver made for *Luftwaffe* use. Troops could gather round this to listen to faint crackly programmes transmitted from the homeland.

below While there was an official list of what should be carried in the breadbag, most men found space for extra personal items as well.

right Food supply was a constant concern of every soldier. Insulated boxes were used to transport cooked food to the frontline trenches. If it didn't necessary arrive piping hot, it might at least still be warm.

below A selection of comfort items such as cigarettes, tobacco, matches, soap, needle and thread, and aspirin.

right A flint and gasoline cigarette lighter was an essential part of the soldier's kit.

ZELTBAHN

All armies seek to produce equipment which combines a multitude of uses in one simple, lightweight design and few have succeeded as well as did the German Army with its *Zeltbahn* (bivouac sheet). This ingenious item – in essence nothing more than a triangular-shaped piece of waterproofed cotton fabric – could be used as a poncho, groundsheet, windbreak, multi-occupant tent, stretcher or as a flotation aid for crossing rivers. Each soldier carried one, which was normally rolled up and suspended from the yoke, while the associated 6-foot length of rope, pole section and three tent-pegs were carried in a small pouch. The sheet had three edges, each 8 feet 2 inches long, one of which was the baseline while the other two each carried a row of metal hooks and eyes, inset into a reinforced strip, which enabled the sheets to be joined together in various patterns to make up four-,

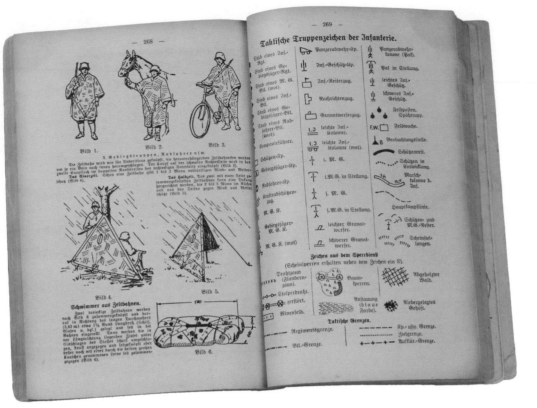

above An infantry instruction manual showing how to fold a *Zeltbahn* and construct a shelter.

eight- or sixteen-man tents.

A slit in the center enabled it to be worn as a waterproof poncho and the fastenings were so placed that it could be worn either by a man marching on foot, riding on horseback or seated on a motor-cycle. The bottom edge had a series of grommets, with larger grommets at either end for pegs; there was an even larger grommet at the apex for the pole. Two men could combine to lay their weapons and equipment on their two *Zeltbahns* and then wrap, fold and tie them in such a way that they produced a watertight container which not only kept their equipment dry but also had sufficient surplus buoyancy to support them during a river crossing.

Introduced in 1931, the *Zeltbahn* was originally dark gray in color but by 1939 was being issued in a splinter camouflage pattern. Totally nondescript in appearance and very cheap to manufacture, it was, rather like the Swiss Army knife, a masterpiece of design, and it served German soldiers well.

left A superbly effective design, the *Zeltbahn* could be a poncho, a ground sheet, windbreak, stretcher or part of a shelter.

PERSONAL IDENTIFICATION

There were two items which every soldier was obliged by law to have about his person at all times. The first of these was the Identity Disk (*Erkennungsmarke*), a small oval metal disk, with three longitudinal slits dividing it in two, and two holes in the top half to enable it to be hung around the neck by a strong cord. The disk was stamped with sufficient information to identify the soldier, usually (but there were variations) his name, the title of the unit where he was first enlisted, the last four digits of his army number and his blood group. This information was duplicated above and below the slits, so that if the soldier was killed the burial party could break off the lower half and send it to an army records office for the death and grave location to be registered, while the upper half remained with the corpse to enable it to be identified later, if required.

The second item was the Pay Book (*Soldbuch*), a small booklet which served as a combined identity document and as a record of units served in, equipment and clothing issues, pay grade, important medical information, and medals or other distinctions awarded. The soldier was obliged to carry this on his person at all times, except when in actual combat when it would be in a government-issue waterproof cover in his large pack,

He was obliged to produce it on demand, for example, when challenged on seeking to enter a secure area, or, of great importance, to identify himself to military, civilian or railway police when on leave. In the early years of the war no photograph was required but from about 1943 onwards one was added as an additional security measure.

above A soldier's pocket book containing tips and hints on living in the field.

above, left and below A selection of identity discs showing how the top and bottom halves could be separated.

MEDICAL EQUIPMENT

above A well-equipped medical post with a Medical Officer and field medic tending a casualty. Note the prominent Red Cross markings on the medic's tunic and helmet.

Until the supply situation began to break down, the German military provided reasonably effective medical support to its combat soldiers. Field dressing stations were normally well forward, close to the front line; although the continual lack of motorized transport often made repatriation to the rear a slow and unreliable process. And as the war progressed, medical support became much more primitive and unreliable.

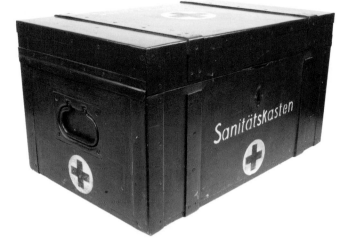

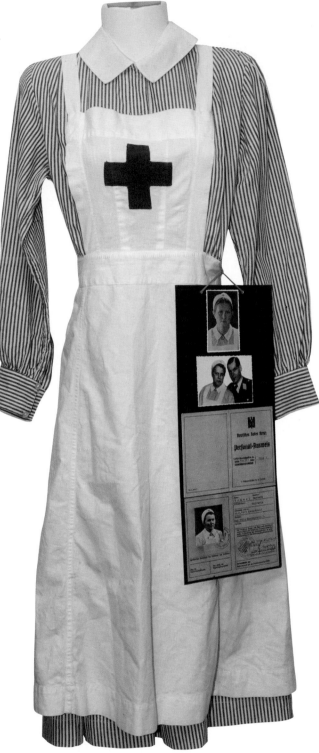

above A nurse's uniform, complete with photographs and ID certificate of the woman who wore it. Female nurses normally operated in field hospitals which were some distance behind the front.

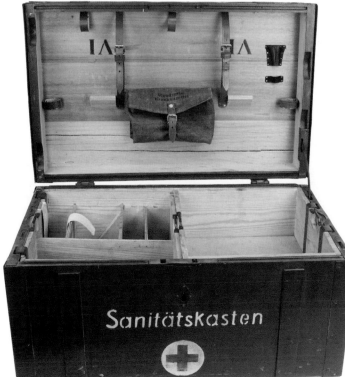

left and above left A typical box holding medical supplies and equipment for a field dressing station.

MEDICAL SUPPLIES

left and below A *Truppenbesteck* was a standard medical pack with all the items needed for a front line field dressing station. This is the 1943 pattern, and with the lid open, it can be seen that it still has all the original contents. Note the contents list and book of first aid procedures inside the lid of the box.

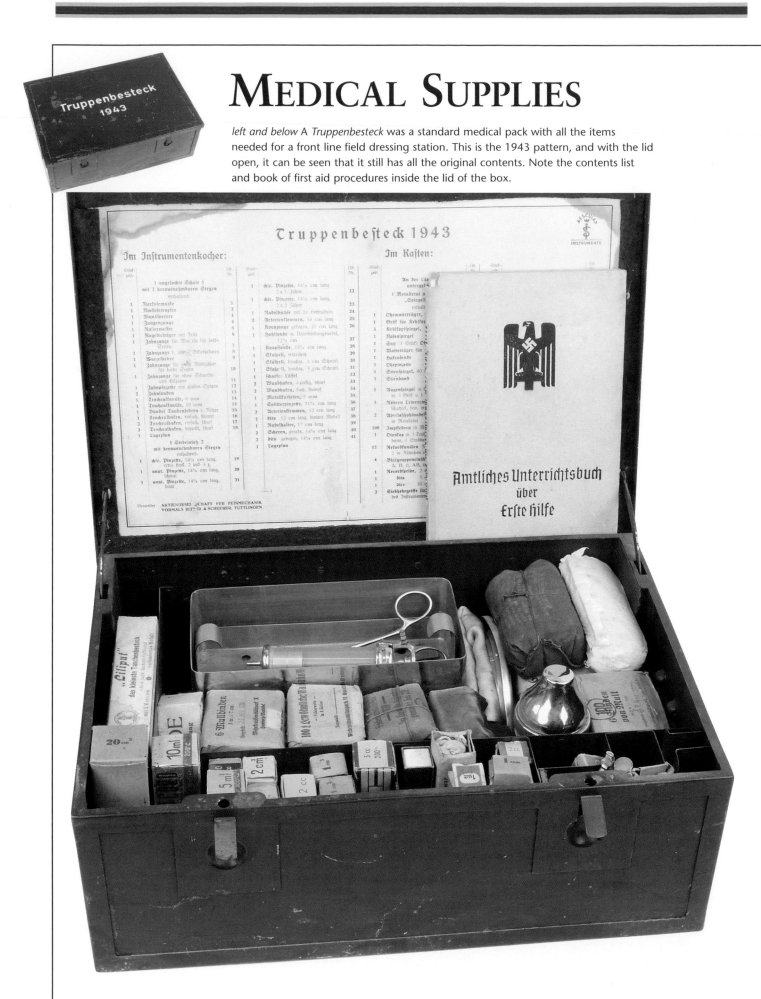

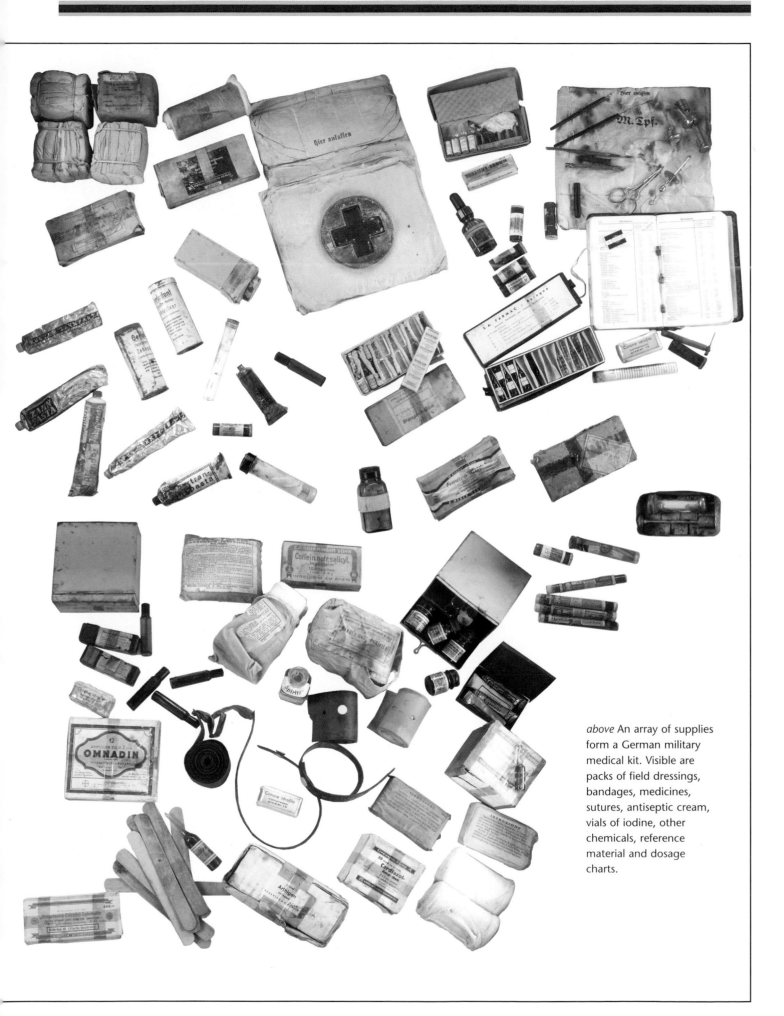

above An array of supplies form a German military medical kit. Visible are packs of field dressings, bandages, medicines, sutures, antiseptic cream, vials of iodine, other chemicals, reference material and dosage charts.

COMMAND IN THE FIELD

Command was exercised at a lower level in the German army than almost any other. In peacetime all ranks were trained to do the jobs of the leader at least two ranks above them, and this attitude persisted throughout the war. NCOs and officers at any grade were expected to respond quickly to events and take command decisions without reference to higher authority.

right A prismatic compass is essential to field navigation, where it allows the user to take a bearing from the map then sight on a terrain feature on the correct bearing and march towards it.

left Industrialized armies run on paperwork and the German military was no exception. This pouch was used by despatch riders, officers and headquarters staff to carry documents.

NICHT IN FEINDESHAND
FALLEN LASSEN!

right and above A folding wooden mapboard with map and pencils inside. It could be easily carried then opened up to consult the map.

right Signaling in the field could be difficult when units were out of voice range. One method was to use colored flares from a pistol such as this.

6
Sternsignalpatronen
Rate 44
dag
Untersucht
Mai 1941

above A smaller set of binoculars in sand-yellow paint.

below German optics were universally admired, and their binoculars were made to such a high standard that captured ones were prized by Allied soldiers.

left Another set of binoculars with a brown leather case and strap. Note the double cap for the eyepieces.

PIONEERS & SAPPERS

A key military role is that of the pioneer or sapper. He can slow enemy progress by mining or blocking routes and preparing defensive positions, or can aid friendly assaults by demolishing enemy positions.

Splinter camouflage helmet cover and combat smock

MP 40 and ammunition pouches

Pioneer's sack containing explosive demolition charges

Pioneer shovel

Folded entrenching tool.

Case for Teller anti-tank mine

Above A heavily-laden pioneer with camouflaged suit, helmet cover and gloves is ready to place explosives or an anti-tank mine.

below The shovel is one of the most basic of infantry tools. Shown here are two versions with different handle lengths and styles.

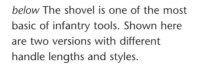

above Sappers hide behind a wrecked Soviet T34 tank, ready to dash forward with their Teller mines.

above The case for a single Teller anti-tank mine.

right An electrical ignition device used to trigger the detonators in explosive charges and demolitions.

left Short-handled wire cutters of the type issued to assault teams when they were tasked with breaking through enemy defenses.

right The Goliath was a tiny remote-controlled vehicle which could be driven up to an enemy position where its large explosive charge could be detonated by the operator.

above and below Powerful, long-handled wire cutters likely to be used by pioneers when clearing an attack route, usually under cover of darkness.

above A pioneer saw used to cut wood for defensive or general construction work. Note the leather "scabbard".

INFANTRY WEAPONS

The following sections cover the main types of weapons to equip an infantry regiment of an infantry division between 1939 and 1945 as well as parachute, mountain and *Waffen-SS* units. It cannot be totally comprehensive as such a multitude of designs saw service at some stage during the war, but it gives a flavor of the equipment in the hands of the German infantryman.

The German infantryman's armory in World War II was a curious mixture of the advanced and the obsolete, as well as incorporating a bewildering variety of national and foreign designs, all of which created immense logistical and training problems, which were never solved. The *Luftwaffe*, the *Kreigs-*

above The Kar98 rifle was reliable, effective and was the equal of any other bolt-action rifle. Its only weakness was the small magazine capacity. The soldier behind the rifleman is aiming an MG15, a machine gun designed for aircraft use but also pressed into service as an infantry weapon.

above The MP40 provided a useful degree of close-range firepower while being compact and easily carried in a vehicle.

marine, the *Waffen-SS* and the *Panzer* force all had priority for production resources and raw materials, which meant that when the war started in August 1939 the infantry was equipped with many very elderly weapons.

One outcome was that once the fighting began in earnest deficiencies in both quantity and quality quickly became very obvious. The initial signs of such problems were disguised from all but the most perceptive by the success of the early campaigns. To take just one example, the antitank guns in service in 1939 were never tested at all in the Polish, Norwegian or Yugoslavian campaigns, and it was only in the fighting in France and North Africa that it became clear that they were ineffective against the most modern enemy tanks. As a result, the anti-tank guns equipping the infantry in the attack against the Soviet Union performed really badly and not only were crash programs set in train in Germany, but foreign equipments, which had been captured in large quantities, were hastily pressed into service.

RIFLES

During the second half of the 1930s the Nazi Party ordered the army to expand as fast as possible and huge sums of money became available for increasingly ambitious weapons projects. Despite this, when war began 1939 the most widely used weapon was the 40-years old *Mauser Gewehr* 1898 with the venerable bolt action and a five-round magazine. During the glory days of 1939 to 1941 as the army swept across Europe and North Africa the basic deficiencies such a bolt-action rifle were not too obvious but they became only too apparent once the invasion of the Soviet Union was under way. Strenuous efforts were made to develop self-loading weapons, but when a satisfactory design was at last available it proved to be too little and late.

right An SS trooper in 'Oak Leaf' pattern camouflage smock, trousers and gloves, complete with helmet cover. His weapon is the G43 Germany's most effective semi-automatic rifle design. As with many weapons produced towards the end of the war, poor quality materials and factory work prevented the G43 from reaching its full potential. Note that this man has black leather ammunition Kar 98 pouches on one side and light fabric G43 types on the other.

MAUSER GEWEHR MODEL 1898

Type: bolt-action, single-shot rifle

Origin: Waffenfabrik Mauser, Oberndorf, Germany

Caliber: 7.92 mm

Weight (empty): 9.0 lb

Barrel length: 29 in; 4-groove rifling; right-hand twist

Ammunition: 7.92 x 57 mm rimless

Feed: fixed vertical box magazine, loaded by five-round charger.

Backsight: Ramped "V," graduated for 100–2,000 m

Foresight: blade, mounted on muzzle.

Designed and developed by *Waffenfabrik Mauser* at Oberndorf-am-Neckar, the *Gewehr Model 98* (rifle, model 1898) or G98 was the most successful bolt-action rifle ever made, having been produced in vast numbers and used, in one form or another, by most armies around the world. It was a strong and reliable weapon employing Mauser's forward-locking lugs and had a five-round, non-removable magazine, the bottom of which was level with the stock. In the original versions the bolt handle stuck out at right angles from the weapon, a clumsy arrangement which proved liable to catch on clothing or foliage – the last thing an infantryman wants to happen – and this was eventually changed to a turned-down design, which was the version used in World War II.

Its only weakness was limited magazine capacity of five rounds, loaded using a metal charger.

It is impossible to work out an accurate figure for the production of G98s but it must have been well over ten million. For the German infantry it was a weapon with a certain mystique which always performed reliably. However, as was found on the Eastern Front, its rate of fire against massed attackers was poor and although its weight was reasonable by World War II standards, by 1940 it was regarded as too heavy.

above The Mauser 98 was a tough, reliable rifle that fought throughout World War I. Many saw service in World War II, although by then the main German infantry weapon was the shortened carbine version.

above For most of the war the core of the German Army was the infantryman armed with a bolt-action rifle. As the war progressed, men like these would be more likely to have automatic weapons.

SNIPER RIFLE

A sniper version of the Gewehr 98 was introduced in 1915 as the Scharf-schützen-Gewehr 98 (sharpshooter, ie, sniper rifle) which continued into use well into World War II. This differed from the standard G98 in only relatively minor details, the most important of which was the mounting for a 4x telescopic sight, which had to be offset to the left to permit continued access to the centrally-situated charger guide. This was also the first model in which the bolt handle was bent down to lie in a new recess in the stock.

left Most German rifle ammunition was of 7.92 x 57 mm caliber. (The first dimension gives the nominal diameter of the projectile, the second the length of the cartridge case.) These are actually inert training rounds, recognizable by the indents along the length of the cartridge case. They are held in the 5-round charger used to load the rounds into the rifle's magazine.

right A sniper in Russia in the winter months. His fur cap provides both warmth and camouflage against the foliage and snow background. He is also wearing a white oversuit.

KARABINER 98K

Various models of the G98 were produced as Karabiner (carbines) for use by cavalry, artillery and engineers in World War One, which were essentially slightly shorter and therefore lighter. In 1935 a new and tidied-up version was introduced as the K98k. Well over 10 million K98ks were produced between 1935 and 1945, and proved very popular. Minor adaptations of the K98k were also developed for paratroops and mountain infantry, but were produced in only small numbers. A simplified, cheaper and easier-to-produce version appeared in 1942.

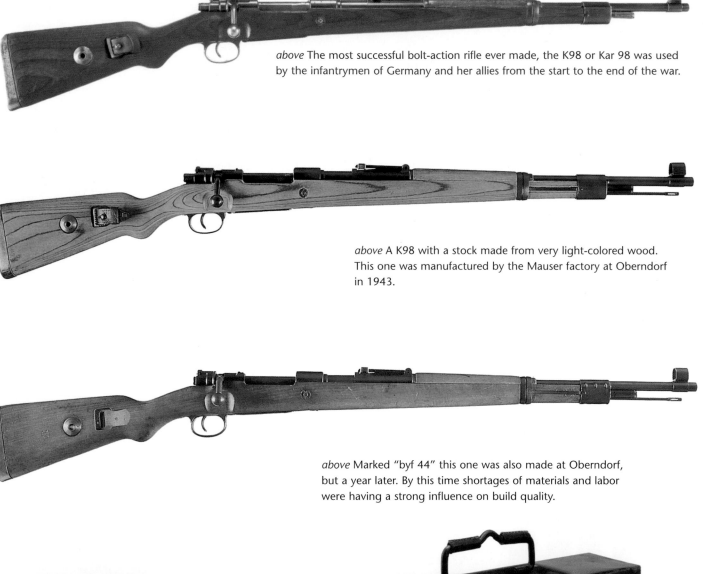

above The most successful bolt-action rifle ever made, the K98 or Kar 98 was used by the infantrymen of Germany and her allies from the start to the end of the war.

above A K98 with a stock made from very light-colored wood. This one was manufactured by the Mauser factory at Oberndorf in 1943.

above Marked "byf 44" this one was also made at Oberndorf, but a year later. By this time shortages of materials and labor were having a strong influence on build quality.

left The stamp detail is from the rifle shown above.

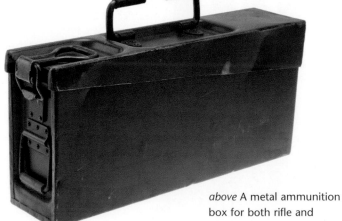

above A metal ammunition box for both rifle and machine gun ammunition.

above This K98 is marked with the production code "bnz 43" and has a single SS rune (see insert detail). These indicate that it was probably assembled from factory-supplied parts by slave labor at a concentration camp.

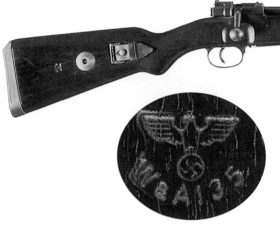

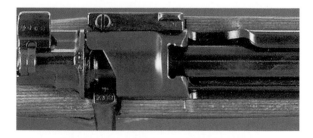

above This Mauser-produced K98 is fitted with the ZF–41 scope, mounted surprisingly far forward from the firer's eye. Details of the scope and carrying case are shown below. Many of these scoped rifles were issued to the best shots in the company rather than to specialist snipers.

right The Mauser mechanism was probably the strongest and most reliable ever fitted to a service rifle.

above and right The markings on this K98 indicate that it was made by the Steyr factory in Austria. Steyr joined the K98 program in 1939 after they became part of the Hermann-Goering-Werke armaments conglomerate.

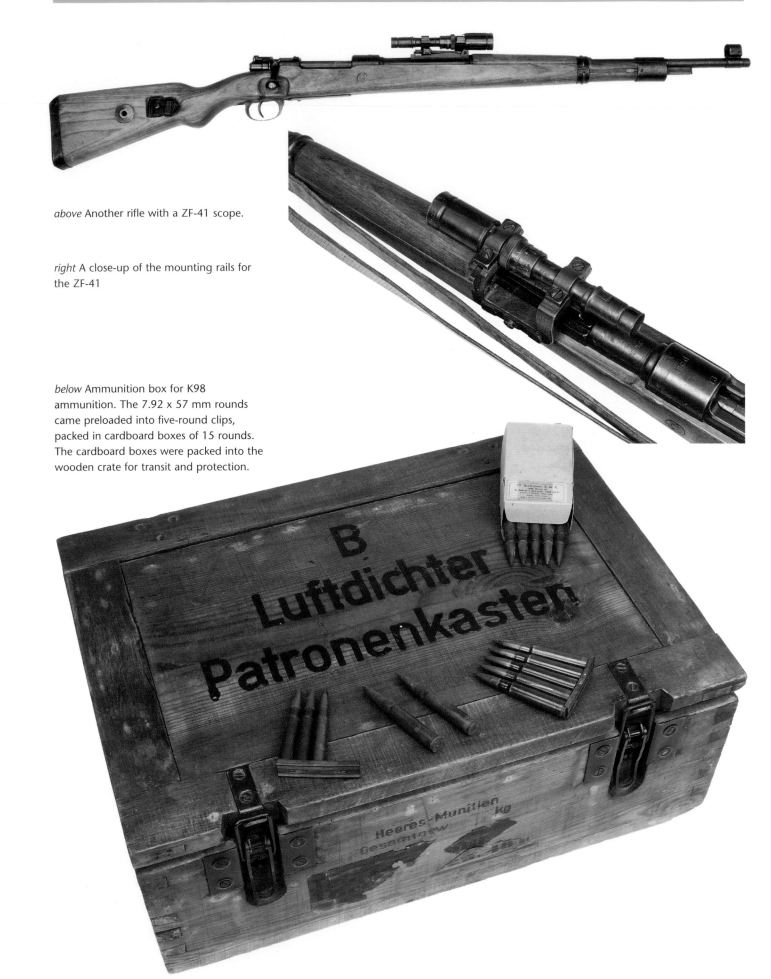

above Another rifle with a ZF-41 scope.

right A close-up of the mounting rails for the ZF-41

below Ammunition box for K98 ammunition. The 7.92 x 57 mm rounds came preloaded into five-round clips, packed in cardboard boxes of 15 rounds. The cardboard boxes were packed into the wooden crate for transit and protection.

GEWEHR MODEL 1898 VK

In the desperate final months of World War Two even cheaper versions were developed by various factories, typical of which was the VK.98 (Volkskarabiner - people's carbine), produced by Steyr-Daimler-Puch. In this weapon, the emphasis was on cheapness and ease of manufacture and the use of non-strategic materials. Some were actually produced and, presumably, pressed into use, but records of those final days of the Third Reich are very sparse.

above Put together quickly from low grade materials, the VK.98 came too late to have any effect on the outcome of the war.

FOREIGN-MADE VERSIONS

Versions of the K98k were in production for their national armies in Austria and Czechoslovakia. When the Germans took over those two countries and not only were existing weapons taken over, but production was reinstated for the *Wehrmacht*. In German service, these were designated Gew 29/40(ö), when made by Steyr-Daimler-Puch in Austria, and Gewehr 33/40(t) in Czechoslovakia.

above Originally made in Czechoslovakia as an "improved" K98, this rifle was taken into German service after the invasion as the Gewehr 24(t).

above Another Czech-built Model 24 drafted into German service, this one has distinctive finger grooves cut into the stock.

right This view of the G24(t) above shows how the sling on all K98 variants sat along the left side of the rifle. A slot cut into the butt enabled the sling to be strapped to the woodwork.

above The Czech Model 33 carbine was slightly shorter than the K98. It was adopted for German service and nearly all examples were issued to mountain troops as the G33/40(t).

RHEINMETALL *FALLSCHIRMGEWEHR* MODEL 1942 (FG42)

Type: automatic/semi-automatic rifle.
Origin: Rheinmetall, Germany
Caliber: 7.92 mm
Weight (empty): 9 lb 15 oz
Barrel length: 20 in; 4-groove rifling; right-hand twist
Ammunition: 7.92 x 57 mm Mauser rimless
Muzzle velocity: 2,500 ft/sec
Feed: removable 20-round side-mounted box magazine.
Cyclic rate: 750 rpm

The *Fallschirmgewehr* (paratrooper's rifle) Model 1942 FG42 was intended to fire in both fully- and semi-automatic modes in a light, easy-to-use package. This was achieved and the weapon's design was well in advance of anything then available in any other army, but it was nothing like as successful as had been hoped.

In order to achieve standardization, the FG42 was chambered for the 7.92 x 57 mm Mauser round, which proved to be too powerful for a lightweight hand-held weapon in automatic mode, causing it to "climb" to the right as the burst continued. An additional problem was that the magazine stuck out at right angles to the left of the weapon, thus upsetting the natural balance when firing, as well as seriously impeding the rifleman when he was carrying it at the "ready." It was also mechanically complicated, and both expensive and time-consuming to manufacture. The army turned it down flat, but Hermann Goering insisted that it be bought for his *Luftwaffe* paratroops, with whom it saw some service. The FG42 was also fitted with a spike bayonet, which folded under the barrel when not in use.

WALTHER GEWEHR 43 (G43)

Type: semi-automatic rifle
Origin: Walther Waffenfabrik, Zella-Mehlis, Germany
Caliber: 7.92 mm
Weight (empty): 9 lb 9 oz
Barrel length: 22 in; 4-groove rifling; right-hand twist
Ammunition: 7.92 x 57 mm Mauser rimless
Muzzle velocity: 2,448 ft/sec
Feed: removable 10-round vertical box magazine.

The Walther brothers began work on a semi-automatic rifle in the 1930s, their system using a muzzle cap which deflected some of the gasses onto an annular piston which drove the working parts to the rear. This meant that the muzzle cap had to deflect the gasses through 180 degrees, leading to considerable fouling and erosion, and when the initial production examples were used in the early stages of Operation Barbarossa as the G41(W) they were quickly withdrawn and the production contract terminated. A much revised design chambered for the new 7.92 x 33 mm Kurz cartridge, the G42(W) was also a failure, but the company persisted and the next version proved to be a great improvement.

In this new weapon, the G43(W), the muzzle-cap was replaced by a more conventional port-and-piston layout,

which was a modified version of that used, with much greater success, by the Soviet Army's *Tokarev SVT*-40. This was placed in production as the *Gewehr Model* 1943 (Walther) G43(W) and the marginally smaller/lighter *Karabiner Model* 1943 (Walther) K43(W). A sniper version was also produced which differed only in having rails fitted on the receiver for a sniperscope, usually a Voigtländer ZF-4.

The G43(W) did reach the German infantry before the end of the war, but by that stage factory conditions were bad, components were of poor quality, workmanship standards had fallen, and overall quality control was abysmal.

above The G43 had a detachable 10-round magazine, usually painted in a semi-gloss black paint. This one shows the paint almost worn away, while there is evidence of black paint or other coating on the wood above the barrel.

above Gustloff Werke were the only major arms manufacturer under direct Nazi party control and were one of the main producers of the G43. This rifle carries the markings associates with Gustloff production, and was likely assembled by slave labor under their control in Buchenwald concentration camp.

above An attempt was made to fit all later G43s and K43s with mounting rails for telescopic sights. But they never became standard. This one has the rail and sports a 4x Voigtlander ZF-4 scope.

above Another K43 with a ZF-4, this time complete with rubber eyepiece and a sunshield over the objective lens.

THE G41

Type: semi-automatic rifle

Origin: Walther Waffenfabrik, Zella-Mehlis, Germany

Caliber: 7.92 mm

Weight (empty): 9 lb 9 oz

Barrel length: 22 in; 4-groove rifling; right-hand twist

Ammunition: 7.92 x 57 mm Mauser rimless

Muzzle velocity: 2,550 ft/sec

Feed: removable 10-round integral box

As they entered the war, the Germans had no automatic rifles in service, so in 1940 a development program was launched to develop a semi-automatic weapon firing the standard 7.92 mm rifle cartridge. The program was known as the *Gewehr 41* (G41). Two manufacturers created competing designs: one was by the Walther brothers and known as the *G41*(W); the other was by Mauser and was called the *G41*(M).

Both rifles used a similar mechanism. Each had a metal cap at the muzzle which trapped some of the gasses expended as the bullet was fired, and deflected them back onto an annular piston. This piston drove the working parts to the rear to eject the cartridge-case, recock the firing pin and load the next round.

The Walther weapon won the competition and was put into production. Field experience in the Russian campaign showed that the mechanism was fragile and unreliable, while the rifle was also badly balanced and distinctly muzzle-heavy. The worst problem was that the gasses quickly eroded the muzzle cap and caused failure of the mechanism, while excessive fouling built up quickly after only a few shots. Some tens of thousands were made and most served with SS units, and as long as it was carefully looked after it was an effective enough rifle.

above The distinctive muzzle-cap redirected the gasses back towards the annular piston to operate the mechanism. Ammunition came from the fixed integral box magazine, which made the rifle slow to reload.

above A G41(W) from the *Berliner-Lubecker Maschinenfabrik*, indicated by the "duv" code stamped on the receiver

above The Walther version of the G41 is easily recognisable from the vertical cocking handle above the ejection post. The distinctive muzzle cap can also be clearly seen.

right A rear view of an SS soldier carrying a G41 over his soldier. Most G41s that remained in service were used by the SS.

This soldier is wearing the side cap or *Feldmütze*, worn instead of the steel helmet when combat was not expected.

The distinctive muzzle cap identifies this rifle as a G41.

Instead of the *Tornisser* large pack, he has a lightweight "A" frame on his back onto which is strapped a camouflaged poncho. The "A" frame was also known as the battle pack

Gas mask cases were carried as standard equipment, even after the threat of the allies using gas had long diminished.

Note the entrenching tool hanging down from the belt, complete with the bayonet frog strapped over it.

Over his *Brotbeutel* bread bag are his mess tins and canteen. This canteen has a woolen cover and a small-sized cup, in this case made from metal.

He is wearing a tunic and trousers in the late-war SS "pea" or "dot" multi-season camouflage scheme.

While he is wearing high marching boots, his trousers are cut to the latewar baggy style which was normally seen with gaiters and low boots.

TRAINING RIFLES

Nazi Germany was a militarized society where all young men were expected to learn the basics of soldiering. Organizations such as the Hitler Youth prepared boys for military service, one aspect of which was learning how to shoot. Rifles firing fullcaliber ammunition were expensive, so smallcaliber training and sports rifles were used. The *Kleinkaliber Wehrsportsgewehr* (KKW) or "small caliber, weapons sports rifle" program saw the procurement of various rifles firing .22 in ammunition but with the same weight, dimensions and mechanism of the standard service rifle.

above This Mauser target rifle reflects the shape, size and weight of the Kar 98 but is in .22 in caliber. It is marked *Deutsche Sport Modell*.

above A Walther factory KKW target rifle which was manufactured before the war but was still in use as late as 1944.

above The Gustloff-Werke manufactured G43 rifles as well as the Volksgerat automatic rifle. This, however, is their KKW training rifle, a .22 in weapon with the same look, feel and weight of the Kar 98.

above The engineering company Simson and Co was based in Suhl and produced rifles and shotguns as well as automobiles and motorcycles. Its owners were, however, Jewish, and the company was forcibly taken over in the late 1930s and renamed the *Berlin- Suhler-Waffenfabrik* (BSW). It was eventually absorbed into the Gustloff company, and one of their products was this .22 in caliber training rifle.

above The *Erfurter Maschinewerke,* or ERMA, is best known for the MP38 and MP40 sub-machineguns. But the factory also produced .22 in conversion kits for Kar 98 rifles and .22 in rifles for the various training schemes. This one is the *Deutsche Sport Modell* 34 (DSM 34) Training Rifle and was made for the *Nationalsozialistisches Kraftfahrkorps* (National Socialist Transport Corps) which trained drivers for the army and provided transport for various military projects.

left As well as shooting, Nazi youth and civilian organisations also taught drill, general field craft and military knowledge. Manuals such as this were widely used.

PISTOLS

$\mathbf{M}$any men in the German infantry carried pistols of various types during the war, some of them of well-known German types, such as *Luger* and *Walther*. There were, however, many others of foreign design, which were either captured in the advances of 1939 to 1942, or the result of arms factories in occupied countries receiving contracts for further production. It was almost unheard-of for a German officer or soldier to carry a revolver and all handguns were semi-automatics firing either 7.65 mm or 9 mm Parabellum rounds.

LUGER 9 MM *SELBSTLADEPISTOLE* PARABELLUM

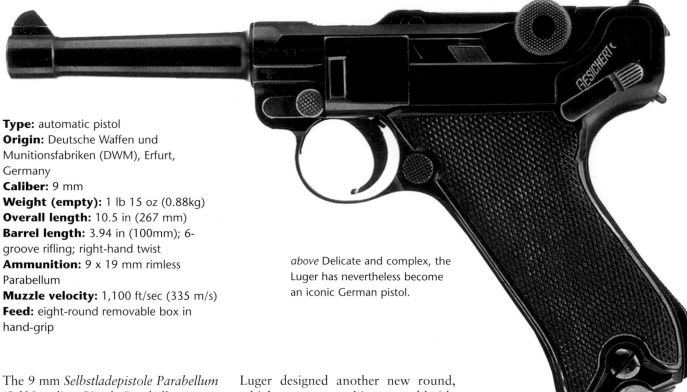

Type: automatic pistol
Origin: Deutsche Waffen und Munitionsfabriken (DWM), Erfurt, Germany
Caliber: 9 mm
Weight (empty): 1 lb 15 oz (0.88kg)
Overall length: 10.5 in (267 mm)
Barrel length: 3.94 in (100mm); 6-groove rifling; right-hand twist
Ammunition: 9 x 19 mm rimless Parabellum
Muzzle velocity: 1,100 ft/sec (335 m/s)
Feed: eight-round removable box in hand-grip

above Delicate and complex, the Luger has nevertheless become an iconic German pistol.

The 9 mm *Selbstladepistole Parabellum* (Self-Loading Pistol, Parabellum) was one of those very few pieces of equipment that has always been instantly identified, particularly in the USA and UK, by its designer's name – "the Luger" – although in Germany it tended to be called the "Parabellum." Georg Johann Luger (b.1849) was a German arms salesman selling Borchardt self-loading pistols and took note of his customers' complaints about the design. He therefore recast the design, simplified the mechanism, improved the balance, increased the angle of the grip and developed a new cartridge, the 7.65 x 21.5 mm Parabellum (known in the USA as the .30 Luger). Some customers considered this round to lack stopping power, so

Luger designed another new round, which was to achieve worldwide acceptance as the 9 x 19 mm Parabellum, in which form the pistol was accepted by the German Army as the *"Pistole M1908 (P.08)."*

It remained in production from 1908 to 1918 and more were manufactured from the mid-1930s onwards to meet the needs of the rapidly expanding German armed forces. Infantrymen used the standard model with a 3.9-inch barrel, although some may have got their hands on Die Lange Pistole 1908 (LP.08) (the "long model, commonly referred to as the "Artillery model."). This had an 8-inch barrel and could be fitted with a combined stock/holster, which, in combination with a 32-round drum magazine,

enabled the weapon to be used as a form of sub-machine gun. Production was phased out in 1942 in favor of the Walther P.08.

Despite its high reputation, the Luger had its drawbacks. It was mechanically complicated, making absolute cleanliness essential and contributing to a lack of reliability in service. It was certainly very powerful and accurate, but in the end there were much simpler, more reliable, and cheaper designs available.

left The Luger was first ordered by the navy as the P.06. This version has a longer 6 in (152 mm) barrel and shows the combined holster/stock which turned the pistol into a carbine substitute.

left With an even longer 8 in (203 mm) barrel, this version was known as the "Artillery" model and was issued to gun crews and the like in World War I. Very few survived into World War II.

left Above: Marked "byf", this Luger was manufactured by Mauser in 1941.

above Another long-barreled "Artillery" model, this pistol has stamps to indicate it has seen both army and naval service.

above A Luger complete with leather holster. This pistol was the personal property of General Maxmilian Fretter-Pico, Commanding-General of Military District IX, who was captured by U.S. forces in 1945.

WALTHER 9 MM SELBSTLADE PISTOLE P.38

left A page from an illustrated training manual showing how the P.38 breaks down into its main components.

above The markings "svw 45" on this P.38 show that it was made by the Mauser factory in Oberndorf in 1945. The crudely-made metal grips and rough finish are typical of late-war production.

Type: automatic pistol
Origin: Walther Waffenfabrik, Zella-Mehlis, Germany
Caliber: 9 mm
Weight (empty): 2 lb 2 oz (.96 kg)
Overall length: 8.38 in (213 mm)
Barrel length: 5.0 in (127 mm); 6-groove rifling; right-hand twist
Ammunition: 9 x 19 mm rimless Parabellum
Muzzle velocity: 1,148 ft/sec (350 m/s)
Feed: eight-round box

The Walther Pistole Model 1938 (P.38) was the outcome of a long line of development models from the Walther Waffenfabrik, which included the Armee-Pistole of 1934 and the Heeres Pistole of 1937. The P.38 was adopted by the German Army in 1938 as the authorized replacement for the Luger P.08. It was produced in vast numbers by the Walther Waffenfabrik itself, as well as by Mauser in Germany, Fabrique Nationale in Belgium, and Waffenfabrik Brunn and Ceska Zbrovoka in Czechoslovakia, but even

so it never totally replaced the venerable P.08. On firing, the barrel and slide were locked together by a wedge-shaped block, but after traveling a short distance they were released by a cam which enabled the slide to continue to the rear while the barrel stopped. A useful feature was that the weapon could be safely carried with one round in the breech and then drawn, safety catch released and fired.

above The P.38 was an effective and reliable military pistol. Positive safety features allowed the user to safely carry the weapon with a round chambered, while the powerful 9 mm Parabellum cartridge had plenty of stopping power. When Germany reformed its army after the war the P.38 went back into production as the P.1.

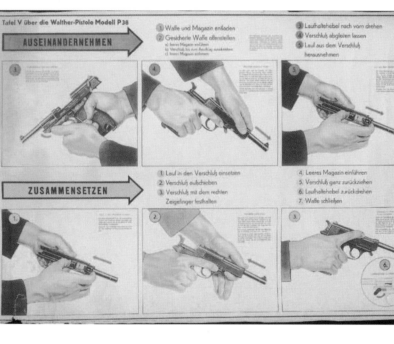

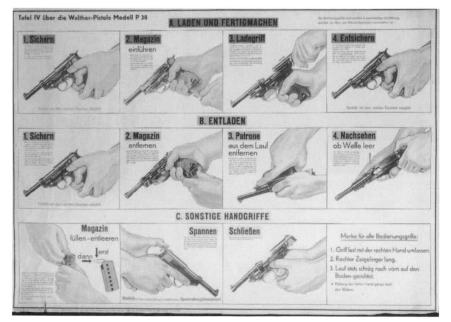

left Training posters such as these can be found on the walls of military establishments anywhere in the world. Shown here are assembly, loading and firing drills for the P.38. Automatic pistols are more complex than revolvers and require the user to master these simple drills and be able to carry them out under combat conditions.

above and below The pistol was originally produced by Walther as the *"Heeres-Pistole"* (HP), or "Army Pistol". After the army asked for some minor modifications the revised design entered service as the P.38. Shown here are both sides and detailed markings on this HP. The army acceptance stamps indicate that it saw military service.

above A P.38 made by Mauser in 1944, shown by "byf 44" stamped on the slide. Initially made for police use, this particular pistol was transferred to military service and was eventually captured by an American soldier during the Battle of the Bulge.

FIGURE 4-74

FIGURE 4-76

FIGURE 4-75

315

left Walther's early production, up to the middle of 1940, had the checkered pattern grips as shown here. This one is resting on an instruction book showing how to disassemble the pistol into component parts.

right Another Mauser-made P.38, this time one manufactured in 1942. The general finish is of higher quality than the 1945 model, and this one has the bakelite plastic grips with the large groove cut alongside the trigger guard.

above The codes "ac 41" indicate that this is a Walther-made pistol, produced in 1941.

above A mid-war (1943) Mauser pistol with engraved bakelite plastic grips. When the P.38 was fired, the slide and barrel recoiled a short distance, held together by a locking wedge. Once this wedge dropped down, the barrel stopped while the slide continued to the rear, ejecting the empty case and preparing to load the next round.

SAUER MODEL 1938-H

Type: semi-automatic pistol
Origin: Sauer und Sohn, Suhl, Germany
Caliber: 7.65 x 17 SR Browning
Barrel Length: 3.2 in (81 mm), 4 or 6 grooves, right-hand twist.
Weight: 1 lb 9 oz (0.71 kg)
Magazine: 13 rounds
Muzzle velocity: 984 ft/sec

The Model 38 was an excellent handgun, being well made, reliable and accurate. Because it fired 7.65 mm cartridge the magazine held 13 rounds, as opposed to the larger 9 mm pistols whose magazines held only six or eight rounds, which might have made the difference between life or death in a close-quarter battle. Even experts are unclear as to the meaning of the suffix "H", which is taken to mean either Hahn, indicating that it was fitted with a hammer rather than a striker, or *Heer*, meaning that it was intended for the Army. It was particularly popular with officers.

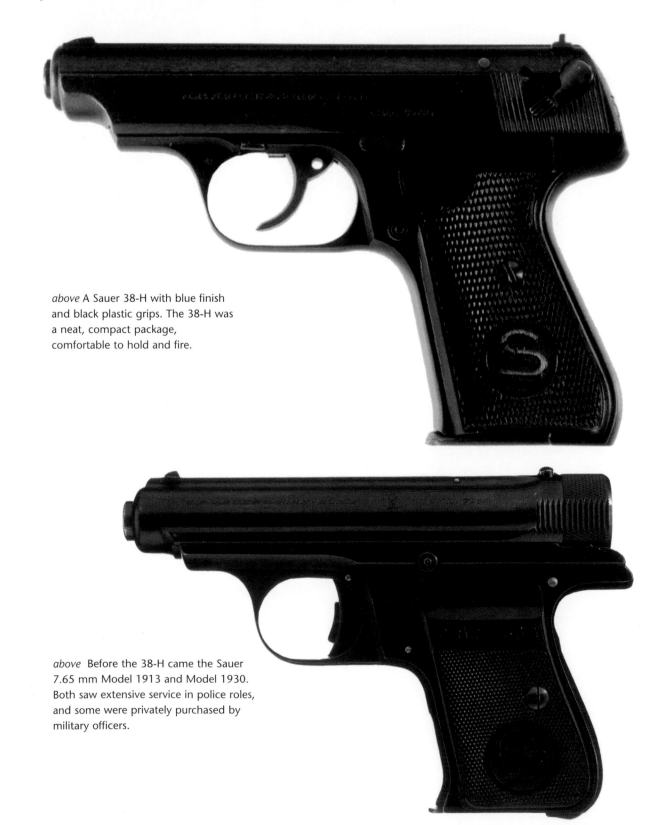

above A Sauer 38-H with blue finish and black plastic grips. The 38-H was a neat, compact package, comfortable to hold and fire.

above Before the 38-H came the Sauer 7.65 mm Model 1913 and Model 1930. Both saw extensive service in police roles, and some were privately purchased by military officers.

FOREIGN PISTOLS

Many foreign pistol designs were pressed into service by the Wehrmacht, some of which found their way into infantry hands. The major models are listed in the table.

above Once Belgium was occupied, Fabrique Nationale put the GP35 back into production under German orders. This is one of the pistols produced at that time as the Pistole 640(b).

FN-BROWNING PISTOLE 640(B)

Type: semi-automatic pistol
Origin: Fabrique Nationale, Herstal, Liege, Belgium
Caliber: 9 mm Auto
Barrel Length: 4.7 in (120 mm)
Weight: 35 oz (0.99 kg)
Magazine: 13 rounds

above The Fabrique Nationale GP35 was probably John Browning's finest pistol design. It saw service with German, Belgian, British, Canadian and other forces, and was a popular choice for the German soldier. This one has a blue finish and dark walnut grips.

This was the last pistol to be designed by the great American, John Browning; indeed, he was still working on it at the time of his death in the Fabrique Nationale factory in 1926. It was a logical development of his M1911, which was manufactured by Colt in the United States for many years, and following his death FN engineers continued to work on it until 1935, when it went into production as the FN/Browning GP35 "High Power." It was an immediate success and was adopted by many armies. Then, when they overran Belgium in 1940 the German Army ordered large numbers which were produced as the *Pistole 640(b)*.

119

above Browning had managed to design a magazine that held 13 rounds of 9 mm x 19 mm ammunition but which didn't require an uncomfortably wide butt. Shown here is a Pistole 640(b) and magazine together with the service issue brown leather holster. Note the pocket for a spare magazine on the outside of the holster.

Country	Manufacturer	Cartridge	Designation	German designation	Comment
Belgium	FN	9 x 7 mm Kurz	Model 1922	Pistole 626(b)	Browning design
Belgium	FN	9 x 19 mm Parabellum	Model 1935	Pistole 640(b)	Browning design
Czechoslovakia	CZ	7.65 x17 SR Browning	Vz/1927	Pistole M27(t)	
Hungary	Fegvergyar, Budapest	7.65 x17 SR Browning	Model 1937	Pistole 37(u)	u = Ungarn (Hungary)
Poland	Radom	9 x 19 mm Parabellum	Model 1935	Pistole 35(p)	Many Browning features
Spain	Astra	9 x 19 mm Parabellum	Model 600	Pistole 600/43	

above The Fegvergyar Model 37M was a 7.65 mm pistol initially produced in Hungary for the Hungarian Army but ordered by the Germans in 1941. Most were issued to *Luftwaffe* personnel (especially aircrew) but some found their way into army hands.

below Another FEG 37M, complete with leather holster. The FEG had a relatively short butt, hence the grip extension protruding below on this one. The markings "jhv 43" indicate a weapon made in Hungary for the German military in 1943, while the marks on the holster indicate that this was a German (not Hungarian) made item.

above The Ceska Zbrojovka arsenal was established in 1919, almost as soon as Czechoslovakia became a nation. They quickly developed and produced a range of pistols, including the 7.65 mm CZ Model 1927 seen here. The CZ 27 was a simple but reliable design and was taken into service by the *Wehrmacht* once they had occupied Czechoslovakia.

above This CZ 27 has an extended barrel and comes complete with a lightweight brown leather holster

right The French MAB Model D took its inspiration from Browning's designs and was an effective 7.65 mm pistol. This one was made during the occupation of France for German use.

above The Spanish Astra 300 was made in both 7.65 mm and 9 mm Short calibers. The 7.65 mm was bought by Germany for army and navy use.

above The Astra 300 (previous page) was modified to fire 9 mm x 19 mm Parabellum as the Astra-Unceta 600. It was produced for the German armed forces from 1943 to 1944.

above Another Astra 300 with a very worn finish. Markings indicate it was made in 1943 in Guernica, Spain.

above Another Browning-inspired design, the Polish Radom
Vis-35 was designed to shoot 9 mm x 19 mm Parabellum.
Originally made for Polish military use the Radom was
adopted by German forces once they occupied the country.
This one has a crude finish and simple replacement grips.

above Another Radom, this time with the
factory-supplied grips. In German service it
was known as the Pistole 35(p).

right This Radom has a higher-quality finish
and is complete with leather service holster
and spare magazine.

OTHER PISTOLS

German industry struggled to keep up with the demands for combat pistols and could never supply enough P.08s or P.38s for all the armed forces. Foreign-made weapons were also taken into service wherever possible but even they weren't enough. Obsolete weapons were often to be found in use, especially in second line, reserve and support units. Pistols intended for police use also found their way into service, while many individuals made private purchases of last-ditch backup weapons. We show a selection of this widely-varied group of weapons.

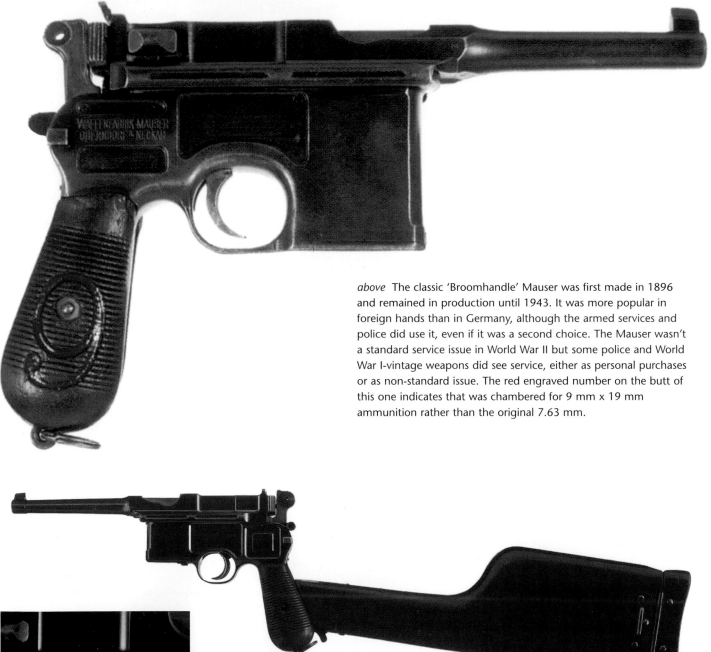

above The classic 'Broomhandle' Mauser was first made in 1896 and remained in production until 1943. It was more popular in foreign hands than in Germany, although the armed services and police did use it, even if it was a second choice. The Mauser wasn't a standard service issue in World War II but some police and World War I-vintage weapons did see service, either as personal purchases or as non-standard issue. The red engraved number on the butt of this one indicates that was chambered for 9 mm x 19 mm ammunition rather than the original 7.63 mm.

*above*The Mauser was often used with a wooden holster which could be attached to the rear of the frame to make a short carbine. The low-velocity pistol ammunition and small magazine capacity (6 or 10 rounds of 7.63 mm) prevented it from being an effective combination.

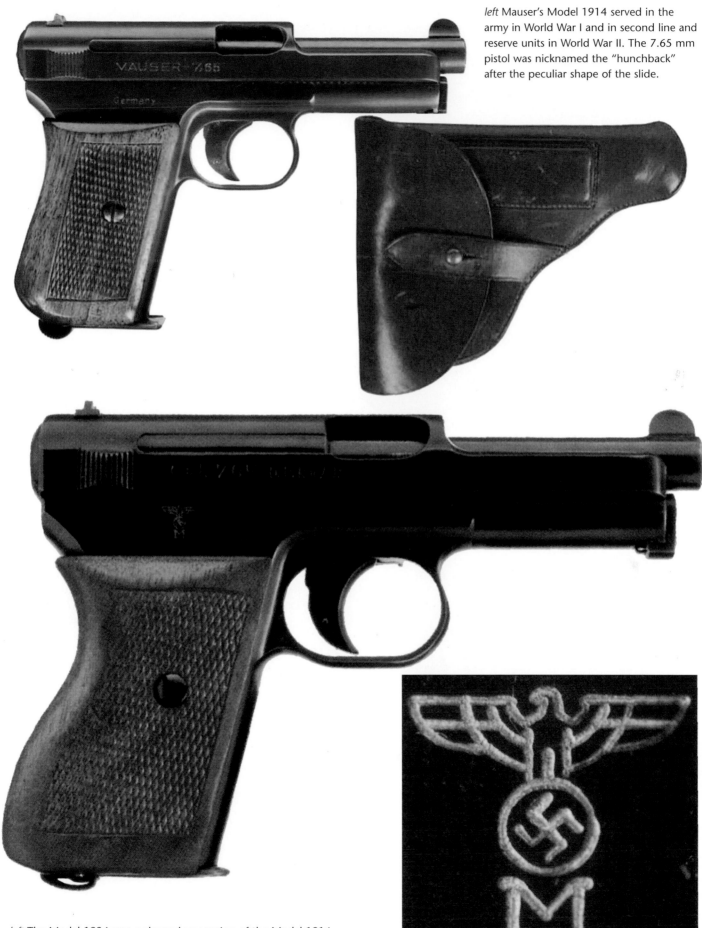

left The Model 1934 was a cleaned-up version of the Model 1914, with a more contoured grip and a polished finish. This one saw naval rather than army service.

above The Walther PP (*Polizei Pistole*) was introduced in 1929, and was the first truly successful automatic to use a double-action mechanism with an external hammer. The user could safely carry the pistol with a round chambered, ready for quick use. It saw service with police and military units, mainly in 7.65 mm caliber. The butt was quite short so many had grip extensions fitted to the bottom of their magazines (as seen here).

above Another Walther PP, this time with a wooden grip and no magazine extension. The PP held 8 rounds of 7.65 mm ammunition.

above In 1931 Walther produced this smaller version of the PP, known as the PPK (*Polizei Pistole Kriminale*), intended for concealed use by police and security personnel. The PPK had similar safety features to its larger brother and held 6 rounds of 7.65 mm ammunition. It proved to be a huge success, the combination of compact size, quick shooting and reasonable firepower proving popular with both police and military officers. This one has the Nazi eagle on its bakelite grips.

above Another PPK with plastic grips in an imitation wood pattern. Almost all PPKs are seen with grip extensions under the magazine.

LIGHT PISTOL

The infantry introduced the Walther Light Pistol in 1928 to fire a cartridge for signaling by day or illuminating by night. It had a smooth-bore, 26.7 mm (1 in) long barrel and was fairly heavy 2.9 lb (1.32 kg). Like all such weapons (for example, the British Verey pistol) the German weapon was loaded by breaking the weapon open, inserting a flare cartridge and then closing. The firer then cocked the hammer, held the pistol over his head pointing in the general direction of the sky, and pulled the trigger. During the war the weight was reduced to 1.7 lb (0.77 kg) by using a lighter metal, resulting in the *Leuchtpistole Model* 1942.

There were also two rather more offensive conversions, the first of which was the *Kampfpistole* (fighting pistol) in which the caliber was reduced to 23 mm (0.9 in) by means of a rifled insert. The original munition was a *Sprengranate*, which carried a 1 oz (30 gm) warhead and was quickly found to be ineffective. This led to the development of the *Wurfkorper* 358 LP round which combined the warhead of the *Stiehlgranate* (stick grenade) with a 23 mm (0.9 in) shaft which was inserted into the barrel. This time the warhead was too heavy, resulting in such a short range that the firers became seriously discouraged. Next came the *Wurfkorper* 361 LP round, which consisted of a *Eihandgranate* (egg-grenade) mounted on a sub-caliber shaft with a wooden sabot which was jettisoned as soon as it left the muzzle. The shaft was originally made of wood, then of steel and finally of plastic. The steel-shaft version weighed 12 oz (0.34 kg)and had a muzzle velocity of 131 ft/sec (40 m/s) which gave it a theoretical range of 93 yd, (85 m) while the plastic-shaft version was marginally lighter and added just over 11 yd (10.1 m) to the range. Over 250,000 of these were manufactured between 1941 and 1942.

An anti-tank round was also developed, with a hollow-charge warhead. Designated the *Wurfgranate* 326

above Before the advent of the lightweight tactical radio, a flare pistol was an essential tool for a small unit commander. It could be used to signal to his own units, to flanking units or to fire support units such as artillery, armor or even aircraft. At night they were also useful for illuminating the battlefield.

above The same pistol broken open for loading. The vertical lever at the front of the trigger guard is operated to unlock the barrel, which hinges forward rather like that of a shotgun.

Hohlladung/Leuchtpistole (HP/LP) this had a 0.8 oz (20 gm) hexogene warhead and was capable of penetrating up to 2 in (51 mm) of armor. Some 400,000 of these grenades were manufactured in 1941–2. The main problem was accuracy, since the chance of hitting a tank at a range of 100 yards (91 m), let alone the theoretical maximum of 300 yards (274 m), even if it was sideways on, was remote, to say the least. Finally, there was a whistling cartridge *(Pfeifpatrone)* whose sole use was as a gas warning signal.

above A less common double-barreled flare pistol. By enabling different combinations of colored flares to be fired at once, this pistol allowed more complex signal patterns, where different combinations meant different messages.

above and right: Another single-barreled pistol, this time with the blue finish almost completely worn away. Next to it is a metal ammunition box which could hold up to 24 cartridges of various color and pattern.

131

MACHINE PISTOLS

The German Army of World War One was the first to introduce a new type of weapon, known variously as the machine pistol, sub-machine gun or machine-carbine. These were light automatic weapons firing pistol-type ammunition which resulted in a weapon which was easy to carry but capable of producing a high volume of fire at close ranges. Their effect was heightened by the characteristic noise. The first of these, the Bergmann MP18 entered service in the last months of World War II and so impressed the Allies that its manufacture was formally banned in the Versailles Treaty.

In World War II the German Army issued such weapons on a very wide scale, particularly in the infantry, where they were carried by platoon and section commanders. Further weapons were issued from 1943 onwards, increasing the scale to two per squad, and on occasions whole platoons were issued with the weapons for specialized, close-quarter fighting missions.

above The first German sub-machine gun was the MP18 which entered service during World War I. A later version, known as the MP28, served in World War II, mainly with SS and police units.

Erma MP38

Type: machine pistol
Origin: Erma-Werke, Erfurt, Germany
Caliber: 9 mm
Weight (empty): 9 lb 0 oz
Overall length (butt extended): 32.8 in; butt folded: 24.8 in
Barrel length: 9.72 in; 6-groove rifling; right-hand twist
Ammunition: 9 x 19 mm rimless Parabellum
Muzzle velocity: 1,250 ft/sec
Feed: thirty-two round box; 23 oz when filled.
Cyclic rate: 520–540 rpm

above The MP38 was a classic design which became the iconic image of the German Stormtrooper. Made from metal and plastic, and with a folding metal stock, it set the pattern for most future sub-machine guns.

above A weary *Gebirgsjager* with his MP40. He wears the triple magazine pouches for this weapon and displays both an Iron Cross 2nd class and the Infantry Assault badge.

The Erma-Werke at Erfurt won a contract in the late 1930s to design and develop a new sub-machine gun, principally for use by the armored and airborne divisions then being formed. Such was the pressure on the defense industry at the time that the new weapon was developed in a matter of months and was issued in late 1938 as the *Maschinenpistole* Model 1938 (MP38). It was the first weapon of its type to be fabricated entirely from metal and plastic, with no woodwork of any kind. The traditional heavy butt was replaced by a folding, tubular metal stock, while the usual machined receiver was replaced by a steel tube, slotted to reduce weight. The MP38 proved to be an excellent weapon, but despite the innovative design it was still expensive to produce. Its one major operational shortcoming was that it did not have a safety device and it was possible for a sharp jolt to bounce the bolt back and fire a round, a design problem it shared with the British Sten gun. All this led to a re-examination of the design and production processes which led to the MP40; this made much greater use of pressings, spot-welding and brazing, and also had a safety-catch. Known to the Allies by its designer's name as the "*Schmeisser*" it was greatly respected by the Allies.

Officers and soldiers armed with the MP38 or MP40 carried seven magazines. One was on the gun and six were in specially designed pouches which were part of the wearer's field harness. The cyclic rate of fire was around 500 rounds per minute but the weapon tended to jam if fired in bursts of more than about 8–10 rounds.

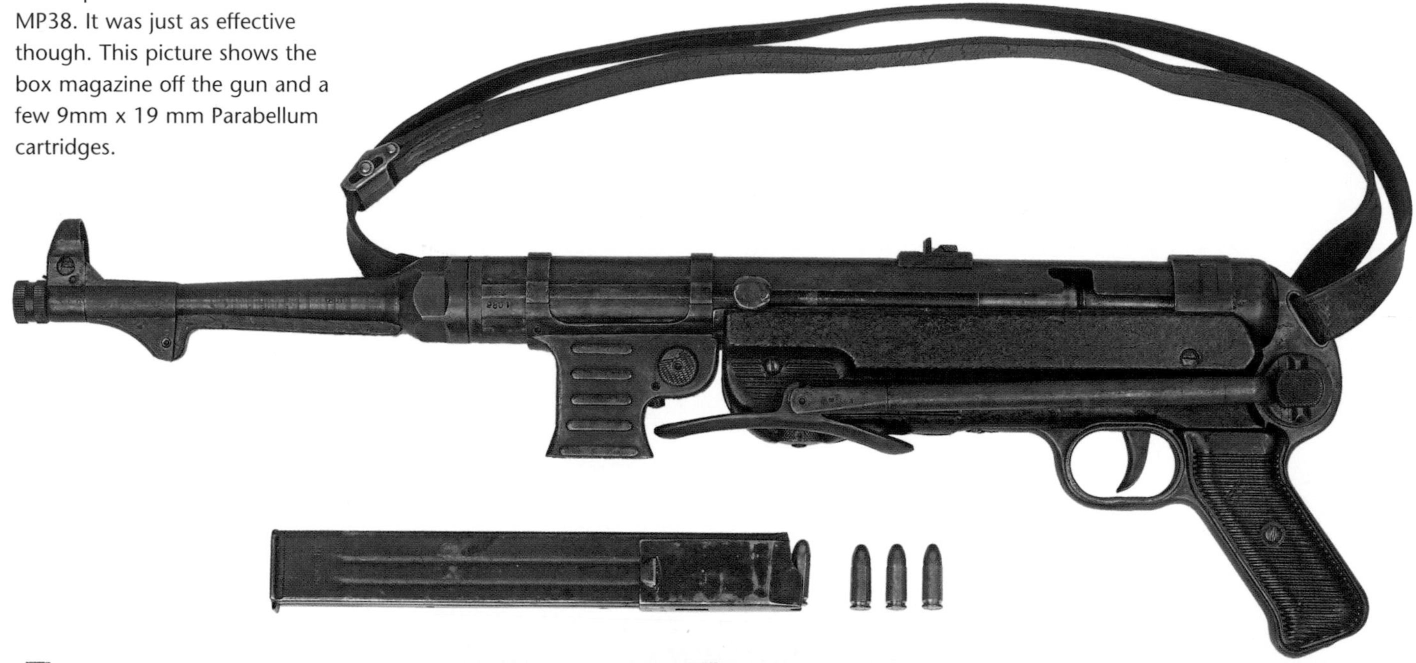

below The MP40 was made using simpler manufacturing techniques than the earlier MP38. It was just as effective though. This picture shows the box magazine off the gun and a few 9mm x 19 mm Parabellum cartridges.

above and right The MP41 was a modification to the original MP38 design to use wooden furniture and stock. The ensuing weapon was heavier, took longer to make than the MP40 and was not a success.

M.P.41
PATENT SCHMEISSER
C. G. HAENEL, SUHL

HAENEL MP44

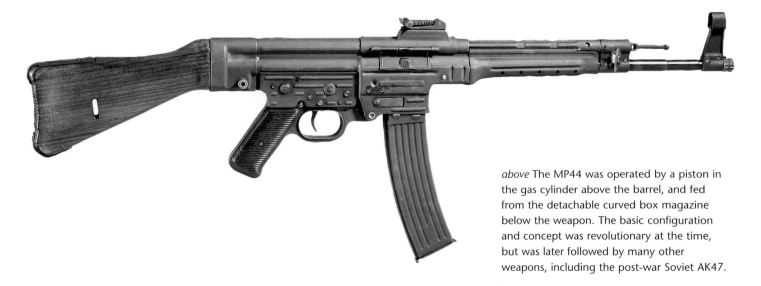

Type: machine pistol/assault rifle
Origin: Haenel Gewehrfabrik, Suhl,
Germany
Caliber: 7.92 mm
Weight (empty): 11 lb 4 oz (5.10 kg)
Overall length: 37 in (0.94 m)
Barrel length: 16.5 in (419 mm); 4-
groove rifling; right-hand twist
Ammunition: 7.92 x33 mm Kurz
Muzzle velocity: 2,125 ft/sec (648 m/s)
Feed: 30-round box
Cyclic rate: 500 rpm

above Regarded as the first modern assault rifle, the MP44 was designed to fulfil the roles of both rifle and sub-machine gun. By using a shorter and less-powerful 7.92 mm cartridge than the K98 it allowed for fully-automatic fire from a rifle-sized weapon which remained effective over the combat ranges that mattered.

The great majority of weapons fit neatly into one of the four categories of pistol, sub-machine gun, rifle or machine gun, but a few straddled the divide between two categories. One such was the MP44 which lay almost exactly midway between rifle and sub-machine gun. It was the outcome a of a long development program, which dated back to World War II, to produce an entirely new type of weapon for the infantry, which was to be much lighter than traditional rifles such as the G.98, with a much greater rate of fire, but still possessing good effective range, accuracy and stopping power.

This program led to the 1942 appearance of the 7.92 x 33 mm *Kurz* (short) round and a new weapon, the *Maschinenkarabine* Model 42 (Haenel) MK 42(H), of which some 8,000 were

manufactured. A competing design by Walther was dropped, but the MK 42(H) had some shortcomings, and as the army wanted to input its extensive combat experience in Russia in 1941–2, the design was reworked by Hugo Schmeisser, resulting in the MP43, which was immediately placed in production. Like the MK42(H), the new weapon was of pressed steel construction with the piston moving in a gas-cylinder above the barrel, but with a longer barrel and a shorter gas cylinder, and while it seems heavy today it was a revolution by World War II standards. In 1944 the designation was changed to MP44, although there were no known advances in the design and then the weapon was reclassified as a *Sturmgewehr* (assault rifle) StG 44, an expression allegedly coined by Hitler

himself. It was manufactured by Erfurt, Erma, Haenel and Mauser, but for reasons never clearly explained production waned from early 1944 onwards and it failed to have the front-line impact it undoubtedly should have had.

One version of the MP44 which has always captured the imagination is the device for "shooting around corners" – the *Krummlauf* (curved barrel). Quite how the requirement arose is a matter of dispute: one suggestion is that it was intended for tank crews to fire at enemy infantry on the outside of their vehicle, another that it was for infantry involved in street fighting to fire around the corner of a house without exposing themselves. Whichever is correct, the result was two versions: the first turned the bullet through thirty degrees and worked, while the second turned it

above The MP44 was operated by a piston in the gas cylinder above the barrel, and fed from the detachable curved box magazine below the weapon. The basic configuration and concept was revolutionary at the time, but was later followed by many other weapons, including the post-war Soviet AK47.

through a full ninety degrees and did not. The device consisted of a curved extension which was clamped onto the muzzle, and there were a number of gas-escape holes at the start of the curve to slow the bullet down slightly.

This barrel extension was small and neat, but the sight, which was brazed onto the extension, was large and bulky. The device worked very satisfactorily with the 7.92 mm Kurz round, but not at all well with the normal 7.92

mm round. Unsurprisingly, the erosion was considerable and the operational life of even the thirty degree version was relatively short.

above Most of the structure was made from simple stampings and pressings spot-welded together, although it still had a fixed wooden stock. This one is the SLG 44 version, converted to fire single shots.

below Detachable magazines could hold up to 30 rounds, although the wise soldier would only put 27 or 28 in to avoid compressing the magazine spring too much. The bullet was the same as that fired by other German rifles, but here it was matched to a shorter cartridge case containing less propellant.

above An MP44 fitted with the legendary *"Krummlauf"* attachment on the end of the barrel. The sighting mirror on the *Krummlauf* is missing from this example.

above An MP44 and *Krummlauf* device together. For a device that was barely usable in most combat situations, great effort was spent developing and manufacturing the *Krummlauf*.

above The *Krummlauf* device diverted the bullet through 30 degrees as it left the barrel. It allowed vehicle-mounted personnel to engage targets who were close to the side or underside of the vehicle.

OTHER MACHINE PISTOLS

While the MP40 and MP44 weapons are the best known of German machine pistols, the armed forces used a range of other weapons too. Some were obsolescent German designs, others were foreign weapons taken into service.

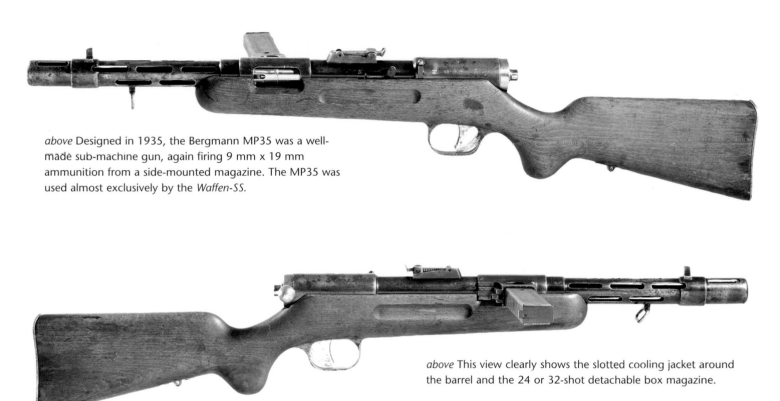

above Designed in 1935, the Bergmann MP35 was a well-made sub-machine gun, again firing 9 mm x 19 mm ammunition from a side-mounted magazine. The MP35 was used almost exclusively by the *Waffen-SS.*

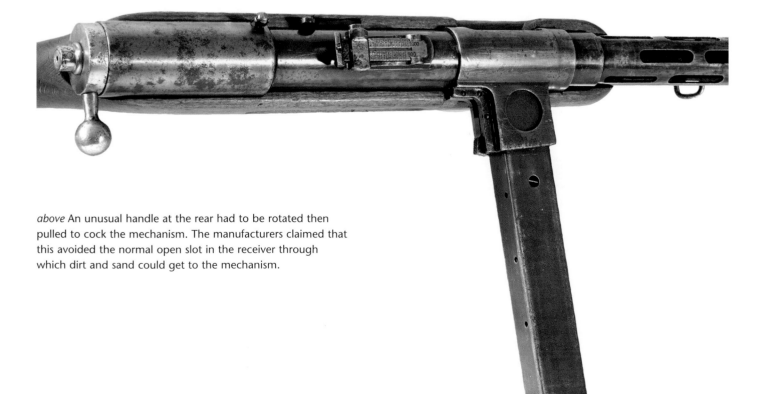

above This view clearly shows the slotted cooling jacket around the barrel and the 24 or 32-shot detachable box magazine.

above An unusual handle at the rear had to be rotated then pulled to cock the mechanism. The manufacturers claimed that this avoided the normal open slot in the receiver through which dirt and sand could get to the mechanism.

above German soldiers crouch down behind cover as shells detonate over the slope. Behind them, on top of the ammunition box, is a captured Soviet PPSh sub-machine gun.

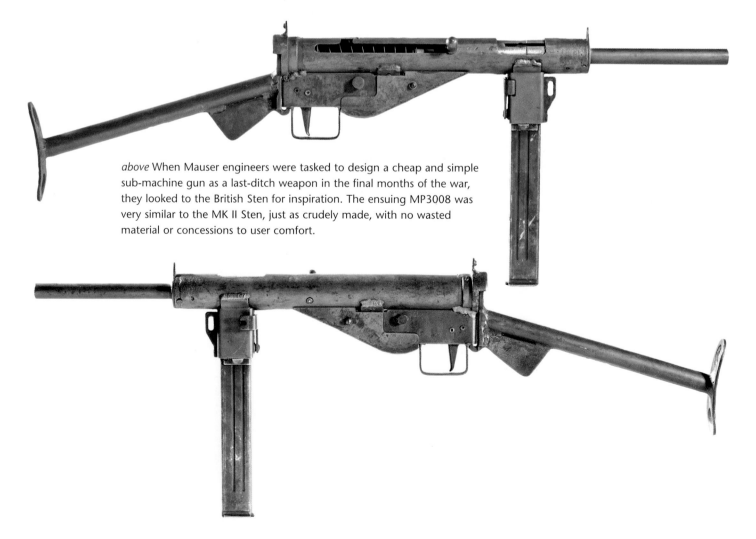

above When Mauser engineers were tasked to design a cheap and simple sub-machine gun as a last-ditch weapon in the final months of the war, they looked to the British Sten for inspiration. The ensuing MP3008 was very similar to the MK II Sten, just as crudely made, with no wasted material or concessions to user comfort.

left The Soviet PPSh was another simple, but effective sub-machine gun which stood up well to the rigors of combat. This simplicity, combined with a 71-shot drum magazine, made captured weapons popular with German soldiers.

right A *Waffen-SS* NCO with an Italian Beretta Model 38/42, a 9 mm sub-machine gun used extensively by German forces. The Beretta was well made, with a wooden stock and muzzle compensator to prevent muzzle climb on automatic fire. This solder has a map case hanging from his belt as well as a single triple pouch for the Beretta's long 30-shot magazines. He is not wearing the full harness and has a black SS sidecap in place of a steel helmet. He is wearing late-war "Pea" style camouflage uniform, although he has full-length boots rather than the late-war shorter boots.

above While otherwise based on the Sten, the MP3008 followed the MP38 in having a vertical magazine feeding from underneath.

MACHINE GUNS

Its experiences during World War I made the German army fully aware of the battlefield value of machine guns *(Maschinengewehr)* and development continued during the inter-war years, resulting in a very effective new weapon, the MG34, but this only began to enter service in 1939. As a result, several earlier models remained in service well into the second or third year of the war. In the infantry battalion every squad had a light machine gun, with further weapons available in the Machine Gun Company.

The Germans divided their machine guns into only two categories – light *(leichte)*, which were bipod-mounted, and heavy *(schwer)* which were tripod-mounted. Both categories used MG34s or 42s firing rifle caliber (i.e., 7.92 mm) ammunition. Thus, the MG34, for example, was "light" when used by an infantry squad and mounted on a bipod, but "heavy" when it was used by a Machine Gun Company and mounted on a tripod.

above The MG08 was the German Army's standard machine gun in World War II. A belt-fed water-cooled weapon based on the original Maxim designs, it was usually fired from a heavy "sledge" mount. It remained in use with second line formations through to 1945.

right The MG34 was the first successful attempt to combine the roles of heavy and light machine gun in a single weapon. Here we see one in the sustained fire role, mounted on a tripod and with the gunner using the tripod screw thread to adjust elevation and range.

Maxim *Maschinengewehr* Model 1908

Type: water-cooled heavy machine gun
Origin: Königliche Gewehrfabrik, Spandau, Germany
Caliber: 7.92 x 57 mm Mauser
Weight (gun): 58.5 lb (26.54); (tripod) 70.5 lb (32 kg)
Barrel length: 28.3 in (719 mm); 4-groove rifling; right-hand twist
Ammunition: 7.92 x 57 mm rimless
Cyclic rate: 450 rpm
Muzzle velocity: 2,925 ft/sec (892 m/s)
Feed: 250-round cloth belt

above The MG08/15 was an attempt to make a light machine gun out of the MG08.

Large numbers of the MG08 remained in service with the German Army until 1940–1 when they were finally replaced by the MG 34. Based on a design by the British Sir Hiram Maxim, MG08 was a standard Maxim with a plain steel water-jacket, muzzle recoil booster and a conical flash hider. It entered German service mounted on a heavy and complicated, tubular-steel sled, which formed part of the tripod mounting for firing, although the whole contraption was normally moved on a light, horse-drawn cart.

There were also several variants of the MG08 still in service in 1939–40. One of these was the MG 08/15, which was one of the early attempts to devise a bipod-mounted light machine gun for use in the infantry squad. This had the standard MG08 firing mechanism and barrel, but with a lighter water-jacket and receiver casing, a wooden butt, and a pistol grip. Ammunition feed was from a drum mounted on the right of the weapon containing the usual 250-round cloth belt. Weight was reduced to 31 lb, but it was a large and heavy weapon for squad use, especially with the associated water-can and rubber tubing. This was succeeded three years later by an air-cooled version, the MG 08/18 which had the water-jacket removed, with the barrel now surrounded by a thin steel perforated jacket; this, too, was still in service, in 1939–40.

Mauser *Maschinengewehr* Model 1934 (MG34)

above The MG34 in the squad light machine gun role.

Type: air-cooled, light/heavy, bipod/tripod-mounted machine gun
Origin: Mauser AG, Oberndorf/Neckar, Germany
Caliber: 7.92 x 57 mm Mauser
Weight (gun): 26.7 lb (12.1 kg); (tripod) 42.3 lb (19.2 kg)
Overall length: 48 in (1.22 m)
Barrel length: 24.8 in (630 mm); 4-groove rifling; right-hand twist
Ammunition: 7.92 x 57 mm rimless
Cyclic rate: 650rpm
Muzzle velocity: 2,480 ft/sec (756 m/s)
Feed: 50-round metal-link belt or 75-round saddle drum
Range: open sights – 2,200 yd (2012 m); tripod-mounted with dial sight – 3,827 yd.

above Surprisingly light and able to provide heavy fire, the MG34 was made to a very high standard of design and build quality. This precision was its only weak spot as it made the gun vulnerable to stoppages caused by dirt and dust.

The MG34 was the first indigenously-designed and truly modern machine gun to enter service with the German Army and was, in many respects, a remarkable achievement. It worked by the somewhat unusual combination of recoil and gas; when the round was fired the barrel recoiled, additional thrust being imparted by some of the gases which were trapped in the muzzle cone and deflected backwards. The actual recoil of the weapon was short, just three-sixteenths of an inch, which was just sufficient for the bolthead to be rotated through 90 degrees and unlock when the pressure was low enough for this to happen safely. This took place over the next nine-sixteenths of an inch at which point the barrel stopped, while the bolt continued moving to the rear until it hit the buffer and the return-spring was fully compressed, at which point the forward action started. This involved the forward movement of the bolt which fed the next cartridge into the chamber, locked itself and fired the round.

The new weapon had many excellent features including easy stripping and the use of high-impact plastics for the butt and pistol grip. Unusually, the MG34 had no change-lever, there being a simple two-part trigger which fired single rounds or full automatic depending on whether the upper part (marked "E") or the lower part (marked "D") was pressed. The MG34 fired either a belt or from a double saddle-drum. Barrel-changing was necessary

below A close up of the receiver and feed, complete with 50-round ammunition drum. The gun could feed from this, from a 75-round twin saddle drum or from a 50-shot belt. Many soldiers preferred the belt in the ground role as it made the rate of fire slower and the gun more controllable.

after firing about 250 rounds continuously, but was quick and easy.

When used as a heavy machine gun, the bipod was removed and weapon mounted on the tripod (Dreibein), which had two legs forward and one to the rear, and was secured to the cradle by a clamp. The cradle incorporated a buffering device which enabled the gun to recoil as a whole in the mounting. The elevating gear was fitted between the rear of the cradle and the rear leg of the tripod and incorporated the trigger group, a handle and a housing for an oil-bottle. An unusual feature of the mounting was the provision of an automatic "searching device", operated by the recoil of the weapon, which elevated or depressed the weapon by predetermined steps thus increasing the beaten zone against an area target.

On the forward side of the joint of the tripod was a socket for the "anti-aircraft attachment" which was essentially a simple rod some two feet long, which raised the weapon, enabling it to be used against low-flying aircraft.

The MG34 was sensitive to dirt and had to be kept scrupulously clean and well oiled, but that was a small price to pay for such an excellent performance.

Two attempts were made to develop improved versions, including the MG34S and MG34/41. Among the measures tried were a shorter barrel, increasing the rate-of-fire and doing away with the single-round option. But, as good as the MG34 was, there was an even better weapon about to enter service.

above and right German machine guns, especially the MG42, had a high rate of fire and quickly consumed large amounts of ammunition. Resupply was a constant problem for the infantry soldier. This metal-framed carrier allowed two boxes of 300 rounds each to be carried on the soldier's back in a reasonably portable pack.

MAUSER *MASCHINENGEWEHR* MODEL 1942 (MG42)

below The MG42 was much cheaper to make than the MG34 and was more able to cope with irregular maintenance and the dirt and dust of combat.

Type: air-cooled, light/heavy, bipod/tripod-mounted machine gun
Origin: Mauser AG, Oberndorf/Neckar, Germany
Caliber: 7.92 x 57 mm Mauser
Weight (gun): 25.5 lb; (tripod) 42.3 lb
Overall length: 48 in
Barrel length: 21.0 in; 4-groove rifling; right-hand twist
Ammunition: 7.92 x 57 mm rimless
Cyclic rate: 1,200 rpm
Muzzle velocity: 2,480 ft/sec
Feed: 50-round metal-link belt
RANGE: open sights – 2,200 yd; tripod-mounted with dial sight – 3,827 yd.

below Using an air-cooled weapon in the sustained fire role calls for the ability to change barrels quickly as the gun heats up. Here is a metal container for a single MG42 barrel, complete with spare barrel.

Early in the war the German Army established an operational requirement for a machine gun which would combine combat effectiveness with ease and economy of production. Once the basic design had been established the project was passed to Dr Grunow, a well-known authority on mass production using metal stampings, riveting, spot welding and brazing, and any other method which did not require complicated equipment, specialized techniques or highly skilled manpower. The outcome was the MG42, one of the finest and most feared weapons to be fielded in World War II, and which could be produced in half the time of the MG34.

It resembled the MG34 in some ways, using the same principles of short recoil assisted by gas pressure from a muzzle booster, but the main difference was in the way in which the bolt locked. The

MG34 used a rotating bolt with an interrupted thread which locked into the barrel extension, but the new gun used a system originally patented by a Polish engineer named Edward Stecke, in which the bolt-head carried two rollers which were held close together until it was ready to lock when they were forced outwards into grooves in the barrel extension. The firing pin could not move forward until these rollers were fully in their grooves, which ensured that the bolt was locked at the moment of firing. Once recoil started the rollers hit a cam path which forced them inwards out of their recesses, thus unlocking the bolt and allowing the cycle to continue.

The gun fired 50-round, metal-linked belts of standard 7.92 mm ammunition, but it incorporated a new and very effective feed system which has since been widely copied.

left An MG42 crew in a late-war setting. The tripod-mounted gun is using a belt fed from the metal ammunition box on the ground. Both crewmembers are wearing *Waffen-SS* reversible smocks, with winter camouflage on the inside and "Oak leaf" on the outside. Note the open side of the barrel jacket on this side of the gun, enabling the barrel to be removed and changed in a few seconds.

right By the end of the war German squads were built around the firepower of the MG42, with the rifleman mainly there to protect the gun and carry the ammunition for it.

The lightness of the weapon, coupled with its method of operation, led to a very high rate of fire of some 1,200 rounds per minute, resulting in a characteristic "ripping" noise which once heard was never forgotten. This rate of fire also caused considerable vibration which had an adverse effect on accuracy, and although the muzzle brake was ingeniously designed to help stabilize the weapon this was never fully overcome. An additional feature of the high ammunition expenditure was that it placed a considerable load on the logistics system and from 1943 onwards, most German infantrymen in combat were to be seen with one or more belts of ammunition hanging around their necks.

There were a variety of mountings, including the bipod, tripod and anti-aircraft, as for the MG34 In addition, there was a complicated add-on to the rear-end which enabled the gun to be aimed and fired from a fully concealed position some two-three feet below the sight-line

In 1944 a new project for a successor to MG42 was under development. Tentatively designated MG45, it was overtaken by the end of the war.

below Both the MG34 and MG42 could use *Gurttrommel* ammunition drums such as this one. Inside the single drum would be a normal 50-round belt, and the whole unit would be clipped to the side of the gun. Also shown here is a two-drum *Gurttrommeltrager* drum carrier. Later in the war such carriers were made from canvas and leather.

147

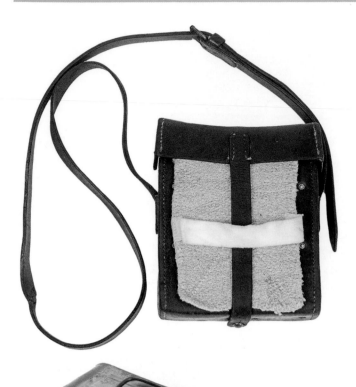

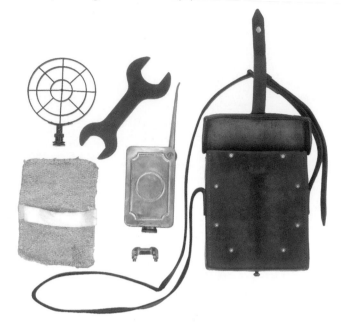

left and below Machine gunners carried this gunners pouch on their belt or on a strap over their shoulder. The closed pouch had a heat pad on the outside, which was used by the gunner to protect his hands when changing a hot barrel. Inside were various assembly and disassembly tools, an attachable foresight for anti-aircraft use, oil bottles, cleaning kit and other equipment.

*below*The MG15 was designed for aerial use, mounted to defend bombers and transport aircraft. When MG34 production failed to keep up with demand the MG15 was fitted with a bipod and issued to ground troops. It fed from a 75-round saddle-drum and used some of the design features of the later MG34. Notice the awkward carrying handle next to the saddle drum.

above Many different styles of can were used to hold the oil essential for weapons cleaning and maintenance. This is a larger one for use with a machine gun, and comes complete with an applicator brush built in to the screw lid.

right As with other weapons, the Germans pressed the best foreign designs into service as they gained control of their munitions factories. This man is carrying a Czech ZB26, a gas-operated light machine gun firing from a box magazine above the receiver. The ZB26 was a remarkably reliable and effective light machine gun, and a version chambered for .303 in ammunition became the Bren, the British and Commonwealth armies' standard section machine gun. Note here that the soldiers' *Tonister* backpacks have been left behind on the bank as the men climb into the rubber boat.

right A saddle drum as used by an MG15. Between them the two drums held 75 rounds, feeding alternatively from left and right to preserve the balance of the weapon. A similar design was also used by the MG34 although this fell from favor in the early war years.

GRENADES

German hand grenades were of two types, but both were offensive in nature. This meant that they had a thin casing and relied on blast rather than fragmentation for their effect, while the fact that they could be thrown to a greater distance than their effective radius of burst meant that they could be used in the open by advancing troops. There were two types, popularly known as "Stick grenades" and "Egg grenades", of which the former was much more widely used.

STICK GRENADES

The *Stielhandgranate* (stick hand grenade) appeared in 1915 and was improved in 1917 and, again in 1924 and 1939. They had a warhead consisting of a metal canister, made of thin iron or sheet steel, containing 6–7 oz (170-200 g) of high explosive. This was secured by a metal collar to a hollow wooden handle, through the center of which ran a double length of cord, which was attached, at the inner end, through a lead ball to a friction-activated igniter-detonator system.

In the Model 24 at the open end, the cord, which included a small length of slack, was attached to a porcelain bead, which was held in place until required by a zinc screw cap. To activate the weapon, the rifleman unscrewed the cap, which allowed the porcelain ball to fall free to the extent of the cord, which he then pulled immediately prior to throwing. In the Model 1939 the porcelain bead was dispensed with, instead of which the cord was secured to the inside of the screw cap. As a (possibly unnecessary) reminder, the warhead was marked with a stenciled notice: *"vor Gebrauch Sprengkapsel einsetzen"* (before use, insert detonator).

These stick grenades were very widely issued and two or more were normally carried by most riflemen, with the handle stuck through his belt until

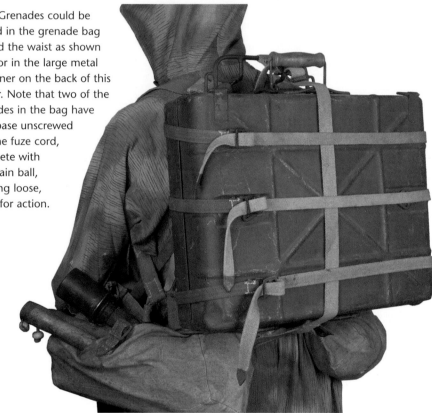

right Grenades could be carried in the grenade bag around the waist as shown here, or in the large metal container on the back of this soldier. Note that two of the grenades in the bag have their base unscrewed and the fuze cord, complete with porcelain ball, hanging loose, ready for action.

just before they were to be used. There was also a special jacket, worn over the normal tunic, which had pockets for ten grenades, five in front and five to the rear.

A particular use, devised in the field, was the *"geballte Ladung"* (demolition charge), in which the warhead canisters of six grenades were detached from their handles and then bound securely around a seventh, which did retain its handle. This then formed a conveniently concentrated and powerful charge for use against targets such as pillboxes and tanks, provided, of course, the thrower could get close enough.

Another wartime development was a cylindrical metal fragmentation sleeve which fitted over the canister and was held in place by three clips and a locking ring. There were two types of sleeve, one smooth, the other scored in a rectangular pattern to enhance the fragmentation effect.

	Length	Diameter (max)	Total weight	Explosive weight
Stick grenade Model 1924	14 in (356 mm)	3 in (76 mm)	21 oz (600 g)	6 oz (170 g)
Stick grenade Model 1939	16 in (406 mm)	3 in (76 mm)	22 oz (620 g)	6 oz (200 g)
Stick grenade Model 1943	16 in (406 mm)	3 in (76 mm)	22 oz (620 g)	6 oz (200 g)
Egg grenade Model 1939	3 in (76 mm)	2 in (51 mm)	12 oz (340 g)	

above The NCO is unscrewing the cap on his grenade, ready to pull the cord and ignite the fuze before throwing. He has another tucked into his belt, behind the magazine pouches. Uniform details suggest that this is a pre-war exercise or during the very early days of the war.

Nebel Handgranate Model 1939 (Nb.Hgr.39)

A modified version of the stick grenade was introduced in 1939, in which the high explosive warhead was replaced by a composition (powdered zinc/hexachlorethane). When ignited, this generated a dense cloud of smoke which emerged through eight holes in the base of the cylinder. This grenade was originally identified by a thin white band painted near the base of the canister, but a later version, the Nb.Hgr39b, had raised ridges on the handle and a much thicker white band.

Stielhandgranate Model 1943

The Model 1943 had a similar external appearance but was very different in operation. In this version the handle was solid and activation was by the same Brennzunder 39 (ignition fuse Model 1939) as in the Eihandgraranate Model 1939, thus making the head self-contained.

above Two Model 24 or 39 stick grenades. These had a reasonable explosive content but very little fragmentation effect, making them useful for offensive purposes (when friendly troops are not in cover) but less so for defensive use.

Egg Grenades

The Egg-grenade *(Eihandgranate)* Model 1939 was, as its name indicates, egg-shaped, with a body of .02 inch 5.1 mm sheet metal; it was 3 in (76 mm) tall and with a maximum diameter of 2 in (51 mm). It had a raised rib around the body at the maximum diameter, where the two body halves were crimped together, but which also aided recognition by feel at night. As originally manufactured, the outer surface of the body was smooth but in 1944 a new version was issued where the surface was scored in a rectangular pattern to aid fragmentation. The egg-grenade was about half the weight of the stick grenade, with the result that most riflemen could throw it further.

The fuse-well extended to the center of the device. To arm the grenade, the wingnut at the top was unscrewed, exposing the well, into which was inserted the detonator, usually the standard Number 8 and the wingnut replaced. In the center of the wingnut was a small porcelain ball retained in place by a boss and screw-thread. Immediately prior to throwing, this ball was unscrewed and it then dangled on a short cord, which, when pulled firmly, activated the fuse. There were various types of delay fuse, which were color-coded: red – 4 seconds; blue – 4.5 seconds (normal use); yellow – 7.5 seconds; gray – 10 seconds.

left A Model 39 'egg' grenade with smooth outer shell. The same fuze unit was used in the top of the Model 43 stick grenade.

BAYONETS AND KNIVES

The vast majority of infantrymen issued with either the *Gewehr 98* or *Karabiner 98* were also issued with a traditional-style bayonet, which fitted on to lugs on the underside of the fore-end of the barrel and was held in place by a spring-loaded catch. These bayonets were the *Seitengewehr* (literally, sidearm) Model S98/05, which were produced in vast quantities over many years by a number of manufacturers; not surprisingly, there were many minor differences in design.

In essence the bayonet consisted of a blade, cross-piece and handle, and when not in use was stored in a metal scabbard, which was carried in a leather or canvas frog. The blade was 9–10 inch (229-254 mm) long, made of good quality steel and running along most of its length was a "fuller," a centuries-old term derived from sword-manufacture, which was a wide, longitudinal groove. Among soldiers, the reputed purpose of this fuller was supposed either to make the blade easier to withdraw from a victim, or to cause internal bleeding and then to close the wound as the bayonet was withdrawn, thus ensuring that the wound was fatal. In reality its purpose was much simpler, being to act as an I-shaped girder to make the blade stiffer and stronger. One version of the bayonet had serrations along the upper edge and was popularly known as the "saw-back;" this was originally intended for use by engineers in World War I, but may have seen wider use in World War II.

above Two Kar 98 bayonets and their frogs and scabbards. The upper frog is the general issue type, made from black leather and with a metal scabbard. The lower one is the webbed fabric tropical variant (also used extensively in Europe) with the same metal scabbard. Note the slots cut into the grip of each bayonet and the long groove (or "fuller") in the blade.

The bayonet handle served two purposes: to enable the device to be grasped while fitting it to or removing it from the weapon (fixing/unfixing), or to enable it to be used as a combat knife. It was originally made of wood, but during World War II handles were made from bakelite or a reddish-brown composition. The end of the handle, the pommel, also contained the spring-loaded retaining catch.

The scabbard was made of mild steel with an insert in the throat which guided the blade when it was being replaced. Swords are generally secured in place in their scabbards by a shaped wood insert, but the bayonet fitted loosely and was held in place and prevented from rattling by a long piece of curved metal which acted as a spring. This scabbard was carried in a frog made of either black leather or canvas, which was attached to the infantryman's belt.

A very long, thin, "screwdriver" bayonet was produced for the *Fallschirmgewehr* 42. This was permanently fitted to the weapon and folded back under the barrel when not in use.

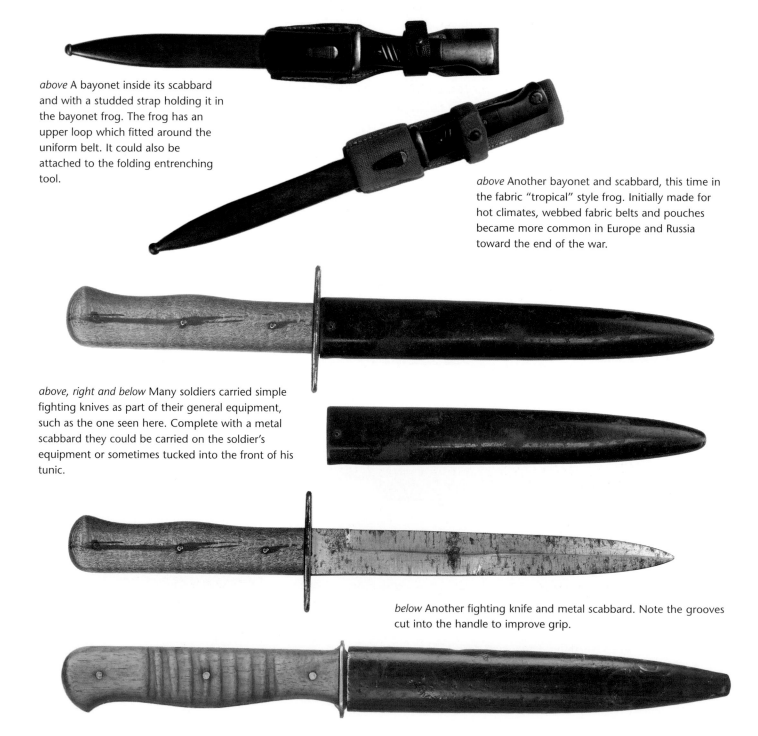

above A bayonet inside its scabbard and with a studded strap holding it in the bayonet frog. The frog has an upper loop which fitted around the uniform belt. It could also be attached to the folding entrenching tool.

above Another bayonet and scabbard, this time in the fabric "tropical" style frog. Initially made for hot climates, webbed fabric belts and pouches became more common in Europe and Russia toward the end of the war.

above, right and below Many soldiers carried simple fighting knives as part of their general equipment, such as the one seen here. Complete with a metal scabbard they could be carried on the soldier's equipment or sometimes tucked into the front of his tunic.

below Another fighting knife and metal scabbard. Note the grooves cut into the handle to improve grip.

MORTARS

The German Army was very keen on the use of mortars within the infantry battalion, but, somewhat surprisingly in view of the excellence of their other weapons, their own mortars were not particularly good and were frequently outclassed, particularly by the Soviet designs. As a result, foreign designs were quickly taken into use as they stood, while several Soviet designs were simply reverse-engineered and placed in production.

LIGHT MORTARS

Following World War I many armies developed very light and extremely simple mortars for use at platoon level. Despite their excellence in other types of infantry weapons, however, the German Army's 5cm *Granatwerfer* 36 (50 mm Mortar Model 1936), although widely deployed, was too heavy, too complicated and had insufficient range and accuracy. The barrel and the baseplate were carried separately, but once assembled there were two leveling handles, a traversing handwheel and elevating screw, all of which made it a complicated equipment and the complete weapon weighed 30.75 lbs (13.95 kg) – three times that of its British counterpart, the 2 inch (51 mm) mortar. There was only one munition, the *Wurfgranat* 38 (Mortar Bomb, Model 1938) , and one charge, giving a maximum range of 515 yards (471 m). Designed and manufactured by Rheinmetall, the 50 mm mortar had a crew of two and remained in production until 1943.

FOREIGN LIGHT MORTARS

A number of foreign mortars were taken into use by the German Army. As with many other items of Soviet military equipment, the Germans found that their 50 mm mortar was an excellent design and many captured weapons were pressed into service. Designated *Granatwerfer* 205/3(r), it weighed only 26 lb (11.8 kg) and fired a 2 lb (0.91 kg) bomb to a maximum range of 875 yd (800 m), a somewhat better performance than the German Gr.W.36.

Other foreign designs were also taken into use; some were undoubtedly used only in training, but others may well have been allocated to second- or third-line infantry units, particularly late in the war.

above and top Two views of the 5 cm Model 1936 light mortar, showing the baseplate, elevation and traversing mechanism and firing tube. Note the painted while line along the tube to help with quick aiming in poor light or darkness.

above Storage and transport case for 5 cm mortar bombs. One problem with portable infantry mortars was the difficulty of carrying enough ammunition on foot in a mobile battle.

right The crew of an 8 cm medium mortar in a well-dug firing position. Organic regimental and battalion mortars were popular with infantry commanders in that they were light, simple, effective and usually available without having to ask for support from another (artillery) organization.

above The carrying case open to reveal a load of 5 cm mortar bombs. Light mortars such as the 5 cm had marginal high-explosive capability but were more effective for laying smoke screens or providing illumination rounds at night.

MEDIUM MORTAR

The standard infantry mortar throughout the war was the 8cm *Granatwerfer* Model 34 (Gr.W.34) which was in continuous production from 1934 through 1945. Of 81 mm caliber, it was known as a heavy mortar, but when the 120 mm mortar entered service midway through the war, that was given the designation "heavy" and the 81 mm mortar redesignated a "medium."

Total weight was 125 lb (57 kg), but for manhandling it broke down into three elements: tube 42 lb (19 kg); baseplate; and the bipod, complete with traversing, elevation and cross-leveling mechanisms. It was manned by a crew of three. The tube was 81.4 mm caliber (3.2 in) and 45 in (1.14 m) long, and fired the Wurfgranate 34 bomb to a maximum range of 2,078 yd (1900 m), although the effective range was 440-1,300 yd (400-1189 m). To load and fire, the bomb was simply dropped down the tube until it hit the fixed firing pin at the base. Maximum rate of fire for a well-trained crew was six rounds in 10 seconds, but this could not be maintained for long. There were four charges; basic Number One in the central tube at the base of the bomb, and up to three more could be added between the vanes. This weapon was designated "*schwer*" (heavy) until early 1943 when the new 120 mm mortar entered service, when the 8 cm weapon became a "medium" mortar.

A special version of the Gr.W.34 was produced as the 8cm *Granatwerfer* 42 Kurz (=short), which was intended initially for use by paratroops, although some other infantry units are also believed to have received it. The weight reduction was achieved mainly by shortening the barrel from 45 in to 30 in (1.143 m to 762 m), but while this reduced the maximum weight from 125 lb to 62 lb (56.7 kg to 28 kg) it also cut the maximum range from 2,078 yd to 1200 yd (1,900 m to 1098 m). It was known to its users as "*Stummelwerfer*" (= stump projector).

right The 8 cm Model 34 was an effective and mobile medium mortar which served reliably throughout the war. The metal spike shapes under the heavy baseplate kept the mortar bedded in and stable, especially after the first few shots. The barrel and bipod could be swung quickly within a reasonable arc before fine aiming was done with the dial sight and traversing screw.

right Front view of the 8 cm mortar. It could be split into three loads (tube, baseplate and bipod) each of which was man-portable. The sight and ammunition also had to be carried.

below The mortar sight in its protective case. The sight would be used to measure the angle and distance from a known and surveyed point to the firing position.

below A metal storage and carrying case for 8 cm mortar bombs. Note the protective caps over the fuzes in the tips of each bomb.

The standard munition was the *Wurfgranate* 34, which was 13 in (330 mm) long, weighed 7.7 lb (3.5 kg) and carried 19 oz (0.54 kg) of explosive. Maximum range was 2,100yd (1920 m). Other rounds included:
the *Wurfgranate* 38 and *Wurfgranate* 39, which had a special charge in the nose which exploded on impact with the ground, throwing the bomb several metres into the air before exploding, thus ensuring maximum casualties at head and torso level.

There was also the *Wurfgranate* 40, which was longer (22.2 in - 560 cm) and carried a larger 11 lb (5 kg) warhead, but which had shorter range (1,040 yd – 951 m).

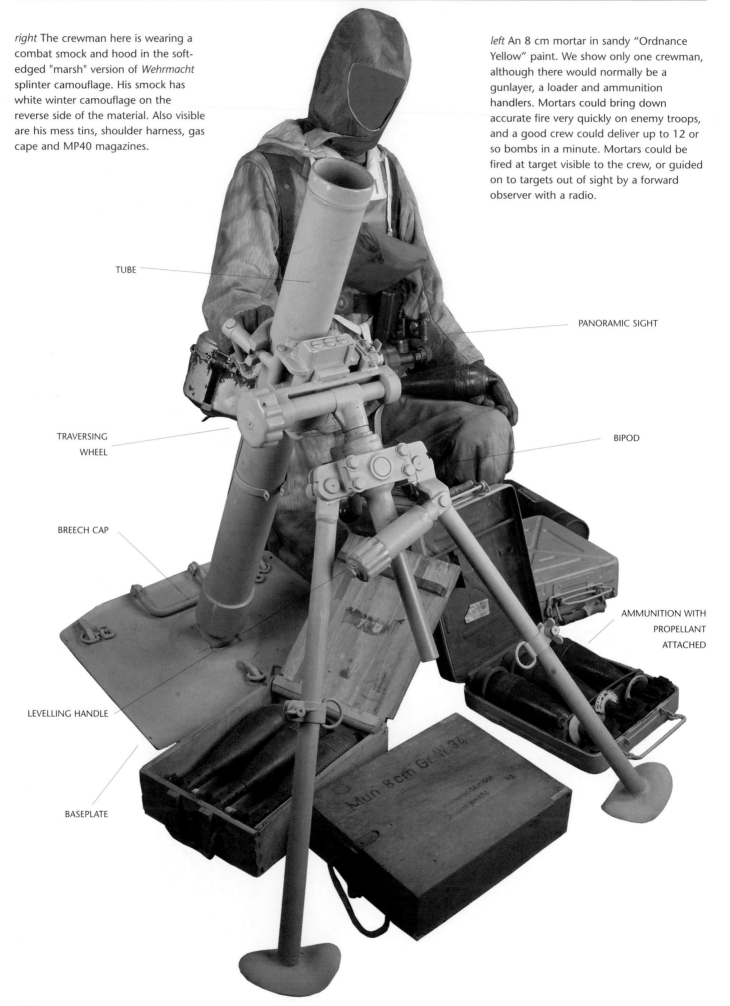

right The crewman here is wearing a combat smock and hood in the soft-edged "marsh" version of *Wehrmacht* splinter camouflage. His smock has white winter camouflage on the reverse side of the material. Also visible are his mess tins, shoulder harness, gas cape and MP40 magazines.

left An 8 cm mortar in sandy "Ordnance Yellow" paint. We show only one crewman, although there would normally be a gunlayer, a loader and ammunition handlers. Mortars could bring down accurate fire very quickly on enemy troops, and a good crew could deliver up to 12 or so bombs in a minute. Mortars could be fired at target visible to the crew, or guided on to targets out of sight by a forward observer with a radio.

TUBE

PANORAMIC SIGHT

TRAVERSING WHEEL

BIPOD

BREECH CAP

AMMUNITION WITH PROPELLANT ATTACHED

LEVELLING HANDLE

BASEPLATE

HEAVY MORTARS

Until 1941 the German infantry's heaviest infantry mortar was the 8cm Gr.W.34 but on the invasion of the Soviet Union they encountered the Red Army's excellent 120 mm HM38. Not only were captured weapons immediately taken into service as the 12cm Granatwerfer 378(r), but the design was placed in production virtually unchanged as the 12cm *Granatwerfer 42*. Total weapon weight was 628 lb (285 kg) and it fired the 120 mm round which carried a 6.8 lb (3.1 kg) high-explosive warhead to a maximum range of just over 6,560 yd (6000 m). The bomb was usually fitted with a fuse which detonated the warhead at some 6 ft (1.83 m) above ground level. The weapon had its own two-wheeled carriage which could be either towed directly by a vehicle or with a two-wheeled limber carrying the ammunition between the two. The Gr.W.42 could be fired at a maximum rate of some 10 rpm for a short period before crew fatigue set in, following which the sustained rate was about 6 rpm. This was a most successful weapon, which was produced in Germany, together with its ammunition, in very large numbers.

above The 12 cm mortar could be attached to a neat wheeled carriage and towed behind a vehicle.

right Individual 120 mm bombs were packed in these protective cardboard cylinders before being put into ammunition boxes. A mortar positon would soon be surrounded by empty cases once firing began.

left and below 120 mm bombs. Range could be adjusted by the addition of extra propellant charges around the tail shaft of the bomb.

right and below Ammunition crates for 12 cm mortar bombs. Note how the stencil markings identify both the Gr.W.378(r) and Gr.W.42 versions of the Soviet design.

ANTI-TANK WEAPONS

As with other nations, German anti-tank weapons made use of both kinetic energy (high velocity solid shot) high explosive anti-tank (HEAT), which used a directed explosion combined with a molten metal slug to penetrate the armor.

ANTI-TANK RIFLES

From the appearance of the tank in 1916 through the mid-1930s the main anti-tank weapon in most armies was a specially developed high-velocity rifle. The first to appear was in, in fact, a German weapon, the *Mauser M1918 Tank Gewehr* (*T-Gewehr 18*), developed as a hasty response to Allied tanks in World War I. Firing a newly-developed 13 mm round, the weapon was large and heavy, had considerable recoil and needed a bipod; it was by no means popular with those who had to use it, but it was all they had and was reasonably effective against the thin steel plating of the contemporary tanks.

PANZERBÜCHSE 38

above The PzB38 was a complex and heavy piece with minimal anti-armor performance.

In the mid-1930s Rheinmetall developed a new anti-tank round, the *Patrone 318*, a 7.92 mm round with a steel core, and a new anti-tank rifle was developed to fire it. This was the *Panzerbüchse 38* (PzB38), a single-shot, manually-loaded weapon, which weighed some 35 lb (16 kg). Having fired a round, the barrel traveled to the rear, ejecting the spent case and was then held open for the firer to insert a new round. He then pressed the release catch, which allowed the working parts to move forward, cocking the action as they did so. The firer then aimed, pressed the trigger and the cycle recommenced. The weapon had a folding butt and a bipod (identical to that on the MG34), but was complicated and difficult to maintain and only a small number were produced in 1939–40, although some of these were carried during the invasion of Poland.

PANZERBÜCHSE 39

above Lighter than its predecessor, the PzB39 was no more effective against tanks.

Gustloff quickly set to work to overcome the shortcomings of the PzB38, which resulted in the PzB39. In reality this was little different, retaining the barrel and working parts of the earlier weapon, but it was slightly lighter. One minor change was the inclusion of two cartridge boxes, each holding ten rounds, which could be attached to the weapon near the breech. These were not magazines but rather ready-use trays, which enabled the gunner quickly to put his hand on the next round before inserting it into the open breech. The weapon entered service in 1939 in time for some 600 to be in the hands of troops for the invasion of Poland and by late 1941 some 25,000 were in service.

Once the Germans came up against a serious armor threat, especially the Russian T-34, they quickly realised that the anti-tank rifle was almost completely ineffective, and began to withdraw them from service. Once it became obsolete in the anti-tank role the PzB39 was modified for infantry use as a grenade launcher, when it was known as *Granatbüchse 39*, although it was quietly taken out of service in 1944.

PANZERBÜCHSE 41

The *Panzerbuchse* 38 and 39 were not the end of the anti-tank rifle story as a totally different weapon had been developed by Solothurn of Steyr, Switzerland, working as sub-contractors to Rheinmetall. Under company designation S18, this was a large, self-loading rifle, firing a specially developed 20 mm round from a box magazine which housed either five or ten rounds. It was large and heavy – it weighed 97 lb (44 kg) – and had both a bipod and a monopod under the butt to assist the firer. Some mystery surrounds this weapon in German use, but it is claimed that it entered production with Rheinmetall as the PzB.41, and examples were certainly captured by the Soviet Army in Russia and the US Army in North Africa, and an Axis publicity photograph showed two Italian Bersaglieri manning one in the Western Desert. If it did enter service with the German Army, it does not appear to have lasted long.

SCHWERE PANZERBÜCHSE 41

above High muzzle velocity and a tungsten penetrator gave this lightweight weapon a remarkable performance against light armor.

From mid-1941 onwards the German Army strove to deal with the ever-increasing tank threat, particularly from the outstanding Soviet tanks on the Eastern front. Thus there was a constant search to develop new and more powerful weapons for the infantry, among which were those relying on kinetic energy to "punch" a hole through the armor. The infantry weapon built on the tapered bore principle was the 2.8 cm *schwere Panzerbüchse 41* (sPzB 41) which had a chamber caliber of 2.8 cm and a 170 cm (66 in) long barrel which tapered to 2 cm (0.78 in) at the muzzle. This gave it the exceptional muzzle velocity of 4,600 ft/sec (1402 m/s) and very good armor penetration of 53 mm at 3500 m (2.1 in at 3,830 yd). This weapon was fielded in two forms, one with normal sized wheels and pneumatic tyres for conventional infantry, the other with small radius wheels and other weight-saving measures for use by para- and mountain troops. Even in its heavier version, the sPzB41 was easily handled by a two-man crew and if its effectiveness against tank armor decreased as the war went on it retained an excellent performance against all other types of vehicle and field emplacements such as bunkers. It also had an H.E. shell, which increased its versatility.

The sPzB 41 had two major drawbacks. The first was the high wear-and-tear on the barrel, which had to be made of high-grade materials to absorb the forces created by the squeezing of every round but even so had to be replaced every 500 rounds. The other drawback was much more pressing which was that tungsten carbide for the penetrators became increasingly difficult to obtain as the war progressed. Nevertheless, the weapon remained in service right up to the end in May 1945.Tungsten penetrators were used in many different anti-tank weapons. The Germans' problem was that almost all of their supply came from Portugal and Spain. Allied political pressure and the interdiction of supply routes after the Normandy landings eventually caused the flow of raw material to Germany to dry up.

PANZERBÜCHSE 35(P) / PzB770(P)

Despite the Nazi-engendered nationalist pride, the German Army was never reluctant to adopt weapons used by its enemies, one of the first being a Polish anti-tank rifle. Developed in the mid-1930s as the *Maroszek WZ35*, this was pressed into German service as the *Panzerbüchse* 35(p), although it was also known as the *Panzerbüchse* 770(p). By the standards of the late 1930s this rifle was a satisfactory weapon with some good design features, but its major drawback lay in the projectile, which lacked a hardened core to penetrate armor, relying, instead, on simple velocity. It was issued to German troops taking part in the attack on France but thereafter, like most other anti-tank rifles, it faded rapidly from the scene.

The concept of an anti-tank rifle became quickly outmoded as armor thickness increased. Even where the projectiles managed to penetrate vehicle armor, they were so small that unless they hit something vital like a crewmember or fuel tank, they were unlikely to stop a fighting vehicle.

PANZERBÜCHSE 783(R) AND 784(R)

The Soviets had two excellent anti-tank rifles in use, and captured versions were impressed into German service. Both used the excellent M41 14.5 x 114 mm round, which had a steel core and could penetrate approximately 1.6 in of armor plate at a range of 100 yards. The first of these weapons was designed by Degtyarev and had the Soviet title PTRD-41. Like the German-designed PzB.38 and .39, the PTRD-41 was a single-shot, manually loaded weapon whereas the Simonov weapon, designated PTRS-41 was self-loading, with a five-round magazine.

Weapon	Country	Company of origin	Cartridge /Model	Length mm	Barrel in (mm)	Weight in (mm)	mv lb (kg) (m/s)	Feed ft/sec
Panzerbüchse 38	Germany	Gustloff	7.92 x 94	51mm (2 in)	43 in (1.1 m)	35 lb (15.9 kg)	3,795 ft/sec (1157 m/s)	Single round
Panzerbüchse 39	Germany	Mauser	7.92 x 94	62.3 mm (2.43 in)	42.8 in (1.09 m)	27 lb (12.25 kg)	4,150 ft/sec (1265 m/s)	Single round
Panzerbüchse 41	Solothurn, Switzerland	Solothurn S18/100	20 x 105	83mm) (3.24 in	35.4 in (0.9 m)	97 lb (44 kg)	2,400 ft/sec (731 m/s)	Self-loading, 5/10 round box
schwere Panzerbüchse 41	Germany	Rheinmetall	28 x 187.5		66 in (1.7 m)	496 lb (225 kg)	4,593 ft/sec (1400 m/s)	
Panzerbüchse 35(p)	Poland	Maroszek WZ 35	7.92	69 mm (2.7 in)	47.2 in (1.2 m)	21 lb (9.5 kg)	4,200 ft/sec (1,280 m/s)	
Panzerbüchse 783(r)	USSR	Degtyarev PTRD-41	14.5 x 114	79.5mm (3.1 in)	53.1 in (1.35 m)	33.7 lb (15.3 kg)	3,314 ft/sec (1,010 m/s)	
Panzerbüchse 784(r	USSR	Simonov PTRS-41	14.5 x 114	83mm (3.24 in)	47.8 in (1.21 m)	43.9 lb (20 kg)	3,264 ft/sec (995 m/s)	Self-loading

ROCKET LAUNCHERS

88 mm RPzB 43 with RPzBGr 4322 Rocket

The Germans received the idea for their recoilless rocket launcher from early models of the US M1 Bazooka which they captured during the North African campaign. The Germans rapidly developed an equivalent system, which was identical in principle, but larger and heavier (see table) and with a different ignition system. This was fielded within a few months under the official designation 88 mm *Raketenpanzerbüchse* 43 (anti-tank rifle, rocket), although, as always, the troops found different names for it, including *Ofenrohr* (stovepipe) and *Panzerschreck* (tank terror).

This very simple system consisted of two elements: the projectile and a launcher. The projectile *(Raketenpanzerbüchse Granat* 4322) was a fin-stabilized missile powered by a small rocket motor in the tail with a 3.46-inch (88 mm) diameter, hollow-charge warhead at the front end. It was 25.25 in (641 mm) long, weighed 7 lb (3.18 kg) and had a theoretical maximum range of about 400 yd (366 m), although effective range on the battlefield was about 130 yd (119 m).

The launcher was a mild steel tube, open at both ends, with a skeletonic rest which sat on the firer's shoulder and rudimentary sights. It was 3.7 in (94 mm) in diameter, 64.5 in (1.64 m) long and weighed 20.5 lb (9.3 kg). The underside of the tube included a hand-

above This operator has neither face protection nor shield and would be vulnerable to the rocket exhaust if he fired his Panzerschreck.

guard, pistol grip, trigger, electrical housing, and the shoulder rest; there was also a sling for carrying. Unlike the US weapons which used batteries, the Germans used a magneto to generate a spark, which ignited the rocket motor.

In a two-man team, the Number One was the firer, while the Number 2 carried five ready-use rockets in a special haversack. The weapon was not prepared for firing until the target was almost within range, whereupon the firer placed the weapon on his shoulder and the Number 2 inserted a rocket in the rear end of the tube until a retaining catch secured it in place. He then connected two wires. To launch, the firer aimed the weapon, cocked it and

then pulled the trigger which generated a spark to fire the rocket motor. The projectile then left the tube, which was immediately ready for the next round to be loaded.

The RPzB 43 was not an immediate success with the troops as the motor was still burning as the rocket left the tube, which meant that the firer needed some protection. This was initially achieved by giving him a fireproof jacket and a respirator with the filter removed, which was not really practical for a two-man hunter/killer team carefully stalking their target. However, as the result of a suggestion from a combat unit on the Eastern front, the original launcher was superseded in mid-1944

Nationality		German			US
Launcher Model		RPzB 43	RPzB 54	RpzB 54/1	M9A1
Rocket model		RPzBGr 4322		RPzBGr 4922	M6
Rocket	Warhead	Hollow-charge (HEAT)			Hollow-charge (HEAT)
	Caliber	3.4 in (86 mm)			2.36 in (60 mm)
	Length				19.4 in (493 mm)
	Mv	361 ft/sec (110 m/s)			270 ft/sec (82.3 m/s)
	Range	164 yd (150 m)	164 yd (150 m)	197 yd (180 m)	120 yd (110 m)
	Weight	7.2 lb (3.27 kg)			3.38 lb (1.53 kg)
Launcher	Length	65 in (1.65 m)	65 in (1.65 m)	60 in (1.52 m)	54 in (1.37 m)
	Weight	20.9 lb (9.48 kg)	24.2 lb (10.98 kg)	20.9 lb (9.48 kg)	15.9 lb (7.21 kg)

by the 88 mm RPzB 54 which introduced a small shield to protect the firer's face with a small mica clear-view insert for sighting. The resulting RPzB 54 was slightly heavier, but fired the same rocket. By the end of the year, however, an even better model was being fielded – 88 mm RPzB 54/1 – which launched an modified rocket, the RPzBGr4992, with an improved rocket motor which completed all its combustion before leaving the tube, which was also shorter and lighter.

By 1944 the anti-tank companies of infantry regiments held 36 each, together with three 75 mm Pak 40s.

above Transport and storage case complete with two RPzBGr 4992 shaped-charge rockets.

left A member of an SS assault gun unit out of his vehicle and equipped with a *Panzerschreck*.

RAKETENWERFER 43

Launcher Model		RW43
Rocket model		**RPzBGr 4922**
Rocket	Warhead	Hollow-charge (HEAT)
	Caliber	3.4 in (86 mm)
	Length	
	Mv	361 ft/sec (110 m/s)
	Range	197-220 yd (180-201 m)
	Weight	7.2 lb (3.27 kg)
Launcher	Length	9 ft 2 in (2.79 m)
	Weight	270 lb (122.5 kg)
	Elevation	-18? to +15?

The *Raketenwerfer* 43 consisted of rocket launcher tube mounted on a simple two-wheeled carriage, which fired an 88 mm hollow-charge rocket. Unlike virtually all other rocket launchers, however, the tube was closed and fitted with a simple breechblock, which hinged sideways and included a striker. A small shield was mounted transversely to protect the crew, which included a rectangular, unplated gap for sighting. The rocket was similar to that for the RPzB 43 but had a rimmed base which fitted over the tail ends of the fins and a flash cap in the center, which was hit by the striker and then ignited the rocket motor. This rimmed base remained in the tube after firing and had to be removed before the next rocket could be loaded. As the tube was closed, the weapon was not recoilless and jumped noticeably on firing. The weapon was sighted from 195 to 765

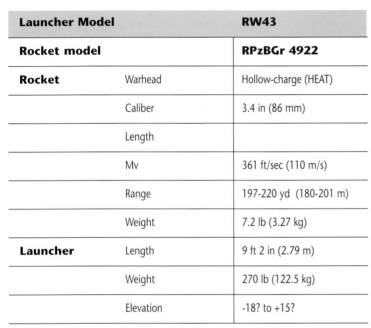

yd (178 to 700 m), although the latter was very optimistic and battle experience showed that 220 yd (200 m) was the maximum effective range.

The weapon was designed to be as low as possible and the wheels could be removed to make it lower still and there were rudimentary skids to enable it to be dragged by its two-man crew. Although fitted with wheels, the weapon was rarely moved long

distances on them but was so light that it could easily be loaded onto a truck or horse-drawn wagon.

The *Raketenwerfer* 43 was known to its crews as *Püppchen*, a small girl's affectionate name for her little doll.

PANZERWURFMINE (PWM)

The *Panzerwurfmine* (anti-tank, throwing bomb) was very much a weapon of last resort, and was developed by the *Luftwaffe* for its infantry units, including the paratroops. It consisted of a hollow-charge warhead mounted on a stick and, at least in theory, was capable of penetrating 3 in (76 mm) of armor plate, if hit at 90 degrees. Its most unusual feature were four cloth fins which were normally folded against the stick and retained by a cover. When ready to use it, the thrower put his hand around the folded vanes and withdrew the cover with the other hand; the vanes were then held closed until the device was thrown whereupon springs deployed the vanes to assure a steady flight. The safety device was a loosely seated metal pin to which was attached a length of cloth. This cloth was released when the vanes deployed and air-resistance then made it pull out the safety pin and the device was then armed. The weapon weighed 3 lb (1.36 kg) and was 21 in (533 mm) long. Over 200,000 were manufactured during 1943, a prime illustration of how valuable production resources were often wasted on useless weapons systems.

PANZERFAUST

below Cheap to make and easy to use, the Panzerfaust became a common close-range weapon, effective against tanks and all vehicles and even usable against infantry in buildings.

The *Panzerfaust*, originally designated Faustpatrone, was a very simple weapon intended to provide the infantry with a highly effective anti-armor weapon, which could be carried and operated by one man, albeit at very short ranges.

The *Panzerfaust* weapon was composed of two elements only: the projectile and the launch tube. The projectile had a bulbous fore-end containing the hollow charge and a spigot which fitted into the launcher, which was a steel tube containing explosive and fitted with a rudimentary shoulder rest and trigger. On pulling the trigger the explosive in the tube was ignited and the projectile was ejected from the tube and after flying about five yards the warhead armed itself. As with all such weapons, there was a

above The *Panzerfaust* was fired from the shoulder or underarm, as shown here. The firer had to be careful not to catch his comrades with the rocket backblast.

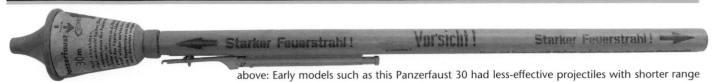

above: Early models such as this Panzerfaust 30 had less-effective projectiles with shorter range

danger area to the rear of the tube, the Germans calculating that the flame was fatal up to ten feet from the venturi. It was also important that the danger area be clear of any obstacles such as walls, which would reflect the flame back onto the firer.

There were four versions, the figure suffix indicating the range in meters.

The projectile was virtually the same in all four cases, consisting of a 5.5-inch (140 mm) diameter head weighing 6.4 lb (2.9 kg) and containing a warhead made of equal parts of RDX and TNT and weighing 28 oz (0.79 kg). This missile had a wooden tail rod fitted with wrap-around, spring-loaded fins which deployed on leaving the launch-tube.

The launch tube was open at both ends, contained gunpowder propellant and had a danger area extending some 10 ft (3.1 m) behind the weapon. Instructions for use and danger information were printed pictorially on the tube and could be used, at least in theory, by any infantry soldier with minimal (if any) training.

Model	Length	Weight	Effective range	Penetration	In-Service date	Remarks
	in/mm	lb/kg	yd/m			
Panzerfaust 30	16.5/420	24.7/11.2	66/30.1 @ 90 degrees	7.9 in (200 mm)	October 1943	
Panzerfaust 60	16.5/420	24.7/11.2	66/60.3		September 1944	Most widely used
Panzerfaust 100	16.5/420	33/15	110/101		November 1944	
Panzerfaust 150	16.5/420	33/15	164/150		March 1945	Pistol grip, reuseable tube

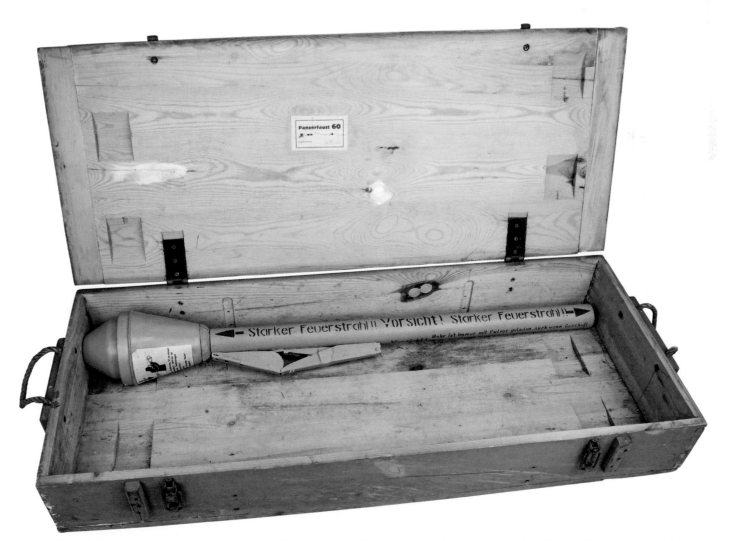

above Each Panzerfaust was effectively a single round of ammunition, with the launch tube being discarded after use. The grooves cut into this case show that it held up to four weapons.

SCHIESSBECHER

Another attempt at a last-ditch defensive device against armored vehicles for the infantryman was the *Gewehrgranategerät* (rifle grenade device) also known, more descriptively, as the *Schiessbecher* (shooting cup). This was an adapter, in effect a barrel extension topped by a cylindrical cup, which fitted over the muzzle of any rifle or carbine chambered for 7.92 mm ammunition. There was also a special sight, graduated up to 300 m (328 yd), which fitted to the left of the normal backsight. Both were clamped in place. A small firing tripod for greater accuracy was also available, although there appeared to be no reason why the rifle should not have been fired without it. The grenade was placed in the 30 mm diameter cup and launched by firing a special ballistite cartridge from the breech in the usual manner, one complication being that each type of grenade needed its own type of cartridge. Well over one million *Schiessbecher* were manufactured, the last in May 1944.

Many varieties of grenade were produced, a few of which are listed in the table. The anti-tank round had, of necessity, to have a hollow charge (also known as High Explosive Anti-Tank (HEAT)) in which the armor penetration is directly proportional to the diameter of the charge. Thus, the original *Gewehr Panzergranate* 30, with its 30 mm (1.17 in) diameter, was quickly found to be inadequate and as enemy

left A rifleman fits a grenade into the *Schiessbecher* (grenade cup) fitted to the end of his Kar 98. A special ballistite cartridge was used to launch the grenade.

above A standard rifle with the grenade cup fitted. It could be attached or removed in a matter of seconds.

Designation		Payload	Fuse	Diameter	Range
German	**English**				
Gewehr Sprenggranate	Rifle grenade, explosive	Fragmentation	Impact or time	30 mm (1.17 in)	15 yd (13.7 m)
Gewehr Sprenggranate mit Gesteigerter Reichweite	Rifle grenade, explosive, extended range	Fragmentation	Impact	30 mm (1.17 in)	25 yd (23 m)

tanks were being fielded with ever thicker armor, so the anti-tank round had to be increased in diameter, first to 40 mm (1.56 in) and eventually to no less than 60 mm (2.34 in).

A 1944 development introduced a totally novel feature. This was the *Doppelschussgranate* (double-shot grenade) in which the base of the round contained additional propellant which was activated as it left the *Schiessbecher*, somewhat similar in concept, if on a much smaller scale, to a twin-stage rocket. Several such grenades were developed and some even put into production. The largest, and typical of the over-complication that characterized many parts of the Nazi war machine in the final months of the war was double-shot grenade with a warhead weighing 1.35 kg (2.9 lb) and a diameter of 100 mm (3.9 in), with 250 g (0.55 lb) of additional propellant for the second-stage propulsion. In theory it could penetrate 360 mm (14 in) of steel, but whether it would ever have hit a target – even one as large as a tank – is a different matter.

The *Gross Gewehr Panzergranate* 40 (large rifle tank grenade/GGP40) was another novel device. The previous grenades had fitted inside the cup launcher, but the GGP40 fitted over it, thus enabling a much larger and heavier warhead to be carried. The complete projectile weighed 520 g (1.15 lb), was 23.4 cm (9.13 in) long, and was fitted with six small stabilising fins.

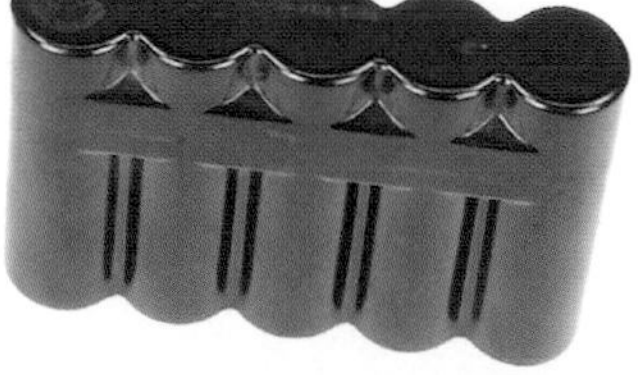

below A wooden carrying case for rifle grenades. The grenades were usually further packed in groups of five inside the container shown below the box.

right This figure is holding an anti-armor grenade, about to insert it into the launching cup on his rifle. He also has a bag of Model 24 hand grenades over his shoulder and two more in his belt. His smock is in softened splinter or "marsh" style camouflage.

Gewehr Panzergranate 30	Rifle grenade, anti-tank; 30 mm	Hollow charge	Impact	30 mm (1.17 in)	15 yd (13.7 m)
Gross Gewehr Panzergranate 40	Rifle grenade, large, anti-tank; 40 mm	Hollow charge	Impact	40 mm (1.56 in)	200 yd (183 m)
SS Gewehr Panzergranate 46	Rifle grenade, anti-tank; 46 mm	Hollow charge	Impact	46 mm (1.79 in)	200 yd (183 m)
SS Gewehr Panzergranate 61	Rifle grenade, anti-tank; 61 mm	Hollow charge	Impact	61 mm (2.38 in)	200 yd (183 m)
Gewehr Fallschirmleuchtgranate	Rifle grenade, parachute illuminating	Illuminating flare	Timed	30 mm (1.17 in)	500 yd (457 m)
Gewehr Propagandagranate	Rifle grenade, propaganda	Leaflet	Timed	30 mm (1.17 in)	500 yd (457 m)

(The 46 mm and 61 mm were designed by the Waffen-SS War Academy; hence the SS prefix)

ANTI-TANK GUNS
3.7 CM *PAK 36*

The first of Germany's post-World War I anti-tank guns, the 3.7cm *Panzerabwehrkanone 35/36* (PaK 35/36 antitank gun), was designed and produced by Rheinmetall, and entered service in 1936 in time for examples to be taken to Spain by the Condor Legion, Germany's contribution to Franco's army.

For its day it was an impressive weapon with a good performance against existing tanks and it was exported to several foreign armies, and also produced under licence in several others. Like all German PaKs, it also fired an HE shell.

It was a relatively small weapon with a 66-inch (1.68 m) barrel in 37 mm (1.46 inch) caliber. It was light and easily handled by the infantry, and had few problems in the early months of the war, because enemy tank forces were minimal. Its shortcomings became very apparent in the French campaign where its crews gave it the all too descriptive nickname of *"Türklopfer"* (door-knocker) since all it seemed to do was to bang on the outer armor, thus drawing the enemies' attention without actually doing them any damage. Two new rounds, the AP40 and the stick bomb, *Stielgranate* 41 hollow-charge, were hastily developed, which gave a theoretical penetration of 1.9 in and 6 in (48 mm and 152 mm) and 6 in respectively at 400 yd (366 m), but the gun was superseded as soon as feasible by the *Pak* 38. Despite this, the *Pak* 36 remained in service with the *Fallschirmjäger* (paratroops) and 2nd- or 3rd-line infantry units until then end of the war.

above Even with its limited anti-armor capability, the light and portable Pak 36 served throughout the war.

5 CM *PAK 38*

As the German rearmament program gathered pace the Rheinmetall company began development of a new 5 cm weapon to replace the *Pak* 36. Prototypes were produced under the designation *Pak* 37, but the *Waffenamt* (weapons office) requested several modifications, mainly involving improvements to the carriage to increase stability when firing, and this led to the *Pak* 38, which entered service just after the France signed the armistice. This was a larger and heavier weapon but with improved performance (see table).

right The 50 mm Pak 38 was a much more effective anti-tank gun than its 37 mm predecessor.

The original armor piercing round had a muzzle velocity of 2,740 ft/sec (835 m/s) and could penetrate 2.4 in (61 mm) of armor at 546 yd (500 m), of armor at 546 yd, but a new round with a tungsten carbide core was also developed which could penetrate 3.7 in (94 mm) at the same range, but the crippling shortage of this critical metal brought this promising development to an end. With the lack of the tungsten carbide round a new hollow charge, known to the Allies as the "stick round", was developed which entered service in 1943. This weighed 29.8 lb (13.5 kg) with a 5 lb (2.3 kg) with a 5 lb hollow charge, which could penetrate 7 in (178 mm) of armor plate.

7.5 cm *Pak* 40

Despite the urgency of the requirement, the first of the new 7.5cm *Pak* 40 guns did not reach the troops until February 1942. It was generally similar in appearance to the *Pak* 38, with a split tubular trail, metal disk wheels with solid rubber tyres and a torsion-bar suspension. A twin-layer shield, consisting of two 4 mm (0.16 in) thick armor plates about 1 in (25 mm) apart, protected the crew. The 11-feet long barrel was of monobloc construction and fitted with a muzzle-brake. It proved to be highly effective and by 1943 was the most widely used anti-tank gun in the German Army and remained so until the end of the war. Utilizing the new Armor-Piercing, Capped, Ballistic

above At the limits of infantry portability, the 75 mm Pak 40 gave effective anti-tank performance until the end of the war.

Capped (APCBC) round it could penetrate 4 in (102 mm) of homogenous armor, angled at 30°Δat a range of 1,000 yd (914 m).

Model	Pak 36	Pak 38	Pak40	Pak 97/38	Pak39
Origin	Germany	Germany	Germany	France	Soviet Union
Caliber	37 mm	50 mm	75 mm	75 mm	76.2 mm
Barrel	66 in (1.68 m)	9 ft 10 in (3 m)	11 ft 4 in (3.45 m)	9 ft 8 in (2.95 m)	11 ft 5 in (3 .48 m)
Weight	970 lb (440 kg	2,204 lb (1000 kg)	3,136 lb (1435 kg)	2,624 lb (1,190 kg)	3,360 lb (1524 kg)
Muzzle velocity (anti-armor)	970 lb (440 kg)	2,204 lb (1000 kg)	3,136 lb (1435 kg)	2,624 lb (1,190 kg)	3,360 lb (1524 kg)
Traverse	60?	65	65?	60?	57?
Elevation	-8? to +25?	-8? to +27?	-5? to +22?	-8? to +25?	-6? to +45?
Ammunition	HE, AP, AP40, Stick	HE, AP, Stick	HE, APCBC, AP, HEAT	AP, HE, HEAT	APCBC, AP40, HE

CHEMICAL WARFARE

Like most armies, the German army took extensive anti-gas precautions. All front-line soldiers carried either a GM30 respirator, or its replacement, the GM38, at all times. There were special versions of both for cavalry, combat engineers and casualties with face/head wounds. These GM 30/38 respirators were housed in an instantly recognizable cylindrical container with longitudinal corrugations, which was painted in standard green and had a long carrying strap. The mask itself was of "whole face" design with two eyepieces and a detachable cylindrical filter in front of the wearer's mouth. The GM30 respirator was made of five layers of treated canvas and had seven attachment points for the harness which fitted over the head, while the GM38 was made of synthetic rubber with five attachment points. Both used the same canisters,

the FE41, which was 2.5 inches deep and 4.4 inches in diameter, or its successor, the slightly larger FE42. This gas mask container was carried at all times in the field, usually on the wearer's back. The infantry regiment's pioneer platoon was equipped with decontamination powder and all infantry companies were capable of forming reconnaissance patrols who were equipped with protective clothing and marker flags to identify and mark contaminated areas.

In addition to the respirators there were various other protective items, including both lightweight and heavyweight suits, the difference being in the degree of protection offered and the length of time a man could continue to wear them. There were also protective goggles, which although designed for protection against gas were so convenient that they came to be commonly worn under field con-

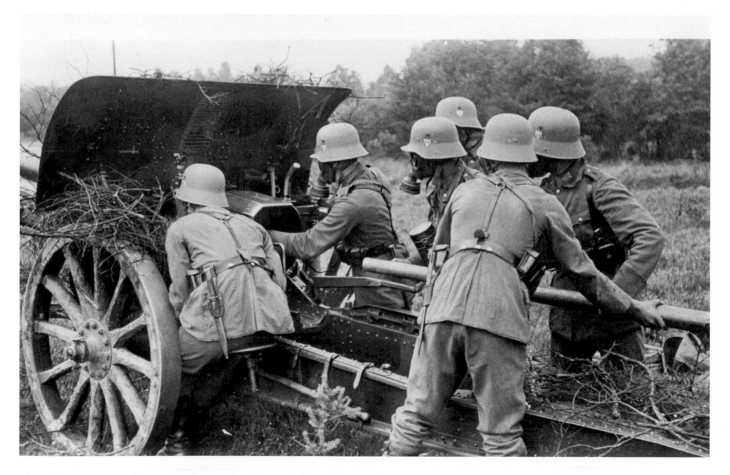

above This late-1930s photograph shows a gun crew wearing gas masks during a field exercise. They also have pre-war helmets. The gunners have no equipment on their backs, revealing the rear strap of the "Y" harness.

right An FE41 respirator case and gas mask. The gas filter at the front of the mask could be unscrewed for a quick change.

above A front view of the gas mask and how it fitted under the helmet. This figure is wearing a (rather tatty) greatcoat and has a breadbag hanging from his leather belt.

below Two pouches for gas capes. The pouches came in a variety of materials and colors and were normally carried on the chest, strapped to the "Y" harness.

ditions, particularly in North Africa. Four sets were carried in a special container, two with opaque eyepieces and two with either amber of green tinted lenses.

Each soldier was issued with a comprehensive personal chemical kit. In the early war years this included a supply of Losantil (calcium hypochloride/chlorinated lime) in tablet form but this was replaced by a protective ointment from 1941 onwards. There were also salves for decontaminating the eyes following exposure to blister agents, and ampoules containing an inhalant to overcome the effects of toxic smokes.

In addition to these individual items there were special vehicles and trailers for collective decontamination of both personnel and their clothing and equipment.

The many animals to be found serving with the German infantry were by no means forgotten.

There were specially-designed respirators for horses together with an oversuit and leggings, and eye-shields, which were carried in a special container which also held a supply of decontaminating powder. There were similar masks, oversuits, leggings and decontaminating powder for dogs, and there was even a special box which gave collective protection to four carrier pigeons.

FLAME THROWERS

The Germans had been the first to use flame throwers *(Flammenwerfer)* in World War I and they also used them in World War I. These were, by definition, very close-range weapons and were, therefore, used in infantry operations against trenches, bunkers and fighting vehicles. They were almost invariably operated by engineer troops or assault pioneers. .

Because of the vulnerability of the operators on foot, by the middle of the war most armies had devised vehicle-borne installations, which gave

above The morale effect of flamethrowers was just as useful as their destructiveness. A few flame shots could often cause defenders to surrender quickly.

much enhanced protection, enabled much more fuel to be carried and, because a more powerful pressure could be generated, achieved a much greater range. In the campaigns in Western Europe German infantry used flamethrowers in their attacks in 1940 but very infrequently thereafter, but in the East they were employed by both sides and throughout all phases of the war.

FLAMMENWERFER 35 (FMW35)

The *Flammenwerfer 35* was in production from 1935 to 1941 and was based on World War I designs. It consisted of a large tank containing 3.1 gallons of oil and a smaller tank containing compressed nitrogen. The hand-held nozzle included a trigger and a hydrogen-gas igniter, and produced a jet of flame with a maximum range of about 30 yards, and, depending on the length of individual bursts, a skilled operator could produce about fifteen. It was fitted with a quick-acting self-closing valve for the operator's protection. This equipment weighed a very substantial 80 pounds and was at the extreme limits of one-man operation.

above A FmW35 in ordnance yellow camouflage. While relatively portable and compact, it still made the operator a highly visible target for enemy fire.

FLAMMENWERFER 41 (FMW41)

A *Flammenwerfer* 40 was developed in an attempt to reduce weight, principally by reducing the size of the tank and thus of the fuel carried. It certainly reached prototype stage and a few pre-production models may have been tested under field conditions, but it never entered service. Instead, the real replacement for *Flammenwerfer* 35 was the *Flammenwerfer* 41. This possessed two cylindrical containers, one holding 2 gallons of oil, designated *Flammöl* Nr 19, the other 0.8 gallons of pressurized nitrogen. The entire outfit weighed 48.5 pounds and could fire up to eight short-length bursts to a maximum range of some 33 yards. As initially produced, the *Flammenwerfer* 41 had a hydrogen ignition system, but this did not work in the extreme cold of the Russian winter and had to be

above Flamethrowers only worked at very close ranges. A flamethrower team waits to cross a crestline to engage an enemy position.

replaced by a cartridge ignition device, named a *Strahlpatrone*, which proved very reliable. This remained the stan-

dard flamethrower to the end of the war, although prototypes of more advanced designs were tested.

EINSTOSS FLAMMENWERFER 46

All previous flamethrowers were reusable, requiring only that the reservoirs of oil and propellant be refilled before being ready for further use. The *Einstoss Flammenwerfer* 46, however, was a one-shot, throw-away device, designed originally for paratroops, but later used by conventional infantry, as

well. It consisted of a cylinder 20 inches long and 2.8 inches in diameter, which held 0.45 gallons of inflammable liquid. The nozzle was built into the end of the cylinder; there were no rubber tubes. The only control was a trigger. There was also a sling and the device was carried and fired with the

sling over one shoulder and the cylinder tucked under the arm. The device was activated by pulling the trigger which broke a small gas-generator to build up pressure in the cylinder and push out the liquid which was then ignited. Range was about 30 yards and it fired one single "hot" shot.

ABWEHR-FLAMMENWERFER 42

One of the many surprises for the Germans when they invaded the Soviet Union was the Red Army's use of dug-in, remotely controlled defensive flamethrowers. This was quickly copied,

although there was little use for such a device as long as the Germans were advancing. The German version, *Abwehr-Flammenwerfer* 42 (defensive flame-thrower Model 42) consisted of

a dug-in tank and projector, and the flame could cover an effective area some 50m long by 15m wide; it was fired in 3 second bursts from a remotely-positioned operator.

	Flammenwerfer 35	Flammenwerfer 41	Einstoss Flammenwerfer 46
Length	n.k	15.7 in (400 mm)	23.6 in (600 mm)
Diameter	n.k	23.6 in	2.8 in
Height	n.k	23.6 in (600 mm	2.8 in (71 mm)
Weight	79 lb (35.83 kg)	49 lb (22.23 kg)	4 lb (1.81 kg)
Compressed gas	Nitrogen	Nitrogen	Nitrogen
Flammable liquid	3.1 gall (11.73 litres)	2 gall (7.57 litres)	0.45 gall (1.7 litres)
Maximum number of bursts	15	8	1
Effective range	27 yd (24.7 m)	22 yd (20 m)	30 yd (27.4 m)
Maximum range	33 yd (30 m)	33 yd (30 m)	44 yd (40.2 m)

INFANTRY GUNS

Infantry regiments had their own infantry-manned artillery resource in the shape of the *Infanteriegeschütze* (infantry guns) which were grouped in each regiment's 13 Company.

These guns were intended for fire missions in close support of the regiment's infantry battalions, and to enable them to meet this mission were wheel-mounted, light, and easy-to-move and man-handle on the ground; they were towed by either horses or light trucks.

The concept of the infantry gun demanded a light, easily portable weapon that could deliver high explosive shells big enough to attack dug-in defensive positions and fortifications. They would be under the direct control of the infantry commander without him having to bid for resources from centralized artillery assets.

In practice they were never as effective as hoped. The guns and ammunition could often not be moved quickly enough to keep up with the infantry, and their direct fire role made them vulnerable to enemy fire. Most armies eventually came to rely on lighter, cheaper and more simple mortars for organic infantry fire support.

right Most infantry guns were light, simple and easily moved by their crew. The German sIG 33 was powerful and effective but was a large, heavy weapon which needed a towing vehicle to move it.

7.5 CM *LEICHTES INFANTERIEGESCHÜTZ* 18 (7.5 CM LEIG18)

Maker: Rheinmetall
Caliber: 2.95 inches (75 mm)
Barrel length: 35 in (889 mm)
Weight in action: 880 lb (400 kg)
Maximum range: 3,900 yd (3566 m)
Muzzle velocity: 725 ft/sec (221 m/s)
Traverse: 12 degrees
Elevation: -10 degrees to +73 degrees
Ammunition: HE – 13.2 lb; hollow-charge – 6.6 lb (3 kg)

The smallest of the infantry guns was the 7.5 cm leIG18, which was developed and produced by Rheinmetall,

starting in 1927. The barrel was very short, just 35 in (889 mm) long and did not have a muzzlebrake. The gun-crew were protected by a small shield. The carriage had a box trail and the ordnance could be elevated between –10 degrees and +73 degrees. There were solid-disc wheels with pneumatic tires.

A variant was produced for mountain troops as the 7.5 cm *leichte Gebirgsinfanteriegeschütz* 18 (7.5 cm le.IG 18), which could be divided into a number of packs, the heaviest of

which weighted 165 lb (75 kg). This variant had a split trail and the wheels had wooden spokes; there was no shield. These were usually assigned on a scale of two per battalion.

Another variant was produced under *Luftwaffe* auspices for the parachute troops as the 7.5 cm le.IG 18F (F = *Fallschirmjäger*). A total of six was produced, all in 1939. This had much smaller wheels and no shield, and could be broken down into four loads, the heaviest of which weighed 309 lb (140 kg).

15 CM SIG 33 (SCHWERE INFANTERIE GESCHÜTZ 33)

Caliber: 5.9 inches
Barrel: 65 in (1651 mm)
Weight in action: 3,360 lb (1524 kg)
Maximum range (HE): 5,140 yd
(4700 m)
Muzzle velocity: 787 ft/sec (240 m/s)
Traverse: 11 degrees
Elevation: 0 to 78 degrees
Ammunition: HE; smoke; anti-tank.

The 15cm *schwere Infanterie Geschütz* 33 (sIG 33) was the heavier of the two infantry-manned artillery pieces to be found in an infantry regiment. It was a very sturdy piece with a box trail and split protective shield, mounted on large metal wheels with solid rubber tyres. It had three types of ammunition: a conventional high-explosive shell for use against soft targets, a smoke shell and an anti-tank shell. Allied intelligence initially described this, quite wrongly, as a "stick shell" for use against

barbed wire and minefields. In fact, it was an anti-tank rocket with a hollow-charge warhead, which was loaded at the muzzle and fired using a sub-caliber charge to ignite the rocket motor. This was intended to be used against Soviet T-34 tanks, but proved to be so inaccurate that it could only be used against concentrations of soft-skinned vehicles, a type of target which was seldom presented by the Soviet Army, anyway.

ANTI AIRCRAFT WEAPONS

Early in the war most of air defense weaponry was provided by the *Luftwaffe* for whom it was not the highest priority mission. Nevertheless, the air force did field some mobile units armed with *Flugzeugabwehrkanone* (air defense cannon or Flak, for short), ranging in caliber from 2.0 cm to 8.8 cm - the famous "88" and there were a small number of *Heeres Flak Abteilungen* (army anti-aircraft units). The numbers of both army and air force AA units rose rapidly as the enemy threat to forward units escalated.

One aspect that assisted in this process was that in many cases the actual weapons and ammunition were common to all three armed services, the identical weapon being used by the *Kriegsmarine* for shipboard defense, and by both the army and the *Luftwaffe* for ground-based defense. Further, where land-based systems were concerned, virtually all models were available on static mounts, on wheeled mounts, on truck or self-propelled tracked chassis, and also on armored trains.

The light weapons listed here were all to be found, at one time or another, as organic to infantry regiments, but there were many other guns systems of 5cm caliber and greater which were operated by artillery regiments, controlled at divisional level and above.

MACHINE GUNS

At battalion level, all MG34 and MG42s in the Machine Gun Company (i.e., in the heavy role) were supplied with a *Dreibein* (tripod) to enable them to be used in the sustained fire role against ground targets. Adapting them for the anti-aircraft role was very simple, since all that was required was for the legs of the tripod to be extended and then a simple rod used to attach the gun to the tripod. The result was a short-range anti-aircraft weapon with an exceptionally high rate-of-fire, but as it was operated under visual control and there were no special sights, their effectiveness, particularly against the much faster Allied aircraft in 1944–45, was questionable. Nevertheless, the noise probably gave great comfort to troops under attack.

2CM *FLAK* 30

The 2cm Antiaircraft Gun Model 1930 (2cm Flak 30) was a recoil-operated weapon that was in service at the outbreak of World War II with both the army and the *Luftwaffe*. It was mounted on two wheels for travel and three feet were lowered for firing. It had a 20-round magazine and could be fired in either full automatic mode at 120 rounds per minute or in semi-automatic mode (single rounds) and had an effective ceiling of some 3,500 ft (1067 m). Like most German flak artillery it could also be used in the ground mode. Although its rate-of-fire was quickly shown to be too slow for modern aircraft it remained in service until 1945. The two-wheel carriage was designed for high-speed towing.

2CM *FLAK* 38

The 20 mm Antiaircraft Gun Model 1938 (2cm *Flak* 38) entered service in 1940 and was operated by short-barrel recoil, which gave almost double the rate-of-fire of the *Flak* 30. It was produced in four versions:

- 2 cm *Flak* 38. The standard, single-barrel version.

- 2cm *Geb Flak* 38. A special version, developed for mountain troops, which, together with its ground mount weighed 0.5 tons (510 kg). The complete weapon system could be broken down into a number of loads, each of which could be carried by an individual soldier.

- 2 cm *Flakzwilling* 38. Twin-barreled version (*Zwilling-twin*) with the barrels side-by-side.

- 2 cm *Flakvierling* 38. Even though the Flak 38 was a great improvement on the *Flak* 30 its rate-of-fire was also too slow for modern aircraft. To overcome this Mauser developed a four-barreled version, originally in a static mount for the Kriegsmarine where it provided close-in air defense for battleships, cruisers and destroyers, but it was then produced in various mounts for land-based use. It proved to be an excellent weapon, very reliable and greatly respected by all enemy airmen who came within its range, although its prodigious ammunition consumption necessitated an increase in crew numbers from six to eight.

above An improvised sledge mount and pony motive power for this 20 mm Flak gun illustrates the improvisations needed to move military equipment in the extreme Russian winter.

above A mobile four-barreled Flakvierling 38 battery mounted on half-tracks sets up in a wooded copse in western Europe.

3.7 CM *FLAK* 18, 36, AND 37

These three weapons all used the same elevating mass and had identical ballistic characteristics, differing only in their mounts. The first model, 3.7cm Flak 18, was, in essence, an enlarged 2.0 cm Flak 30, with the same automatic action involving barrel recoil and residual gas pressure. The one-piece barrel was fitted with a muzzle brake, to bring the recoil with acceptable limits. The mount consisted of four legs which opened out and were leveled using screw jacks. It was produced in relatively small numbers.

below Two *Luftwaffe* cleaning kits for light flak guns. Visible is a spiral wire cleaning brush, cleaning rags, oil bottle and a chain "pull-through" for cleaning the inside of the barrel.

	2cm Flak 30	2cm Flak 38	2cm Flakvierling 38	3.7cm Flak 18, 36, 37	3.7cm Flak 43
Caliber	20 mm	20 mm	20 mm	37 mm	37 mm
Barrel length	56.6 in (1.44 m)	56.6 in (1.44 m)	56.6 in (1.44 m)	10 ft 9 in (3.28 m)	9 ft 8 in (2.95 m)in
Weight in action	0.535 tons (540 kg)	0.45 tons (460 kg)	1.68 tons (1710 kg)	1.93 tons (1960 kg)	1.37 tons (1390 kg ns
Weight, travelling		0.82 tons (830 kg			
Effective ceiling	3,500 ft (1067 m)	3,500 ft (1067 m)	3,500 ft (1067 m)	5,000 ft (1524 m)	5,000 ft (1524 m)
Maximum horizontal range	5,230 yd (4782 m)	5,230 yd (4782 m)	5,230 yd (4782 m)	7,200 yd (6584 m)	7,200 yd (6584 m)
Practical rate of fire	120 rpm	220 rpm	800 rpm	80 rpm	150 rpm
Muzzle velocity	5,230 yd (4782 m)	5,230 yd (4782 m)	5,230 yd (4782 m)	7,200 yd (6584 m)	7,200 yd (6584 m)
Traverse	360°	360°	360°	360°	360°
Elevation	-12° to +90°	-20° to +90°	-10° to +100°	-5° to +85°	-6° to +90°
Crew	4	6	8	7	7
Effective ceiling	2200 m (7220 ft)	2200 m (7220 ft)	2200 m (7220 ft)	4800 m (15,750 ft)	4785 m (15,700 ft)
Ammunition types	HE, AP, AP40	HE, AP, AP40	HE, AP, AP40	HE-T, HE-I, AP-HE, HE	HE-T; HE-I; AP-HE, HE

below Italian colonial troops are shown the workings of a *Luftwaffe* 3.7 cm single-barrelled Flak gun.

below A single-barreled 20 mm Oerlikon gun in *Luftwaffe* service. Ammunition is fed from the large, upright box magazine on the left of the gun, while another one is on the ground in front. This is a short-range weapon, normally aimed by the gunner using a simple optical sight and making his own estimate of target range, speed and altitude.

3.7 CM *FLAK* 43

In external appearance the 3.7cm Anti-aircraft Gun 43 looked like the Flak 18, 36, 37 series but was, in fact, a completely different weapon. One of the basic factors in the design was to achieve ease and economy of production; it also incorporated a new, gas-operated, breech fed by a fixed loading tray, filled with eight-round clips. The result was a weapon with twice the rate of fire of its predecessors. There was also a twin barrel version, 3.7 cm *Flakzwilling* 43, in which the two barrels were mounted one above the other, and which could be fired either together or independently. It was a very effective weapon but less than 300 had been completed by the time the war ended in May 1945. As with other anti-aircraft mounts, the Flak 43 could be fired in the ground role, using either HE or armor-piercing rounds.

THE *WAFFEN-SS*

Even 60 years after the end of World War II, the *Waffen-SS* remains a difficult subject to discuss. On one hand, there can be no doubt that some *Waffen-SS* formations and units displayed considerable courage and fought with a determination on the field of battle which any soldier can admire. On the other hand, however, elements of the organization achieved a notoriety that will never be lived down and the *Totenkopfwachtsturmbanne* (death's head guard units) which operated the concentration camps, and soldiers like those from the *Der Führer* Regiment of the 2nd *SS-Panzer* Division *Das Reich* who murdered 642 men, women and children in the small French town of Oradour-sur-Glane on June 10, 1944, have besmirched its reputation for all time. Similarly, some of the non-German divisions, particularly those employed on anti-partisan missions, behaved with great brutality.

The abbreviation SS derived from the original organisation, the *Schutzstaffel* (protection squadron), a 200-strong self-protection organiza-

above and top Waffen-SS peaked caps. The upper is an NCO's cap with leather band and in field gray material. The lower is an officer's in black dress uniform color and with silver braided strap.

above and top Waffen-SS belt buckle and eagle badge. The buckle has the SS motto *Meine Ehre Heisst Treue* (My Loyalty is True) under the eagle.

tion for Adolf Hitler and other Nazi party leaders before they came to power. Once the Nazis were in government this small organization was expanded to become the *SS-Stabswache* (headquarters guard), a group of armed Nazis of "pure Aryan" descent. When the unit was officially embodied on Nazi Party Day in September 1933, its title was changed yet again to SS-Leibstandarte Adolf Hitler (*SS-Lifeguard Regiment*, Adolf Hitler). Thereafter, it developed for several years as just one of the myriad Nazi party organizations, with a status mid-way between the police and the armed forces. Its role was defined as being "exclusively at

above A *Waffen-SS* trooper in the field. Note the runes on his helmet and collar, and the eagle on his sleeve. He has a Germania cuff band on his left sleeve.

above and top Two views of an SS helmet with the early rolled edge. The runes can be clearly seen on the right side of the helmet in place of the *Wehrmacht* eagle.

above A late-war SS trooper in "palm tree" camouflage smock and equipped with a G-43 semi-automatic rifle. Underneath the smock he wears a field-gray uniform and high "jackboots". Note the combat dagger tucked into the front of his tunic.

the disposal of the *Fuhrer*," although it was always intended that it should come under army command in the event of war. At this time the body as a whole was known as the *SS-Verfügungstruppen* (armed reserve troops – *SSVT*) and it followed another Nazi trait by adopting its own uniform, essentially a copy of the standard army uniform but in a very striking and smart combination of black clothing with white or silver accoutrements. It also adopted its own ranks and unit titles which were, again, based on its Party background, although they were

left A diorama view of an SS machine gun team. The gunner is wearing a reversible summer-pattern "oak leaf" camouflage smock with white snow camouflage on the inside. Unusually for a combat situation he is wearing the peaked field cap under the smock. His weapon is an MG42 set up on a tripod for the sustained fire role. Note how the ammunition belt is fed to the gun directly from metal case on the ground.

above A late-war SS eagle in a triangular patch for sewing on to a field cap. The SS eagle can be recognized by the tapered wingtips – the *Wehrmacht* eagle wing tips have straight edges slanted down and inward.

above A metal death's head badge as sewn on the front of an SS peaked cap. German armor crews also wore a similar badge.

graduated in accordance with the military structure.

The SSVT was under the direct personal control of Heinrich Himmler, one of Hitler's closest associates, and was a tool of the Nazi party and not of the *Wehrmacht*. Nevertheless, it became an increasingly militarized organization and expanded steadily, with some 8,500 men in three regiments (*Standarte*) by March 1935. It also steadily built up a bureaucratic infrastructure to procure new equipment and to provide its own planning, recruiting and training establishments, while it also expanded into supporting arms and services, such as artillery, signals, medical and transport. The organization was headed by the *SS-Führungshauptamt* (*SS-FHA*), a sprawling headquarters of four departments (organization, training, inspection and medical) each with numerous branches. A little-noticed policy at the time was to avoid employing horses for transport and to go straight to motorized formations and units, although, in a somewhat contradictory move, the *Waffen-SS* subsequently formed many cavalry units.

WAFFEN-SS IN ACTION

A combination of careful selection, tight discipline and high motivation, coupled with good equipment, meant that when Poland was invaded there were high hopes of Himmler's embryonic army, now redesignated the *Waffen-SS*, but these were not fully realized and it was quickly appreciated that more military training (as opposed to constant political indoctrination) was required.

Nevertheless, Hitler allowed Himmler to expand "his army" so that by the time of the invasion of Russia in June 1941 the *Waffen-SS* had an overall strength of about 160,000, of whom some 37,000 were in Russia in four divisions, two battle groups and an independent regiment. All the *Waffen-SS* regiments in this force were either *Panzer* or *Panzergrenadier*.

As with many thrusting, ambitious and hard-fighting units in any army, the *Waffen-SS* suffered heavy losses and by mid-1942 the four main divisions had to be withdrawn to regroup, re-equip and absorb new recruits. Nevertheless, they had established a good reputation and even the diehard elements of the army were glad to have them under command. Despite these losses *Waffen-SS* continued its inexorable growth, reaching some 190,000 in September 1942, 350,000 in September 1943, and just under one million by the start of 1945.

Some 41 *Waffen-SS* divisions were eventually formed, of varying quality. Each fighting division, at least on paper, represented two regiments, each of three battalions, plus, engineers, signallers gunners and logistics personnel. Some were well-equipped, well-trained and dedicated, and had first priority for new weapons, vehicles and equipment as they were produced. Some were only cadre units, formed from the remnants of others as Germany collapsed. Others were employed in policing and anti-partisan roles, and some, such as the 36th Sturm 'Dirlewanger' Division earned themselves a uniquely unsavory reputation for harsh treatment of civilian populations.

above Waffen-SS troopers armed with MP 40 machine pistols advance past an abandoned American armored car during the Battle of the Bulge.

WAFFEN SS INFANTRY BADGES

Shoulder boards and left-hand collar patches (soldiers and NCOs)

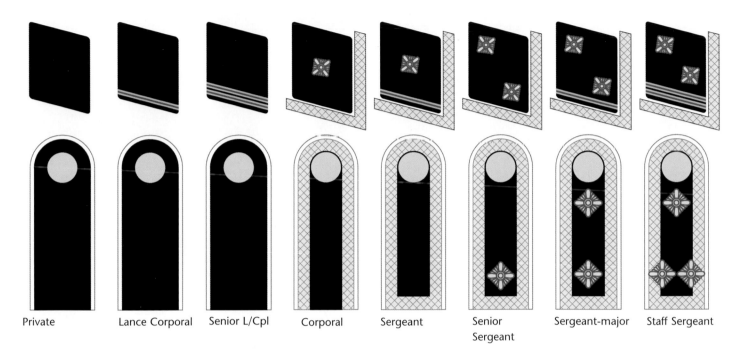

Private   Lance Corporal   Senior L/Cpl   Corporal   Sergeant   Senior Sergeant   Sergeant-major   Staff Sergeant

Shoulder boards and left-hand collar patches (officers)

Right-hand collar patches

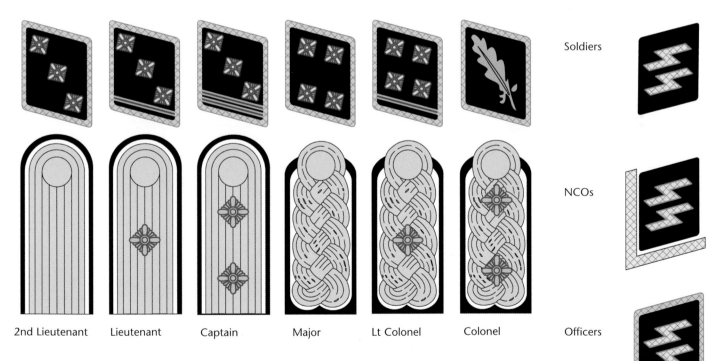

2nd Lieutenant   Lieutenant   Captain   Major   Lt Colonel   Colonel

Soldiers

NCOs

Officers

Sleeve patches (NCOs only)

Private 1st Class   L/Cpl   Senior L/Cpl

above Shoulder boards, collar patches and sleeve badges used to identify *Waffen-SS* ranks.

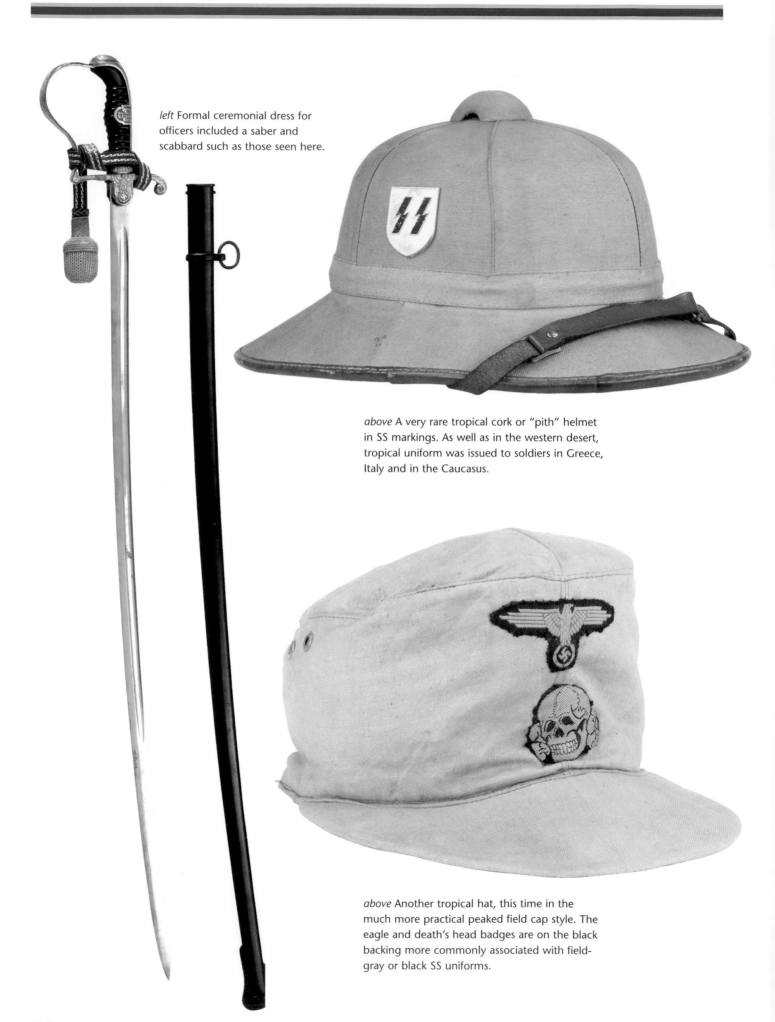

left Formal ceremonial dress for officers included a saber and scabbard such as those seen here.

above A very rare tropical cork or "pith" helmet in SS markings. As well as in the western desert, tropical uniform was issued to soldiers in Greece, Italy and in the Caucasus.

above Another tropical hat, this time in the much more practical peaked field cap style. The eagle and death's head badges are on the black backing more commonly associated with field-gray or black SS uniforms.

left A soldier's or NCO's side cap in field gray with the SS eagle and death's head badge on the front.

below Many *Waffen-SS* units wore unit cuff bands embroidered with their unit name. This one is from the *Totenkopf* division, a unit initially formed from concentration camp guards.

One of the most curious features of the *Waffen-SS* was that not only did the racially-conscious Nazis set out to attract foreign recruits but such recruits were actually forthcoming. Some were undoubtedly pressured into joining (for example, as an alternative to a prisoner-of-war camp), but many were genuine volunteers, and such non-German elements eventually provided approximately 25 percent of its strength. Ethnic Germans from the occupied territories provided another 25 percent and the remainder were Germans from the *Reich* itself. The *Waffen-SS* had virtually no marching infantry regiments, but its very existence had an impact on the army as a whole. First, it was yet another element with loyalties which lay outside the normal army chain-of-command, so that army commanders had to be constantly aware that their *Waffen-SS* subordinates also had a direct line to Himmler and his staff, who, in turn, had direct access to Hitler.

Secondly, the *Waffen-SS* became a parallel and very sizeable army with it own infrastructure, uniforms, customs and regulations, as well as its own procurement system and its own training organisation, all of which resulted in duplication of effort and resources that Germany could ill afford. Thirdly, as with any elite, it took away many good young leaders, both officers and NCOs, who would have been better employed raising the standards in the more run-of-the-mill line infantry regiments. The *Waffen-SS* was, and remains, a unique organization, a parallel army run by a political party. The Italian Black Shirts, although similar in concept were but a pale imitation. Even Stalin, who was determined to impose Communist party control over the Soviet armed forces, did so by means of political commissars appointed to every unit, rather than by setting up a completely separate body.

above Another woven cuff band, this time from *Germania* division, which eventually became the SS *Wiking*, a formation largely manned by nordic and Scandinavian volunteers.

left and below *Waffen-SS* breast eagle and a Corporal's collar patch, both on black background.

above A *Waffen-SS* officer's style belt buckle.

left A ceremonial SS dagger with scabbard, chain, portapee cord and engraved motto on the blade.

above sleeve, eagle and rank badges on a senior Lance-Corporal's tunic. The tunic is in "pea" pattern camouflage.

192

above An SS mortar team preparing to cross a river on an inflatable assault boat. Notice the heavy baseplate carried by the soldier in the middle of the group.

above and right An extremely rare paratrooper helmet with SS markings. A single battalion of SS paratroopers saw service.

MOUNTAIN TROOPS (GEBIRGSJÄGER)

Following World War II, the German Army was maintained at minimal size under the restrictions imposed by the Versailles Treaty, but each of the seven divisions included a Jäger company. These were equivalent to light infantry and in three Bavarian regiments these companies had a mountaineering capability, while 13th Company of 19th (Bavarian) Infantry Regiment, which was nominally a mortar company, was specifically equipped and tasked as a mountaineering unit.

During the expansion of the army following Hitler's coming to power in 1933, this mountain capability was developed rapidly, expanding to a *Gerbirgsbrigade* (mountain brigade) in 1935 and to a full-blown division (*1.Gebirgsdivision*) in 1938. When the *Anschluss* (occupation of Austria) took place various Austrian Army infantry regiments then became *Gebirgsjäger* regiments in the German Army.

These mountain units established a fine reputation and there were eventually five divisions, whose special training, mountaineering skills, high standard of fitness and thrusting attitude made them a true elite. Indeed, the *Gebirsgtruppen* were not only the obvious choice for any fighting in mountainous terrain, such as in Norway or the Caucasus, but they were also often employed effectively in other terrain. It should be noted that despite their special training and fighting in arduous conditions there was no form of special pay or allowance for members of the *Gebirgjäger*.

There were eventually eleven Mountain Divisions and four-highly specialized independent battalions intended for combat at the highest altitudes. The *Waffen-SS* also raised eight mountain divisions, of which one was composed of ethnic Germans and the remainder from people of the occupied territories.

THE MOUNTAIN INFANTRY REGIMENT

The general organization pattern of a Mountain Infantry Regiment was based upon that of the conventional Infantry Regiment, but with a number of differences to match it to the environment in which it was designed to fight.

The Mountain Regiment retained the three-battalion structure, but was larger, with 3,500 all ranks compared to 3,152. The battalions retained their three Rifle Companies and the Machine Gun Company, (twelve machineguns, six 81 mm mortars). Added, however, was a new Heavy Weapons Company, consisting of a Mountain Gun Platoon (two 75mm howitzers), a Heavy Mortar Platoon (four 120 mm mortars) and an Anti-Tank Platoon (four 28 mm anti-tank guns), and with its own Pioneer and Communications Platoons. But, not readily apparent from organization charts and tables is that, particularly in mountain operations, the regimental headquarters played a less important role and the tactical emphasis was more on the battalion. As a result, the infantry guns were permanently allocated to battalions, which were also given a more powerful anti-tank capability.

above Mountain troops but airborne. These men are from the 5th Mountain Division, units of which were landed from Ju 52 transports during the invasion of Crete.

WEAPONS

As in infantry regiments, the basic personal weapon was the *Mauser Karabiner 98k*, but some mountain units were issued with the Czech version, which in German service was designated the 7.92mm *Gewehr 33/40*. Produced under licence from *Mauser* by the *Waffenfabrik Brünn* at Brno, this was very slightly shorter and lighter than the *Karabiner 98k* and also had some minor differences such as a reinforcing plate on the left cheek of the butt and a full-length handguard.

Mountain units were also issued with the self-loading Stg-44 in the last year of the war. Snipers used the same G.33/40, but with a special sight, either the *Zielfernrohr-41 (ZF-41)* or the *ZF-44*, which had x2.5 and x 4 magnification, respectively.

As with the conventional infantry, those officers and soldiers entitled to do so carried either *Luger P.08* or *Walter P.38* pistols, while squad leaders carried the *MP38* or *MP40*, although it was by no means unknown for them to carry a captured Soviet Army *PPSh* sub-machine gun instead.

Among the few weapons developed specifically for use in the mountains were a number of mountain guns and howitzers of 75 mm and 105 mm caliber, all of which could be broken down into loads which could be carried by a pack-animal. Each infantry battalion included a platoon of two 75 mm guns, while the Mountain Artillery Regiment had thirty-six 75mm and twelve 105 mm howitzers. These were excellent designs.

above and below Two examples of the Gewehr 33/40(t) as used by mountain troops. The rifle was originally made in Czechoslovakia as the Vz 33, and was itself a lightweight copy of the Mauser G98. Once the Germans had overrun the country they took the rifle into army service, where it was mainly issued to mountain units who valued the light, handy weapon.

Designation	*leichte Gebirgs-infanteriegeschütze 18*	*Gebirgsgeschüutze 36*	*Gebirgshaubitze 40*
English	light Mountain Infantry Gun (model) 1918	Mountain Gun (model) 1936	Mountain Howitzer (model) 1940
Manufacturer	*Rheinmetall*	*Rheinmetall-Borsig*	*Böhler* (Austria)
Caliber (mm)	75	75	105
Weight of gun (lb)	12 lb (5.44 kg)	13 lb (5.9 kg)	33 lb (15 kg)
Weight of shell (lb)	12	13	33
Muzzle velocity (ft/sec)	725 ft/sec (221 m/s)	1,558 ft/sec (475 m/s)	1,854 ft/sec (565 m/s)
Range (yd)	3,882 yd (3550 m)	9,952 yd (9100 m)	13,834 yd (12650 m)
Entered service	1918	1938	1942
Pack-horse loads	10	8	5

PERSONAL EQUIPMENT

CLOTHING

Much of what the *Gebirgsjäger* wore was standard army uniform, but there were some special items. From the earliest days their working headdress was the *Bergmütze*, a cylindrical cap with a short peak and an integral flap which was normally raised, with two buttons at the front and hooks-and-eyes securing the rear part. In bad weather this flap could be lowered, giving protection to the ears and neck. It was both practical and popular, and the design, albeit with a longer peak, was taken up by the rest of the German Army as the *Feldmütze* in 1942. A white cover for the *Bergmütze* was issued. As with other troops in Russia, the *Gebirgsjäger* were issued with two types of toque, either field-gray for summer use or white for winter. This was a knitted cylindrical item, open at both ends, which slipped over the head and neck which served the same purpose as the British cap-comforter. Both the *Bergmütze* and the toque could be worn under the steel helmet.

There was also a pair of trousers with a reinforced seat and crotch, and which tapered at the bottom, enabling them to be tucked into the top of the boot. The gap was then closed by means of puttees (*Wickelgamaschen*), strips of woolen material, some 29 inches long and 3 inches wide, which tapered to a point at one end, from whence ran a long cotton tape about two-thirds of an inch wide. The wearer wound the puttee around his ankle until the pointed end lay over the outside of his ankle, facing to the rear. The tape was then wound around until it could be secured by means of a metal buckle.

Mountain troops also had various forms of over-clothing designed to combat the effects of high altitude and extreme cold. These included a wind jacket (*Windjacke*), and a loose-fitting anorak, both of which were worn over the usual field blouse. There were also a double-layer winter suit, white on one side, camouflage on the other, and felt overboots, which were based on a design worn by Russian peasants.

above Officers' collar patches in silver thread on the green backing which indicates mountain troops.

above A *Gebirgsjager* with skis and ski-poles. He is wearing a reversible gray/white smock with chest pockets and gray trousers tucked into gaiters and short boots. Note the peaked mountain cap and snow goggles.

MOUNTAIN AND WINTER EQUIPMENT

Naturally, the army issued mountain infantrymen with a full range of specialized mountaineering equipment. Wehrmacht-pattern skis were made of wood and painted white, with a wide green line on the fore-end and which were fitted with contemporary cross-country binding. This consisted of a metal footplate with a raised bracket at the fore-end into which the skier slid the toe of his boot; a leather strap then secured the toe in place. A long loop of metal wire held the boot in place, which had a spring-covered section fitting into a groove on the heel of the skier's boot. This was secured at the front by a clip which could be adjusted to suit various sizes of boot. For downhill skiing, the metal loop could be secured at its mid-point by a series of hooks on the sides of the footplate, which then locked the wearer's boot firmly to the ski. For cross-country skiing (known as *langlauf*) the wire was released from these mid-point clips, enabling the skier to lift his heel, while his toe was still held in the toe-clip. To prevent the ski from slipping backwards when climbing a slope, special waxes could be applied, but there were also long, thin sections of animal skin (*Skifelle*) with the fur all pointing backwards, which could be attached to the under-

above and below Front and rear views of a large Bergen rucksack as used by mountain troops. Note the various straps and loops for attaching other items of equipment.

left The boots, rucksack and grappling hook shown here are all specialist mountain equipment. Note the metal clips wrapped around the soles of the boots for the attachment of crampons etc.

left A heavily-laden soldier negotiates a steep, ice-covered slope. He is roped up to a colleague and is wearing crampons and a winter camouflage smock, while carrying a metal-framed *Bergen* rucksack. Thick snow and ice, high winds, low temperatures and the thin air of high altitude combine to make movement and even just survival an exhausting and difficult business. Mountain troops also operated in extreme heat, and hot, dry summers in Italy, the Caucasus or Greece proved to be just as trying for the fighting soldier as winter.

Combat operations in these conditions pose their own set of tactical problems. Weapons, ammunition and heavy equipment all have to be carried across this rugged terrain, either by man or mule. The difficulty of carrying heavy radio gear and poor reception conditions in rough ground make command and control problematic, demanding high levels of initiative and independence at all levels.

Lack of space makes it difficult to deploy artillery, while limited ammunition reduces its effectiveness further. Tactical air support also struggles to operate and find targets in such rough, high terrain, while rapidly-changing weather can force a change to operational plans within minutes. Men who fight in these conditions need to be supremely fit, with deep reserves of stamina, endurance and determination.

side of the skis. Ski-poles were also issued, together with anti-glare goggles.

Various designs of snowshoe were available, which were strapped to the soldier's boots in order to reduce his pressure on the snow, thus enabling him to move across snowfields.

For mountaineering there were ropes, ice-axe, ice-hammer, pitons (steel spikes for securing ropes) and crampons, which were arrays of short spikes, which were strapped to the soldier's boots for moving across ice.

It is important to note that when wearing these items the mountain infantryman was not lightly loaded, like a tourist, but would usually be wearing his full array of personal equipment. Metal-framed rucksacks were used for load-carrying, while the soldier would also have his weapon and ammunition. He was expected to be able to fight as well as climb and survive in a hostile environment.

above A mountain trooper using his ski-poles to make an improvised rest for his rifle.

left and below The *Eidelweiss* badge was the symbol of mountain troops and the metal example shown would have been worn on left side of the field cap. The two cloth badges indicate a *Waffen-SS* mountain unit.

BADGES

The most noteworthy symbol of the *Gebirgsjäger* was the Edelweiss, a distinction awarded on May 1, 1939. The Edelweiss is a rare and much-prized Alpine plant found at altitudes of between about 6,000 and 9,000 feet; the characteristic white spiky elements are actually powder-covered leaves and the small yellow balls in the center the flowers. A metal Edelweiss was worn on *Gebirgsjäger* head-gear. One form, with a stem, was worn on the left side of the *Bergmütze* above the ear, usually stitched direct onto the cap, although some units added a dark-green cloth backing, to make it stand out better. It was also worn, in a slightly different form (without a stem) on the front of parade-dress peaked cap (*Schirmütze*), between the national cockade and the *Wehrmachtsadler*. This motif was repeated on an oval embroidered badge worn on the right sleeve, which consisted of an Edelweiss

above Mountain operations depended on mules for much of their transport. Shown here on a parade are two mules carrying a disassembled light anti-aircraft gun.

surrounded by a twisted rope and a piton, on a dark-green backing. Both the cap-badge and the sleeve badge were worn by all mountain-qualified members of the *Gebirgstruppen*, regardless of rank.

There was a further badge worn only by mountain leaders who had qualified on a particularly arduous course at the *Heeres Hochgebirgschule* (army mountain school) at Fulpmes in Austria. Worn on the right breast, this metal/enamel badge was the same overall size as the arm-badge, but with a different and slightly smaller design of Edelweiss and with white margin bearing the word *Heeresbergführer* (army mountain leader) in Gothic script.

TRANSPORT

Gebirgsjäger (mountain troops) depended on packhorses and mules for off-road transport, and used these animals in campaigns in Norway, Yugoslavia, Greece and the Soviet Union, particularly in the Caucasus. Although the establishment changed from time-to-time during the war, a Mountain Division normally mustered some 1,400 trucks and about 6,000 pack animals. These were packhorses and mules, which were selected for their hardiness and specially trained in movement in mountainous terrain.

The *Gebirgsjaeger* were always innovative and in the Caucasus they pressed indigenous Bactrian camels into service. These could carry approximately 200 pounds in weight and pull a normal *Infanteriekarre* but their prime advantage lay in their ability to cope with arid desert conditions.

PARATROOPS (FALLSCHIRMJÄGER)

As with other countries, Germany developed doctrines in the 1930s which envisaged infantry and other troops being delivered to the battlefield by air.

One method was to deliver the soldiers and their equipment by aircraft or gliders which actually landed, so that no particular or lengthy training was required other than in boarding and exiting the aircraft and the correct methods of loading and unloading equipment, such as guns and vehicles. This meant that ordinary infantry could be used, but it required a landing field secure from enemy interference.

The other method was by parachute (*Fallschirm*) and here the Soviet Union led the way in the 1930s until in 1932 Herman Goering, then head of the Prussian police, attended a Soviet demonstration which led to him establishing a small parachute detachment in his paramilitary Polizeiabteilung (police battalion). Once the *Luftwaffe* was officially established in 1935, Goering as its head transferred his paramilitary police to the air force as Regiment Hermann Goring. The *Luftwaffe* parachute corps officially came into existence in January 1936, with the small paratroop nucleus now named the *Fallschirmschützen Bataillon* (Parachute Rifle Battalion) although it was still part of Regiment Hermann Goring.

In mid-1936 the Army took alarm at these

top The diving eagle *Fallschirmjäger* badge as worn by paratroopers.

above A group of paratroopers after the attack on Holland pose with a civilian, possibly a fifth columnist or collaborator.

developments and started training its own parachute force, but Goering was far too powerful a figure in the Nazi hierarchy and the nascent army parachute battalion was compulsorily transferred en masse to the *Luftwaffe* in January 1939.

When war broke out, the *Fallschirmjäger* seemed a very potent force and played a significant and very successful role in the brief campaigns in Poland, Belgium, Norway and Greece. They were expanding rapidly and despite the continued existence of an air-landing division in the army, the *Fallschirmjäger* also formed an air-landing component in the form of the glider-borne *Luftlande-Sturm Regiment* (air assault regiment). Then came the invasion of the Mediterranean island of Crete which was led by paratroop assaults on three

left Two *Luftwaffe* figures, the one on the left being a paratrooper. Note the camouflaged smock, the MP44 assault rifle and the netting on the paratrooper's helmet. The rucksack on the ground is in *Luftwaffe* blue, although the *Zeltbahn* strapped to it is in splinter camouflage.

above By the end of the war paratroopers were being used as elite infantry, often being deployed to plug the lines in a crisis. This group are hitching a ride on a Panther tank in December 1944 during the Battle of the Bulge.

airfields, with follow-up support provided by the *5 Gebirgsdivision* (mountain division) which was pressed at very short notice into moving to the island by both air and sea. The Germans succeeded but at such heavy cost that Hitler never again allowed the paratroops to be used in such a role.

There were very occasional parachute operations such as a battalion descent in Yugoslavia in May 1944 in an unsuccessful attempt to capture Tito, but by then parachute units were being used as dedicated, reliable, hard-fighting light infantry.

Fallschirmjäger were rushed hither and thither around Europe as a "fire brigade" to plug gaps and shore up collapsing fronts. Thus, despite the disappearance of their ostensible role they continued to expand and by mid-1944 they numbered some 150,000, although only about 30,000 of these were actually jump-qualified. They were, however, superbly fit, well trained, well-equipped and highly motivated, and could be relied upon to do what they were told, to fight hard and to hold on until any hope of success had to be abandoned.

UNIFORMS AND EQUIPMENT

left and right Front and rear views of a splinter-camouflaged paratrooper's smock. The long smock could be gathered between the legs with the edges clipped together or could be left loose. Early war smocks were in a gray-blue color.

left and right The paratrooper helmet followed a similar outline to the standard army one but had no flared rim to catch on rigging lines.

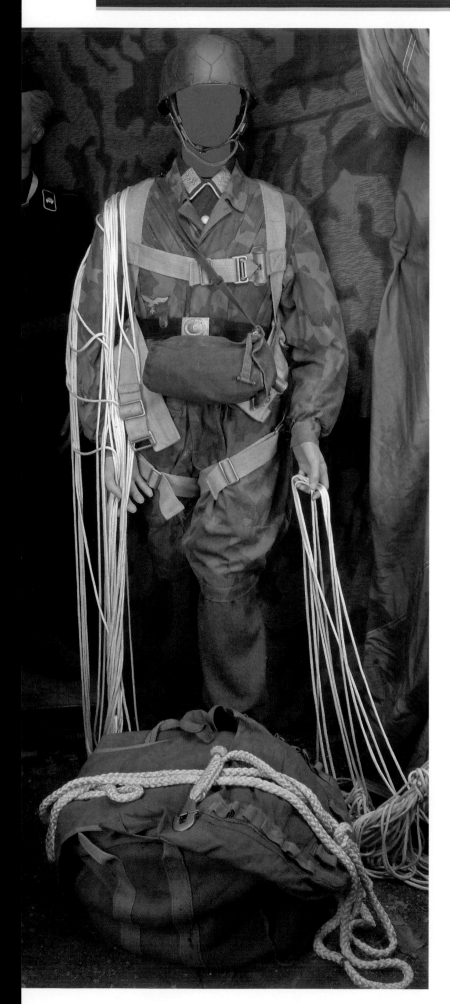

PARACHUTES

The German parachute, known as a *Rücken-packung Zwangauslösung* (literally, "back-packed, automatic release" = RZ) was developed from the early 1930s onwards, the initial models incorporating ideas from pioneers in the field, particularly the Russians, Americans and Italians. Among the models to enter service were the RZ-1, RZ-16 and RZ-20, which differed in detail, but all of which suffered from the same inherent shortcoming, in that, while the Germans based their harness on that developed by Irvin in the United States, they designed their own suspension system.

The parachute operated on the static line principle and there was no separate release for the parachutist; nor did he have a reserve chute. The static line, some 20 feet long, was secured inside the aircraft and as the parachutist fell this pulled the bag containing the canopy from the pack on the man's back; the canopy then deployed and the static line detached itself and the bag.

The problem for German parachutist lay in the single lift web, which forced him to hang in a face forward position. Leaving the aircraft required him to lunge forward into a "spread-eagle" position, which caused the parachute to deploy automatically and quickly. But once in the descent position he had no means of controlling any swing, as did the US or British parachutist with his four lifters. But worse was to come with the landing, which was equivalent to jumping off a sixteen foot wall. His face-forward position meant that he could not use his legs to absorb the shock of hitting the ground, his only recourse being a rapid forward roll. Despite paratroopers being issued with knee- and elbow-pads there were many injuries. A further disadvantage of this system was that it severely limited the amount of equipment the man could carry on his body.

A further danger could arise immediately after landing, if the parachutist was not only unable to control his parachute but also unable to free

above A paratrooper in the process of folding his parachute and gathering in the rigging lines. Notice that he wears *Luftwaffe* uniform and badges under his smock.

above A rare paratrooper's smock in SS "pea" camouflage.

above A pre-war publicity shot of a paratrooper in jump gear, with helmet on and parachute attached. After the jump he would quickly need to find the separate container with his weapon and equipment.

himself. To meet this situation he was provided with a *Fallschirmjäger Messer* (paratrooper's knife), which was popularly nicknamed the *Kapmesser.* This was known in English as a "gravity knife," since, although it looked like a normal clasp-knife, the blade opened automatically as it was withdrawn from its special trouser pocket and was then locked in place by a thumb-catch. This meant that the

above: The gravity knife could be opened with one hand and enabled a paratrooper to cut his way out of tangled rigging lines after landing.

paratrooper could grab the rigging lines with one hand while reaching for and deploying his knife, which could then be used to cut the lines.

The usual aircraft for combat jumps was the tri-motor Junkers Ju-52 with drops usually being made at a speed of about 90 mph at a height of some 400 feet. The system was so designed that the man fell for about 80 feet by which point the parachute was fully deployed and he then continued his descent at a speed of about 16 feet per second. This gave a total time from leaving the aircraft to arriving on the ground of between about 20 and 25 seconds, which was rather less than for US or British paratroops, but any advantage in the air was more than offset by the landing.

CONTAINERS

Weapons and equipment were delivered in specially designed containers, four of which could be carried in a Ju-52 and which were usually thrown out by

above Personal effects of Sgt Major Erwin Haug of the 1st Parachute Regiment. Included are his parachutist badges, Crete shield, Iron Cross 1st and 2nd class, ground assault badge, wound badge, certificates, ID documents and cuff bands.

right Preparing to jump from the door of a Ju 52. He will dive out in a head-down spread-eagle while his parachute opens automatically. Note the padded knee-protectors.

the air dispatchers after the paratroops had jumped. The containers used the same static line system as the men and once the parachute was deployed they fell at a speed of some 18 mph. The most commonly used container was 5 feet long with a square 16 x1 6 inch cross-section, beveled along the long edges to add to the mechanical strength. One side was hinged along its length to form a lid. The lower end of the container was fitted with a shock-absorbing device, and each container had a pair of wheels with balloon tires and a towing handle, so that it could be pulled rapidly away from the landing zone. These containers weighed about 50 pounds empty and could contain loads weighing up to 260 pounds, which were secured by straps with quick-release buckles. These containers could, of course, also be delivered by dedicated aircraft rather than in conjunction with paratroops.

WEAPONS

There were only a very few weapons designed specifically for use by the paratroops and they were normally armed with the usual range of infantry weapons. One such was the FG42 automatic rifle, described in more detail earlier. One of the major disadvantages associated with the German parachute system was that the paratrooper could not carry his rifle with him and had to recover the container before he was properly armed. As a

consequence paratroopers normally carried a pistol for immediate defense on the drop zone, although sometimes one man in four would carry a Machine Pistol MP40.

COMMUNICATIONS

By their very nature, parachute operations presupposed units being widely dispersed immediately after the drop, heavy casualties and a land gap between the parachute headquarters and superior authority. This could only be met by radio and German *Fallschirmjäger* were issued with double

left These men are wearing their smocks both clipped between their legs and hanging loose. One has chest bandoliers for holding FG 42 magazines.

below A group of paratroopers after their daring raid to snatch Mussolini in 1943. They are wearing helmet nets and splinter-camouflaged smocks, and have a mixture of Kar 98 and FG 42 rifles as well as belts for their MG 42 machine gun. The large figure third from the left has bandoliers for FG 42 magazines while the man to his left has a grenade cup on his Kar 98 rifle.

above Paratroopers made extensive use of automatic weapons such as the MP 40. Note the folding stock under the receiver

the normal scale, although the sets themselves were those used by conventional infantry including the *Torn.Fu.b1* (high frequency 3-5 *Megaherz*) and the Torn.Fu.d2 (very high frequency 33.8-38 Mega-herz) manpack sets.

PROVISIONS

When they jumped paratroops carried sufficient rations for three days – two days to be consumed, plus one day's "iron ration." There was no question of the usual mobile kitchen, so the para-troopers carried an Esbit cooker, a very lightweight metal box, measuring no more than 4.7 x 3.5 x 1.2 inches which opened out to form a rudimentary cooking stove burning blocks of hexamine which were stored inside the box. If they had neither been relieved by troops traveling overland nor found local stocks, paratroops needed air resupply. More containers like those described above could be dropped, but there was also the *Versorgungsbombe* (ration bomb), a cylindrical and tailed container shaped like a normal bomb. This was 6 feet long and 18 inches in diameter, and was carried on bomb racks, but contained rations and other supplies for the troops on the ground. It was free-fall and not parachute retarded, which must have added to the excitement for those awaiting its arrival on the ground.

OTHER INFANTRY CONTINGENTS

It is a curious fact of military life in most countries that other parts of an army, or, indeed other services such as the navy and air force, frequently believe that they can take on the infantry role with little or no previous experience or additional training. This attitude certainly occurred in Germany in World War Two where both the *Kriegsmarine* and the *Luftwaffe* fielded specially-formed units to fight in the infantry role, almost always with disastrous consequences.

NAVAL INFANTRY

The Third Reich perceived no need for naval infantry units with an amphibious role equivalent to that of the US Marine Corps or the British Royal Marines. But, as the national situation became increasingly desperate from mid-1944 onwards the *Kriegsmarine* (navy) hastily formed infantry formations from officers and sailors no longer required for purely naval duties. It is noteworthy that, although when raised both divisions were commanded by naval officers, these were both replaced by army officers within a few weeks.

At least two such divisions saw service in the final months of the war. One saw action in February 1945 in north-west Germany against advancing Allied, mainly British and Canadian, troops. The other was formed in March 1945 in the Schleswig-

Holstein area and saw action as far south as Celle before being pushed back past Bremen. It surrendered to British troops in early May. Other divisions were also formed, particularly in the final, increasingly desperate two months of the war, and elements of some may have seen combat, but it was to no avail.

Each of these divisions was supposedly composed of three Naval Infantry Regiments, a Naval Artillery Regiment, a battalion each of Naval Engineers, Communications and *Panzerjaegers*, and a Naval Logistic Support (*Versorgung*) Regiment. There was also one independent naval infantry regiment. All these units were organized on army lines and while they looked good on paper, how many men there actually were, how many and what sort of weapons they were armed with, and how well trained they were is quite another matter.

Officers and sailors of these naval infantry units wore a field-grey uniform generally similar to that of the army, except that the metal buttons were

above Uniform eagle badges came in a wide variety of types, ranging from woven metal thread to simple prints on green triangular patches of material. This one has good quality backing material with a woven gray thread pattern.

stamped with a naval anchor. Personal equipment and weapons, such as the *Mauser K98k*, were identical. However, by the time they took the field in early 1945 there were shortages in every area and it is very unlikely that more than a few were correctly kitted-out or that weapons were fully up to the authorized scale.

far left The tunic is for a naval infantry soldier and has the late-war style of lower pockets, inset into the lining. This tunic belonged to a unit medic, as indicated by the armband and the large pouches for dressings and first aid equipment.

top left A 1943-pattern naval infantry helmet, originally painted in gray and with the gold on black naval eagle decal on the side.

below left Another naval infantry helmet, this time bearing the remains of a camouflage pattern painted over the normal gray color.

right The sleeve badges indicate that these men belong to the RAD (*Reichesarbeitsdienst*), a support organization responsible for field labor and construction. Towards the end of the war many RAD units were pressed into service as untrained infantry.

LUFTWAFFE FIELD DIVISIONS

The Marine Divisions were raised when Germany was in extremis and there may have been some justification for rushing sailors into an army role without adequate training or, perhaps, without even considering transferring them to the army. There was no such excuse for the *Luftwaffe* field divisions. Following its failure to take Moscow in the winter of 1941 the German Army was in desperate straits and one of the non-army elements pressed into service was the *Luftwaffe's* Division *Meindl*, commanded by *Generalmajor* Eugen

below These men from a *Luftwaffe* field division (note the collar badges, breast eagle and Bergmann sub-machine gun) question a Russian woman surviving in the ruins of her home.

LUFTWAFFE FIELD CAP

GAS CAPE IN
GRAY-BLUE COLOR

TONISTOR BACK PACK IN
LUFTWAFFE BLUE-GRAY

LUFTWAFFE TUNIC AND
BADGES

HELMET WITH
LUFTWAFFE EAGLE

STANDARD KAR 98
RIFLE

STANDARD GAS MASK
CASE AND WATER BOTTLE

BLUE-GRAY
BROTBEUTEL
BREADBAG

above and left A Luftwaffe field soldier in full military equipment.

Meindl, a former army officer who had distinguished himself in the attacks on Norway and Crete, and who had formally transferred to the *Luftwaffe* in November 1940. In late 1941 Meindl was on the eastern front, commanding Luftland *Sturmregiment Nr 1*, but in the crisis he was ordered to form *Division Meindl*, which comprised Meindl's own regiment plus four other *Luftwaffe* field regiments, a signals battalion and a ski battalion, all *Luftwaffe* and all in the area at the time. Parts of the division fought very well, because Meindl was an outstanding leader, but overall losses were severe and the division had to be withdrawn to recuperate.

above A soldier from a *Luftwaffe* field division in training. He has camouflage foliage and a face net on his helmet.

At about this time the army high command convinced Hitler that surplus *Luftwaffe* personnel should be transferred to the army and initially he agreed, until a furious Goering managed to make him change his mind and leave them with his beloved *Luftwaffe*. The quid pro quo was a promise from the *Reichsmarschal* that the *Luftwaffe* would form, equip and train 22 infantry divisions, which would fight under army command, but remain under overall *Luftwaffe* control.

In the event, all the promised 22 *Luftwaffe Feld-divisionen* (Air Force field divisions) were actually formed, but despite the title virtually all were considerably smaller than an army division. They normally had four infantry battalions, grandiosely titled *Luftwaffen Jägerbattalionen* (air force light infantry battalions), compared to a minimum of seven in an army division) and only one poorly-equipped artillery battalion, although they did have a full battalion of 88 mm anti-aircraft guns (but these were originally raised by the *Luftwaffe*, anyway).

Other support and logistic units were correspondingly smaller than in the army and were mounted in trucks; they had no horses, which, at least on the Russian front, was by no means an advantage. All of this, combined with their lack of training and battle experience resulted in them marching into one disaster after another.

Most were deployed on the Russian front although there were also several in France and Italy and one each in Greece and Norway. The men wore blue uniforms which made them stand-out from the army and gave the Soviet Army an excellent indication of where a softer than usual target was located.

above A *Luftwaffe* belt buckle with eagle and crest.

ARMORED UNITS

Panzer crews occasionally carried infantry weapons even though their prime role was to fight from their vehicles. This could be to provide security when their vehicles were parked up or to carry out foot reconnaissance before an attack. And in the chaos of the last few months of the war anyone who could carry a rifle was pressed into service, including armor crews who had no vehicle.

below A *Panzer* crewman in military field gear and with a rifle ready to act as a temporary infantryman.

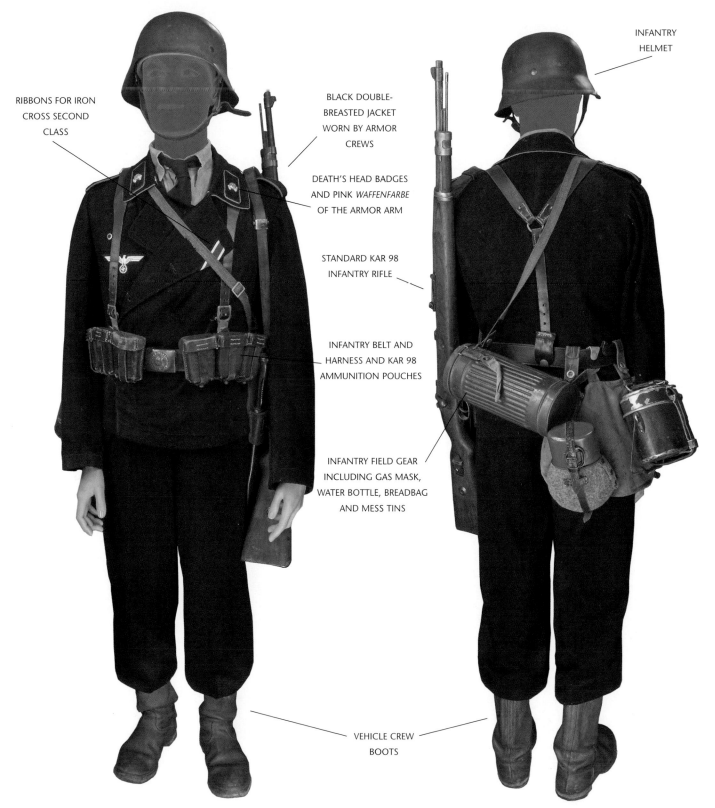

RIBBONS FOR IRON
CROSS SECOND
CLASS

BLACK DOUBLE-
BREASTED JACKET
WORN BY ARMOR
CREWS

DEATH'S HEAD BADGES
AND PINK *WAFFENFARBE*
OF THE ARMOR ARM

INFANTRY
HELMET

STANDARD KAR 98
INFANTRY RIFLE

INFANTRY BELT AND
HARNESS AND KAR 98
AMMUNITION POUCHES

INFANTRY FIELD GEAR
INCLUDING GAS MASK,
WATER BOTTLE, BREADBAG
AND MESS TINS

VEHICLE CREW
BOOTS

217

SPARE BELT FOR THE
MG 42 MACHINE
GUN

STANDARD HELMET
WITH CAMOUFLAGE
NETTING OVER THE TOP

THIS CONFIGURATION WAS
POPULAR LATE IN THE WAR. INSTEAD
OF THE TORNISTOR BACK PACK
THERE WAS A LIGHT A-FRAME ON
THE BACK OF THE HARNESS TO
WHICH WAS ATTACHED THE
BLANKET, *ZELTBAHN* AND MESS TINS

SPARE MG 42
BARREL INSIDE ITS
CARRYING CASE

GRAY DOUBLE-
BREASTED TUNIC
USUALLY WORN BY
ASSAULT GUN
CREWS

WATER BOTTLE
ATTACHED TO
BROTBEUTEL BREAD BAG

MG 42 WITH AMMUNITION
DRUM AND BIPOD IN LIGHT
MACHINE GUN ROLE

above Assault gun crews wore a similar uniform to armor crews but in field gray or sometimes reed green. This man is kitted out for infantry action as a machine gunner

FOREIGN TROOPS

During the war a number of countries provided official and organized contingents which fought alongside the German Army. These were placed under German operational control, but retained a full national identity and structure and wore their own uniforms, and were ultimately the responsibility of their home governments. Thus, for example, the *Corpo de Spedizione Italiano* in Russia (Italian Expeditionary Corps in Russia), which later became the *Armata Italiana* in Russia (Italian Army in Russia) was organized, equipped and trained to Italian standards, and with an internal Italian chain-of-command, but under the operational control of German army and army group commanders. Bulgaria, Hungary and Romania provided similar national contingents, and all these will be discussed separately.

There were, however, a number of bodies which, while the men were grouped together by nationality, the units were actually an integral part of the German Army, wearing German uniform, and armed, dressed and paid as German soldiers. In the case of the Spanish and French, their home governments in Madrid and Vichy took an interest in what happened to their compatriots, but they were by no means in control.

above A Norwegian volunteer in the SS in winter conditions. Such volunteers were often not treated kindly by their own countrymen after the war.

right and below The shield and medal were worn by "East Peoples Volunteers"; men from the Baltic states of Estonia, Latvia and Lithuania who fought in German service against the Russians.

left These badges were worn by Croatian volunteers in a *Waffen-SS* mountain unit fighting against Yugoslav partisans. The red and white shield was worn on a fez-style cap while the other patches were on the tunic collar.

above Spaniards fighting in the Blue Division on the eastern front. Apart from their blue shirts, their uniforms, weapons and equipment were identical to those used by German army formations.

SPANISH BLUE DIVISION

News of the German invasion of the Soviet Union was greeted with such enthusiasm in Madrid that, despite Spain's supposed neutrality, sufficient volunteers, most of them regular soldiers, were forthcoming to enable a complete division to be formed. These volunteers went to Germany where they were kitted out at the Grafenwohr training center with German uniforms and equipment, given the full-range of German weaponry and organized along German lines. The formation came into existence on 25 July 1941 and was designated the 250th Infantry Division of the German army, but was more popularly known as the *Division Azul* (Blue Division), which was the color of the Spanish Falangist shirts they wore.

Organization was almost entirely on the German

pattern, with three infantry regiments, an artillery regiment and the normal engineer, communications, reconnaissance and *Panzerjäger* units. There was the full range of logistic support units, and as with other marching infantry divisions, the 250th used horses rather than trucks. The division was some 17,000 strong when it left for the Soviet Union in August 1941. Organizationally, the division changed little during its period of service, although a Ski Company was added to combat Soviet ski troop incursions in December 1941 and, in line with the rest of the German army, the regiments changed their title from "infantry" to "grenadier" in mid 1943. Officers and men were rotated through the Blue Division, some of them conscripts for the Spanish Army who had not volunteered.

The division suffered such heavy losses in 1943, some 12,776 out of a total of approximately 18,000, that it had to be withdrawn and disbanded in October of that year. This decision was, however, also the result, in part, of very strong diplomatic pressure from Allied governments.

The survivors were ordered home by the Spanish dictator, Generalissimo Franco, but some 2,000 refused and formed the Spanish Legion, also an integral part of the German army, which was organized on similar lines to a *tercio* (regiment) of the Spanish Foreign Legion, with two infantry *bandera* (battalions) and a support bandera with artillery, engineers, communications, and logistics elements. This Legion fought against Soviet partisans in the northern area of the front, but only until April 1944, when, having been pushed back into Estonia, it was decided that they had had enough, the unit was disbanded and the relatively few survivors finally made their way home to Spain.

The officers and men of the 250th Division wore standard German uniform, with three minor variations. First, they wore the Spanish national colors on the right side of the steel helmet and the right sleeve of the field jacket and greatcoat, midway between elbow and shoulder. This was a shield with three horizontal bars of red, yellow and red; the embroidered arm shield also bore the word "ESPAÑA" across the top. Secondly, they wore the Falangist blue shirt under the German jacket, but with the blue collar showing. Thirdly, they wore

both Spanish and German medals and ribbons, which were mounted in the Spanish rather than German manner.

The position of the Blue Division was unusual. Spain was neutral in the war which gripped the rest of Europe, but, as a result of its very recently ended Civil War, many of its people, particularly in the military, were very strongly anti-Communist. Thus, the Spanish dictator, Franco, permitted volunteers to go to Germany to enlist in the German Army, provided that they fought only on the Eastern front and only against Communists. However, although many of the volunteers were actually serving in the Spanish Army, the Blue Division was not a formed unit of that army, but a German unit, which happened to be manned entirely by Spaniards.

LÉGION DES VOLONTAIRES FRANÇAIS (LVF)

The Légion des Volontaires Français contra la Bolshevisme (LVF) was officially *Infanterie-Regiment Nr.638* of the German Army, its title in French being *"638me Regiment Reinforce d'Infanterie Francais."* It was formed from French volunteers in July 1941 and after training in Poland went to the Soviet Union where it formed part of the German 7th Infantry Division. It suffered such heavy losses in the Soviet winter campaign of 1942/43 that it had to be withdrawn and rebuilt, but this time as two semi-independent battalions involved in anti-partisan operations. These were amalgamated in 1943, but the survivors were transferred en bloc from the army to the *Waffen-SS* in September 1944, becoming part of *Waffen-Grenadier Brigade der SS Charlemange.*

As with other foreign volunteer units the LVF was a German unit and not part of the Vichy military forces. The officers and soldiers wore German uniforms, with a helmet transfer and embroidered sleeve badge, consisting of a shield with vertical stripes of red-white-blue, topped by a bar bearing the word "FRANCE."

HILFSWILLIGE (HIWIS)

The German army started the campaign in the East with an inborn contempt for the inhabitants of the Soviet Union, but the enormous losses and desperate supply situation forced them to employ increasing numbers as *Hilfswillige* (volunteer helpers), generally known as "HiWis." They were generally enrolled from the huge numbers of prisoners-of-war, although it was by no means unknown for civilians to volunteer, and they were given non-combatant jobs in the rear areas, such as in the supply and construction organizations, thus releasing ethnic Germans for the fighting units. Some were even employed in the collection and murder of Jews in German-occupied Poland. As these men gained the trust of their captors, they were given jobs ever closer to the forward areas, such as interpreters, horse-cart drivers, stretcher-bearers, etc, but eventually some were formed into combat units, mostly in battalion strength, primarily for employment on anti-partisan duties.

above: Tunic and badges worn by Soviet HiWi volunteers in German service.

Initially unarmed, they were eventually armed with the usual German weapons, primarily the ubiquitous *Mauser 98k*, although some retained Soviet weapons, particularly their machine pistols, which were widely considered to be superior to their German equivalents. Their uniforms went through several stages. At first, they wore Soviet Army uniforms with all badges and insignia removed and an identifying armband marked *"Im Dienst der deutschen Wehrmacht"* (In the service of the German Armed Forces), or sometimes simply *"Deutsche Wehrmacht."* Throughout 1942, as their numbers increased and their reliability came to be recognized, the authorities made strenuous efforts to clothe them in German field-grey uniforms with a shield identifying their ethnic origin. On the collar they wore a dark-green patch with a white stripe, while the epaulette was in dark green with a red border. However, clothing was in ever-shorter supply and these men were at the very

above A Moslem auxiliary in German service in the Balkans

left The *Waffen-SS* recruited many volunteers from different nationalities and ethnic groups although they were never regarded as full members of the SS. Many thousands of Moslems joined, mainly from Soviet territories, in the hope of overthrowing the Communist government. Many wore these fez-style hats adorned with the eagle and death's head badge of the SS.

below Another fez hat worn by an SS volunteer. After Germany surrendered most of the survivors were handed to the Soviet Government where they were either executed immediately or condemned to harsh sentences in Gulag work camps.

left Cossacks had no love for the Soviet Communist government and many willingly served in German uniform. They were employed in both eastern and western theaters.

end of the chain, so it is unlikely that more than a few ever received the proper uniform.

The enrolment of these men and their employment seems to have been left to the individual initiative of field commanders at divisional level and below, and there was certainly no authorized table of establishment. Some undoubtedly helped the Germans because of their hatred of the Soviet regime, while others did so to escape from the rigors of a prisoner-of-war camp, and yet others because it was simply a matter of survival and a way to gain some food and shelter. It should be noted that because the Soviet Union had failed to sign the 1929 Geneva Convention on the Treatment of Prisoners-of-War, German employment of such prisoners on paramilitary, and eventually combat tasks did not strictly contravene international law, although after the war the Soviet authorities simply regarded the men concerned as traitors and either executed them on the spot or sent them to Siberia.

CAVALRY

Despite equipping increasing numbers of *Panzer* and *Panzergrenadier* divisions from 1935 onwards, the *Wehrmacht* continued to employ cavalry units throughout the war. A cavalry brigade took part in the invasion of Poland and was so successful that it was increased to divisional strength in time for the invasion of France. This was, however, the last time a full cavalry formation was employed in western Europe and it then moved to the east where it took part in the invasion of the Soviet Union, but in early 1943 it was converted to tanks, becoming *24th Panzer Division*. In 1942 the army raised an auxiliary force from Cossack volunteers and these were first converted into full-time military units and then, in April 1943, they were amalgamated into *1. Kosaken Kavallerie Division* (1st Cossack Cavalry Division). They were engaged mainly on anti-partisan operations under command of *2nd Panzer Armee*, but were eventually transferred into the *Waffen-SS Kavallerie Korps*. From 1935 onwards, however, infantry divisions included a Reconnaissance Battalion (*Aufklärungsabteilung*) composed of three squadrons, one mounted on horses, one on bicycles and a support squadron armed with light guns and armored cars. These continued in existence on the eastern front, but in 1944 the cavalry squadrons were withdrawn and grouped to form cavalry regiments and at the war's end these were being grouped into army (as opposed to *Waffen-SS*) cavalry divisions.

above: A cavalry unit prepares for a river crossing. Equipment and weapons are being wrapped in Zeltbahn to make reasonably watertight packages.

above: Cavalry units were effective for anti-partisan and security duties in the Ukraine and Byelorussia.

JAPAN

The Japanese soldier was probably the toughest of all of the major combatants, with a willingness to face death that was unparalleled by the soldiers of any other country. But this willingness to fight to the end was squandered by the uncoordinated strategy of his superiors, where an aggressive doctrine and self-belief caused Japan to overreach and end up simultaneously fighting the mightiest industrial power (the United States), the greatest land power (Russia) and the most extensive empire (the British).

A lack of natural resources and industrial power meant that the Japanese soldier was at the end of a very thin supply chain indeed, but that didn't stop him fighting on when all sensible hope of victory had long passed.

THE JAPANESE ARMY

At the time of the attack on Pearl Harbor, the Japanese Army was approximately 375,000 strong with trained reserves of about two million. This army had to serve in areas ranging from the semi-Arctic conditions of Sakhalin to the tropics in the south, and from the open rolling country of Manchaca to the jungles of south-east Asia, as well as undertake assaults on many islands across the Pacific basin.

The army was overwhelmingly infantry-oriented. Japanese tanks, artillery and support equipment were never supplied in the quantities available to US forces, and although much of the artillery was light and reasonably effective, Japanese armor and anti-tank weapons were mostly second-rate designs.

THE INFANTRY SOLDIER

The Japanese soldier's training was thorough and little different from that in any other army except for intense study of the "soldier's code," known as Yamato Damashi, which translates roughly as "the traditional spirit of Japan." This code laid down a number of precepts under which the soldier had to conduct his military life, much of which was unremarkable; for example, obedience to orders, to be brave and to behave correctly.

above At the start of the war, Japanese infantry swept aside almost all opposition in a rapid series of aggressive campaigns.

below Uniform service cap of an infantry soldier with red piping and cap band, and tan interior.

There was, however, one element went far beyond virtually all other codes, especially those in Western armies, which was the welcoming of death on the battlefield in two circumstances. The first was in pursuit of the immediate military objective; for example, in an attack an engineer would deliberately lay on a barbed wire entanglement and blow himself up in order to clear a path for an attack, or a soldier would sit in a hole in a road grasping an aircraft bomb which he would detonate when a tank passed over. The second circumstance was that death was preferable to surrender; indeed, to become a prisoner-of-war brought dishonor not only on the soldier but also on his family.

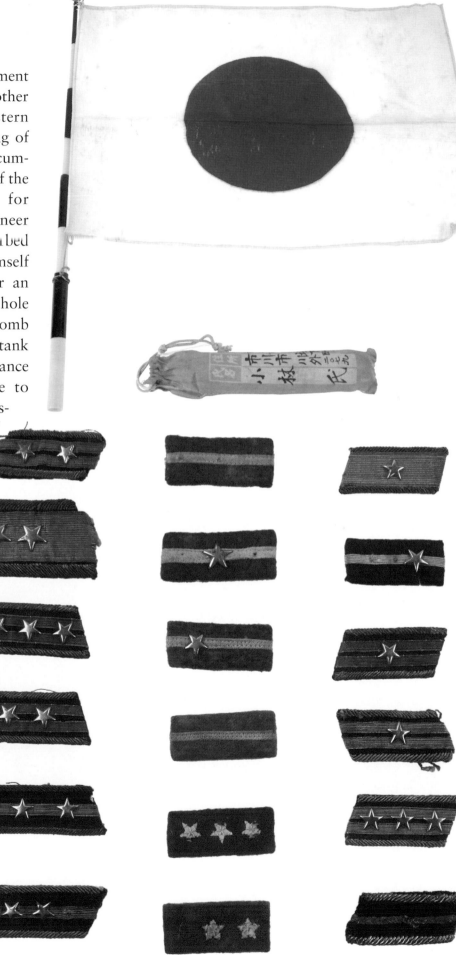

above right Japanese infantry units made great use of flags for communications, identification and to boost morale. This signal flag has a small cloth storage bag.

right Collar badges for NCOs and officers. These were either worn on the high turn-down collar of the Model 98 tunic or on the open front of the tropical uniform. The left hand column shows badges for captain through to lieutenant-general, the center column shows the badges for private to 2nd lieutenant, while the right hand shows more officers badges up to major-general. The diagram on page 235 gives more details of infantry rank badges.

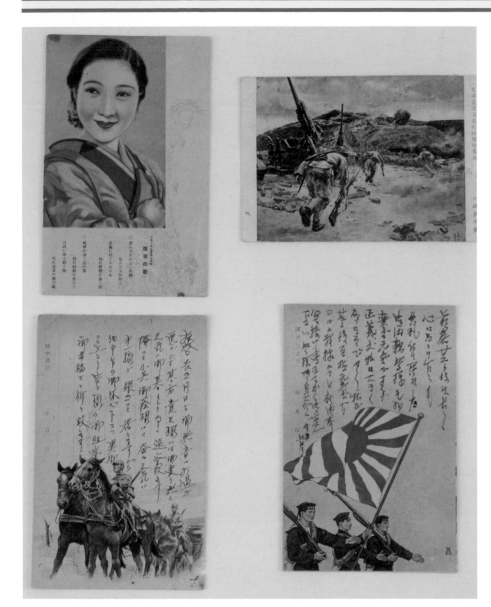

left Postcards used by soldiers to send short messages home. As with most armies these show either uplifting scenes of military valor or images to remind the soldier of home, family and sweetheart.

right An army private in a Type 98 raincoat. Unusually for this rank he has a pair of issue binoculars.

far right A captain in Model 98 uniform demonstrates how the Japanese soldier had to carry individual items with their own shoulder straps rather than have them attached to a harness or load-carrying system.

below Collar of a tunic worn by a Private First Class, showing where the rank badges were fitted.

SPECIAL FORCES

The Japanese Army never saw any need for Special Forces in the way that the US Army had Rangers and the British their Special Air Service. There were Special Naval Landing Forces, but these were effectively sailors who went ashore, and there were both army and navy paratroops and army raiding forces, but apart from a few operations in 1941-42 none of these was particularly successful. Nor was there a need for politically motivated special units on the lines of the German *Waffen-SS* or the Italian Blackshirts, since all Japanese soldiers were fully motivated by love of and obedience to the Emperor.

IN ACTION

The Japanese Army contained many contradictions. Internal discipline was very severe, starting with the premise that every order passed from a superior to

a subordinate came with the authority of the Emperor. Thus, obedience was absolute and unquestioning. On the other hand, the dress, particularly on operations, was untidy and would never have passed muster in a German unit, while when on the move the soldiers simply walked, rather than marched, taking a drink as and when it suited and

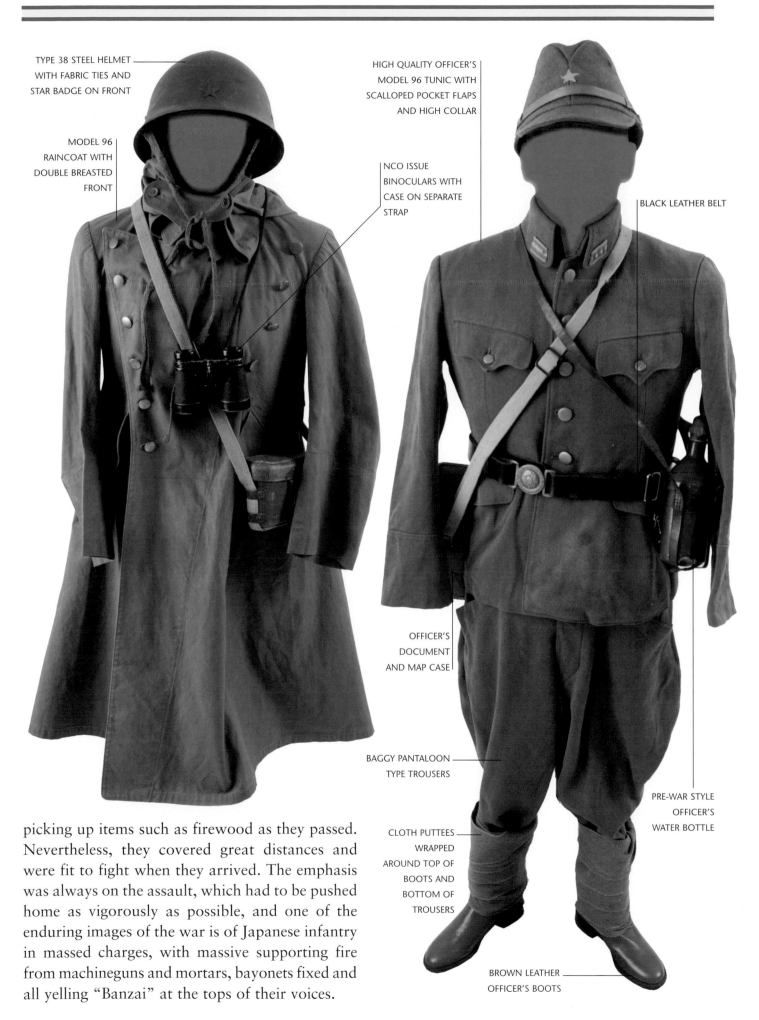

TYPE 38 STEEL HELMET WITH FABRIC TIES AND STAR BADGE ON FRONT

MODEL 96 RAINCOAT WITH DOUBLE BREASTED FRONT

HIGH QUALITY OFFICER'S MODEL 96 TUNIC WITH SCALLOPED POCKET FLAPS AND HIGH COLLAR

NCO ISSUE BINOCULARS WITH CASE ON SEPARATE STRAP

BLACK LEATHER BELT

OFFICER'S DOCUMENT AND MAP CASE

BAGGY PANTALOON TYPE TROUSERS

PRE-WAR STYLE OFFICER'S WATER BOTTLE

CLOTH PUTTEES WRAPPED AROUND TOP OF BOOTS AND BOTTOM OF TROUSERS

BROWN LEATHER OFFICER'S BOOTS

picking up items such as firewood as they passed. Nevertheless, they covered great distances and were fit to fight when they arrived. The emphasis was always on the assault, which had to be pushed home as vigorously as possible, and one of the enduring images of the war is of Japanese infantry in massed charges, with massive supporting fire from machineguns and mortars, bayonets fixed and all yelling "Banzai" at the tops of their voices.

In the opening months of the war they swept all before them and they showed remarkable endurance, doggedness and skill in all their campaigns. They even proved very adept at jungle warfare, even though it was a type of terrain and vegetation for which they had no previous experience. In 1941 and early 1942 this was sufficient and they conquered vast swathes of territory.

Once the Allies had come to understand what was going on the shortcomings of Japanese tactics were quickly revealed and they were forced onto the defensive. Japanese industry could not adequately supply and support their forces, and the supply lines themselves became more and more vulnerable to US and Commonwealth naval, land and air forces. However, if Japanese infantrymen had been determined in the advance, they were even more so in defeat and, as all the Allied armies discovered, they fought – and usually died – for every yard of ground. Thus, every island had to be fought for and there was no question of negotiating surrenders when all was clearly lost. Approximately 1.25 million Japanese soldiers died in the war, the vast majority of them in the infantry.

above Rapid movement, infiltration and sudden aggressive charges were essential elements of Japanese infantry tactics.

opposite right Paper and silk fans were important symbols of status as well as being practical for keeping cool or as accessories in polite surroundings.

above An officer's compass and carrying case, which could be attached to the uniform belt.

right The *Kempetai* military police force were feared for their brutality and use of torture, especially in occupied territories. They wore army-style uniform but with a black collar, and with *Kempetai* badges on collar and headgear.

below Lightweight bamboo sun helmets were also used in tropical climates, usually worn with a fabric outer cover, as seen here.

right A close-up of a *Kempetai* belt buckle, with the English language word "Constabulary" embossed on it.

233

RANKS

When the Model 90 uniform was introduced, rank badges were on the shoulder but from 1938 onwards these were moved to detachable collar patches for all ranks. The system of rank badges was very simple. There was a basic patch for each grade (private, NCO, company officer, field officer and general officer) and steps within that grade were marked by the addition of stars. Later, in 1944, rank badges were added to the cuff of the jacket for warrant and commissioned officers.

A variety of special badges could be earned for particular specializations, (e.g., farriers, blacksmiths), proficiency (marksmen, signalers) and good conduct. In addition, as with the German Army and its *Waffwenfarbe,* the Japanese indicated a soldier's arm- of-service by a colored badge, in this case a small chevron, which was worn above the right pocket. The more common colors were:

right A colonel of cavalry in finely-tailored Type 98 uniform, complete with medal ribbons, high riding boots, spurs and riding crop. The red and white sash denotes he is acting as duty "Officer of the Day" in barracks.

Arm of Service	Color	Remarks
Armor	Crimson	Same as infantry
Artillery	Yellow	Gunners in infantry units were infantry, not artillery
Army Aviation	Sky blue	Land-based air force was part of army (as with USAAF)
Bandsmen	Blue	
Cavalry	Green	Horsed units; i.e., not tanks
Engineers	Maroon	
Infantry	Crimson	
Medical	Dark Green	
Military police	Black	
Transport	Deep blue	

All these badges, apart from those indicating rank, were left behind in barracks when soldiers went on operations.

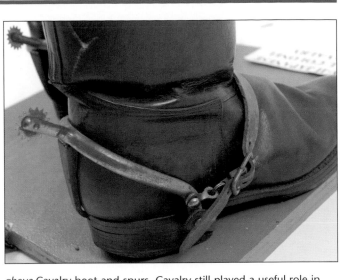

above Cavalry boot and spurs. Cavalry still played a useful role in China and in internal security duties.

left A leather map and document case for use by officers and NCOs.

above Captain's badges on a greatcoat collar.

JAPANESE INFANTRY RANK BADGES

Collar tabs (soldiers and NCOs)

below Collar and sleeve badges for infantry soldiers up to the rank of Colonel.

Private	Private 2nd class	Private 1st class	Superior Private	Lance Corporal	Corporal	Sergeant	Sergeant Major

Collar tabs and cuff badges (officers)

Warrant officer	2nd lieutenant	Lieutenant	Captain	Major	Lt Colonel	Colonel

THE INFANTRY REGIMENT

The basic unit of Japanese infantry was the regiment, with three in both Type A and B divisions. Strengths of these regiments could vary widely, from 3,000 (or less) in a Type B division to almost 6,000 in a Type A division. There were also numerous independent regiments, virtually all of which were designed to meet specific operational situations. Thus, although the following is typical, it should be noted that there was no such thing as a fixed organization.

Infantry units were designated by numbers in a very straightforward system, the regiments being numbered in two series. The shorter of these were the elite imperial guards units, which were designated 1st, 2nd, 3rd, 4th, 5th and 6th Guards Infantry Regiments. All the remaining line regiments were numbered sequentially from 1st Infantry Regiment onwards; there were no territorial or other qualifications in the titles.

An infantry regiment generally consisted of regimental headquarters and three infantry battalions, plus a machine gun company and a communications platoon, both of the latter being manned by infantry and not specialist artillery or signals personnel.

Within each regiment battalions were numbered consecutively from 1 to 3 and companies numbered across the regiment as a whole. Thus,

- 1 Battalion = 1, 2, 3 Rifle Companies; 4 Machine gun Company
- 2 Battalion = 5, 6, 7 Rifle Companies; 8 Machine gun Company.
- 3 Battalion = 9, 10, 11 Rifle Companies; 12 Machinegun Company.

Platoons were numbered consecutively from 1 to 3 within their companies, and sections from 1 to 6 within their platoons.

right Infantry moving forward through light forest. They have netting over their helmets to allow the attachment of foliage for camouflage. They also have sword bayonets fitted to their *Arisaka* rifles.

right An officer surveys the wide-open terrain of Manchuria with his sword hanging by his side. Japanese officers took swords into battle as a matter of course, using them as a badge of rank and even as a weapon when at close quarters.

below A soldier with no rank badges and wearing a lightweight tropical shirt. He has a water bottle, document pouch and the leather case for a sniper's telescopic sight. Also visible are the shoulder straps of his backpack.

Regimental Headquarters. The regiment was commanded by a full colonel, with a major as his principal staff officer, assisted by a lieutenant. Two lieutenant-colonels were attached to a regimental headquarters, one in charge of administration the other of training, and these were assisted by up to six officers "borrowed" from the battalions under command. There were also a number of officers, warrant officers and NCOs from the intendance, medical and ordnance services who dealt with matters such as pay, supply, medical and repair.

Communications Platoon. The communications platoon was commanded by a lieutenant who had passed a specialist course at an infantry school. The platoon was about 40 strong and equipped with telephones and wire; there were very few radios at this level.

Heavy Weapons Company. The Heavy Weapons Company consisted of three platoons:
- One Gun Platoon of two sections, each with one 37 mm infantry gun
- Two Mortar Platoons, each of two sections with one mortar each.

237

THE INFANTRY BATTALION

An infantry battalion consisted of battalion headquarters, with a major in command and a junior captain as adjutant, four rifle companies, a gun platoon and a machine-gun company.

Rifle Company. A rifle company had a strength of 4 officers and 150–160 other ranks, commanded by a captain. Typical strength of the headquarters was 1 officer plus 15–18 NCOs and enlisted; there was no authorized post of second-in-command. Communications were by runners, buglers and visual signals.

Rifle Platoon. A rifle platoon was commanded by a lieutenant, assisted by an NCO, and here, too, the organization was flexible. Early in the war it was organized into six squads, four of them composed of riflemen only (one NCO plus seven enlisted), while the fifth and sixth were armed with light machine guns (LMG).

Later there were three rifle squads of some 12–13 men, in which the LMG teams were an integral part of the squad. The remaining men were armed with four Type 89 Grenade Launchers in three four-man teams, and these could be either grouped together or allocated on a semi-permanent basis of one team to each squad.

Gun Platoon. The battalion gun platoon was normally armed with two Type 92 70 mm Infantry Guns. Although termed a "platoon" this sub-unit was actually about 70 men strong, the large number being needed to move the guns, particularly in hilly or jungle terrain, and to ensure ammunition supply in an army where logistics were nothing like as sophisticated in European armies.

Machine gun Company. The machine gun company of an infantry battalion was commanded by a captain and organized into three platoons. Nos. 1 and 2 platoons, each consisted of two sections of one gun each, for a battalion total of four guns. The third platoon was responsible for ammunition supply.

left Another attack being pressed home. The officer in the lead has his sword drawn while the men are relatively unladen, only carrying the most basic equipment needed to fight and survive in the front line.

above Another view of the prismatic compass, unfolded so the user can march on a particular bearing.

right Radios were not widely issued, and older methods of communication such as this Ichiki bugle were still used. This one was captured by an American soldier in August 1942.

left and right Front and rear views of an infantry sergeant with a simple leather-covered backpack.

below A platoon flag from an infantry unit. As well as a signaling tool, these were also prized souvenirs by Allied soldiers.

Colors

The regimental color consisted of the Japanese military flag (red sun and rays on a white ground) which was bordered by a purple tasseled fringe. This was mounted on a pole, capped by the Imperial crest, a chrysanthemum. On parade and other ceremonial occasions this color was carried by a junior lieutenant. During World War II most regiments took their colors on operations, as well, and even carried them unfurled when circumstances permitted.

All infantry battalions had a distinguishing flag, but its purpose was to indicate the location of battalion headquarters rather than as a traditional symbol. These were made of white cloth and about 36 in (1 m) square with distinguishing zigzagged stripes running horizontally across the center: 1st Bn — one red zigzag; 2nd Bn — one red, one black zigzag; 3rd Bn — three zigzags (red, black, red).

COMMAND AND LOGISTICS

COMMUNICATIONS

With their conquests spread over much of the eastern hemisphere, Japanese long-distance strategic communications depended primarily on radio. They were, therefore, subject to the problems common to that era, including fading, interference from other stations, the need to change frequencies at night – and interception. After a slow start, Allied interception and cryptanalysis of Japanese communications became a very sophisticated operation and an astonishing amount of intel-

above Close-up of a fine leather officer's pouch for documents and maps. Only officers and senior NCOs were expected to be able to read maps. Soldiers were expected to just follow orders and die if necessary.

right A simple signal flag and its wooden box. The box has room for another flag, now missing, which would have been of another color.

above Men and supplies coming ashore. The Japanese Army relied on its soldiers to be able to live and fight with much less supplies and support than a western soldier.

ligence was gained. This not only resulted in strategic successes, but also in tactical battlefield advantages, as well.

At the level covered by this book, radios were used from division back to army level, and from division forward to regiment, but there was little forward of that. As a result, regiments and battalions depended on cable and telephones, runner, whether on foot or motorcycle, visual means (flags), and bugles.

LOGISTICS

The Japanese Army reduced logistic support to what was almost certainly the lowest level of any major army, but, simple as their demands were, even Japanese soldiers had to eat, drink and be given medical treatment when ill. Also, animals had to be fed, watered and treated when sick, or automobiles and trucks supplied with

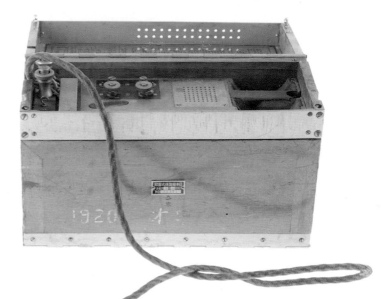

above Field telephones such as this were useful when a static or defensive position was created. They were less so during an attack.

below A clip of five 7.7 mm rifle cartridges. This round was introduced to replace the less powerful 6.5 mm cartridge, although the older ammunition stayed in service throughout the war.

right A wooden box for 100 rounds of 6.5 mm ammunition. Some individual cartridges can be seen in front of it.

gasoline and lubricants. Finally, and by no means the least important, weapons had to be supplied with ammunition, and all forms of equipment maintained, repaired, supplied with spare parts or replaced.

AMMUNITION

The general staff's requirement was that one day's ammunition at standard firing rates should carried within units (either on the man in the case of small arms ammunition or on unit trans-

above and right Leather ammunition pouches and paper packs for 7.7 mm cartridges. The pouches were worn on the front of the belt, one on either side.

left A selection of medicine and drug bottles used by military medics. Japanese medical support was scarce, and wounded men were often left to fend for themselves.

right A superior private in tropical uniform getting ready to prepare a meal.

FIELD CAP WITH NECK PROTECTION FLAPS ATTACHED

TROPICAL TUNIC WITH COLORED CHEVRON SHOWING BRANCH OF SERVICE. (ARTILLERY)

MESS TIN. THE LID DOUBLES AS A PAN, AND THERE WAS USUALLY ANOTHER PAN INSIDE.

PUTTEES AND SHORT BOOTS

port) and that a further one day of fire be carried by divisional transport. This one day of fire amounted to about 500 tons and required about 600 two-wheeled carts, plus 600 horses, or 250 trucks.

RATIONS

All troops were encouraged to make maximum use of local supplies and Japanese soldiers were notorious throughout their occupied territories for purloining meat, vegetables and rice from the inhabitants, almost invariably without payment. However, the army could not rely on this and, as always, there was a staff planning figure, which was that one man consumed 2.75 pounds (1.25 kg) per day, made up of varying amounts of rice, barley, dried fish/tinned meat, salt and shoyu (a form of Soya sauce) to which were added 8 oz (230g) of vegetables or eggs, when available. Every man carried one day's iron rations, plus one day's fresh rations and five day's supply of rice. A further one day's ration was carried in unit transport and two day's aboard divisional transport.

One factor that placed the Japanese Army apart from virtually every other army in the world, was that there were no arrangements for communal cooking. Thus, there no field kitchens and every man cooked for himself, or, at best, in groups of two or three within their squads.

right A lieutenant of cavalry in woolen service dress (note the blue cavalry chevron on his chest).

TRANSPORT

As with most other armies, the Japanese Army started to replace animals with motor vehicles from the 1920s onwards. The process was, however, very slow and military production centered on tanks, armored cars and guns, with logistic vehicles being given a low priority. As a result, by the time war broke out some infantry divisions had vehicle-born support, while most others retained horse and wagons. The army was very avaricious where civilian transport was

above The distinctive split-toe sole of the lightweight *Tabi* boot. This design supposedly gives better grip on difficult terrain or when climbing walls or trees.

above Cloth puttees give protection and support to the lower leg. They were held in place by cotton tapes, which were often tied off in cross pattern over the front of the puttee.

concerned and purloined almost any available vehicle, which was then driven until it fell apart.

A divisional horse-drawn logistic battalion, for example, had approximately 750 men and 650 horses, with 600 two-wheeled carts, each capable of carrying a load of 500 pounds (227 kg) for a total lift of 150 tons. A motorized battalion had 250 trucks, 20 automobiles, 5 gasoline trucks, 75 motor-cycles and approximately 1,500 men, giving a total lift of some 500 tons.

FORAGE

Where horses and mules were used, they had to be supplied with forage and the staff planning figure was 0.013 tons (26 pounds/ 12 kg) per horse per day. Thus for an estimated 4,000 horses in a division the daily requirement was 104 tons.

above A leather forage bag which would be carried on the horse, attached to the saddle.

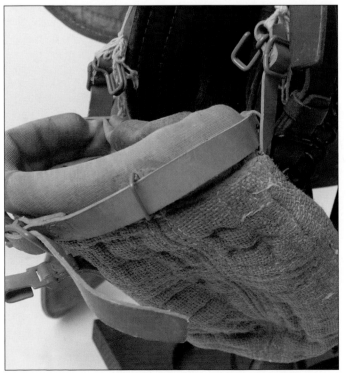

above A close-up of a horse's feed bag, carried by the saddle. The bag would be tied to the horse's bridle to allow it to eat.

right An officer in the veterinary corps – an essential service when an army depends on animal transport. He carries a canvas equipment bag as well as a leather document case. Note also the leather officer's gaiters he wears over his boots instead of cloth puttees.

UNIFORMS AND EQUIPMENT

The uniforms of the Japanese officers and soldiers were among the most simple, least flamboyant and most serviceable in any army, with only minimal distinctions between officers, NCOs and enlisted men. There were five orders of dress, three of which are not strictly relevant here, but are mentioned for completeness.

Full Dress was a blue uniform with frock coat, French-style *kepi* and white plume, and trousers with a vertical stripe in the wearer's "arm color" (crimson for infantry, for example). This was worn only by officers and warrant officers on very special ceremonial occasions.

Number One Khaki, was worn by all ranks on ceremonial occasions, other than those for which blues were worn.

Fatigue Dress consisted of a denim tunic and trousers for training and rough work; it was worn by NCOs and privates and was khaki in color throughout the army except for engineers, who wore white.

Number Two Khaki was the normal working dress in barracks

Field Service Dress was simply Number Two Khaki but with the addition of full personal equipment

above A 1938-type (known as a Model 98) officer's tunic with lieutenant's badges on the collar. This one also has braid on the shoulders and an artillery lanyard. The medals are (from left to right): 1914–1920 World War I; 1931–43 Manchurian "Incident"; and 1928 Hirohito enthronement medal.

right Puttees were worn by many nations, including the Japanese. These strips of cloth were wrapped around the lower leg, usually in a spiral, then tied off with the fabric tape.

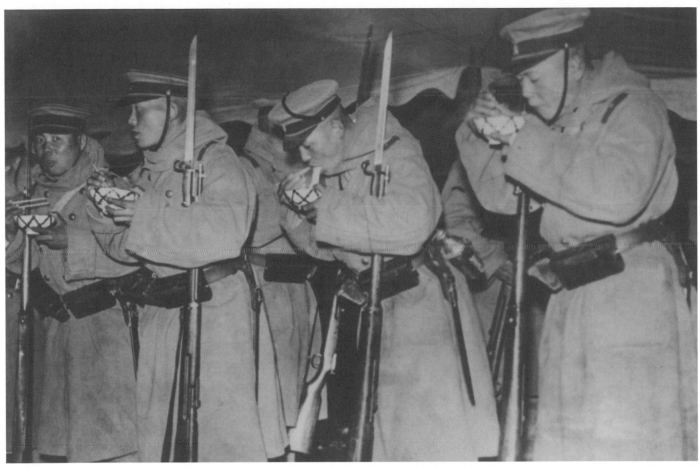

above Eating from a ceremonial bowl, these men are wearing peaked service cap with the red band and a greatcoat with a detachable hood. Their rank badges are over the ends of their shoulders, in the style of the older 1930 (Model 90) uniform design. On their belts they wear leather ammunition pouches for their 6.5 mm *Arisaka* rifles.

right A lieutenant in Model 98 tunic and peaked cap. Officers bought their own tunics so a wide variation of materials and cuts can be found. This uniform is a well-made specimen. He has a cord pistol lanyard over one shoulder, while the red and white sash over the other shows he is acting as duty officer (officer-of-the-day) for his unit.

right A captain from the Special Naval Landing Force in tropical uniform. The lightweight shirt has short sleeves, an open collar and his rank badge above the breast pocket. His lightweight trousers are held up with fabric ties instead of a belt. Note also the shoulder straps for his backpack and the water bottle and carrier at his side.

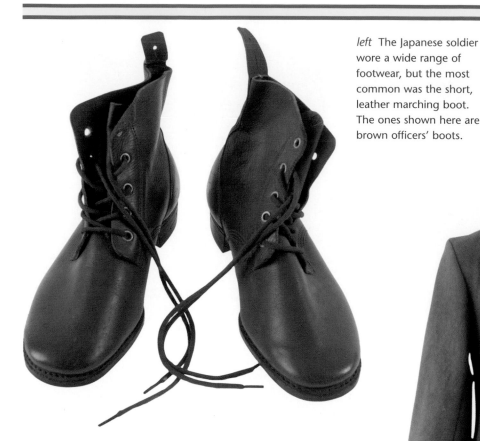

left The Japanese soldier wore a wide range of footwear, but the most common was the short, leather marching boot. The ones shown here are brown officers' boots.

and weapons. This uniform, of which the version in service throughout the war was the Model 98 (i.e., introduced in 1938), was produced in two versions: temperate climates — yellowish khaki wool – and tropical and summer wear — khaki drill, which was lighter in weight and easier to wash.

The basic uniform consisted of a tunic with a turn-down collar, which was normally worn open, over a lighter colored shirt, whose collar was usually worn outside that of the tunic. The rank badges were worn on the lapels of the tunic. Ties were not worn. All ranks wore pantaloons which buttoned below the knee. Officers wore high German-style boots (the so-called "jack boots") or ankle boots with long leather leggings, all in brown leather, while NCOs and enlisted men wore black ankle boots, with puttees worn up to the knee, the tapes always at the top and secured in a criss-cross pattern. These puttees were also sometimes worn by officers.

All ranks were issued with a greatcoat, which had a detachable hood. For really cold weather special clothing was issued. This included a loose serge overcoat, with goatskin-lined collar and which was worn over the greatcoat, sheepskin waistcoat, mittens and nose protector.

right A captain wearing a neat double-breasted Type 3 (1943) greatcoat and brown boots.

A Private First Class wearing the Model 98 uniform in heavy wool, typical of those worn in temperate and winter climates such as in China and Manchuria.

PEAKED FIELD CAP WITH SINGLE STAR (WORN BY ALL RANKS)

PRIVATE FIRST CLASS RANK BADGES ON COLLAR.

HEAVY WOOLEN TUNIC FOR TEMPERATE AND WINTER CLIMATES.

LEATHER PISTOL HOLSTER AND SHOULDER STRAP. NOTE LACK OF LANYARD IN THIS CASE.

BROWN LEATHER BELT

FULL-LENGTH PANTALOON STYLE TROUSERS IN HEAVY WOOL. A PRIVATE SOLDIER WOULD NORMALLY WEAR PUTTEES ON HIS LOWER LEGS WHEN IN THE FIELD, BUT THIS FIGURE DOESN'T HAVE THEM ON.

SHORT MARCHING BOOTS IN BROWN LEATHER.

HEADGEAR

Various forms of headgear could be worn. The Japanese Army's service cap was similar in style but of much inferior quality to that worn in the United States Army. The Japanese model was made of khaki cloth, with black leather visor and chinstrap, and red piping around the rim of the circular crown. There was a 1.5-inch (38 mm) wide red cap band with a gilt yellow, five-pointed star in the center at the front. There were no indications of rank, except that officers' service caps were of a better quality.

below An interior view of the same cap where you can see the separate red capband and leather interior headband. The lining is made from silk and has the manufacturer's symbols printed on it. Note also the black underside to the leather peak and the ventilation holes either side of the crown.

right An officer-quality service cap with red cap band and piping, black leather visor and a black leather chinstrap.

below Army service caps were decorated with a simple metal 5-pointed star at the front.

left A soldier's or NCO's service cap. Of similar design to the officer's cap it is made from inferior materials and to lower standards of workmanship. These caps were worn in rear areas and on garrison duty but not in combat.

above This cap sports the same gilt metal star on the cap band as does the officer's one.

right An interior view of the soldier's and NCO's service cap. Compared to the officer's model: the headband is not as rigid, the lining is of lower quality material, and the black leather peak has a brown underside.

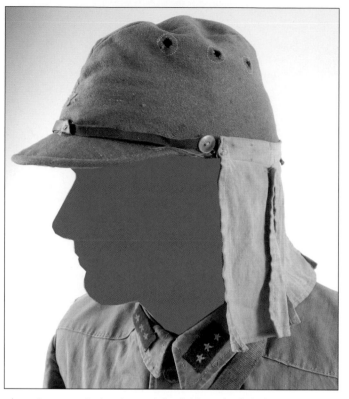

left Officers and soldiers wore this simple field cap made from a variety of materials. For army personnel the only badge was the simple woven star at the front, above the short peak and chinstrap.

above Some tropical variants of the field cap had cloth neck protection and extra ventilation holes as seen here.

left: A sentry with fixed bayonet, in tropical uniform and with puttees, wears neck protection on his service cap.

The Japanese field cap was a unique shape. It was made of olive-drab/khaki cloth, with a high crown topped by a gusset, which gave a flattop. It had a short, stiffened peak in the same material, which was sharply angled downwards, and a brown leather chinstrap. A small star on a circular cloth backing was positioned on the front vertical seam – silver for officers, gold for enlisted men. The field cap could be worn with lowered neck flaps in tropical climes, and there were prominent ventilation holes around the crown.

A winter cap was issued to all ranks in Manchukuo. This had fur-lined ear flaps and a fur-lined visor.

above Winter uniform included a thick coat with fur-lined collar. The fur-lined winter cap gave good protection from cold weather, especially when the side flaps were folded down and tied beneath the chin.

above As with other Japanese headgear the sun helmet was decorated with the five-pointed star, this time stitched to the fabric cover.

above Japanese Army headgear for all ranks had almost no decoration, and usually just sported a simple five-pointed yellow or gold star in front. In this case the sun helmet had a printed star on a patch, sewn on to the front of the fabric helmet cover.

right An inside view of the sun helmet (this one being made from bamboo) showing the structure and fabric ties. Such helmets only provided cover from the sun and gave no protection against fragments or bullets.

Sun helmets (sometimes known as "solar topis") were issued for wear in tropical areas. These were of similar shape to the steel helmet, but made of cork and fitted with a khaki-colored canvas cover which was held in place by two narrow cloth bands, one around the rim, the other where the skirt angled outwards, There was a yellow embroidered star on a circular khaki cloth backing front center. A khaki cloth chinstrap was also fitted. A white cover with light tan cloth bands was sometimes worn by more senior officers.

STEEL HELMET

The Japanese Type 90 steel helmet was of a symmetrical domed design with a slightly turned-out rim. It was painted in a matt khaki color (white in winter) and had a metal five-pointed star at front center. It was often worn over the field cap and often covered with a camouflage net or canvas cover. The built-in liner was of leather, but this rotted quickly in tropical conditions and was often replaced by cloth substitutes.

left The standard Model 90 (1938) steel helmet had a distinctive bowl shape with slightly flared rim.

above The Model 90 had a leather or fabric liner to fix it on to the wearer's head.

above An inside view showing how the net fitted over the rim and the fabric straps which were tied around the wearer's neck. Japanese helmets didn't have leather straps or metal buckles but instead used these simple ties.

left A Model 90 with string netting over the top. This was very common and allowed the wearer to attach foliage and twigs for extra camouflage.

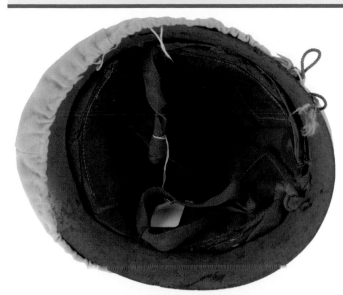

above Another interior view, this time of a helmet with the fabric cover fitted.

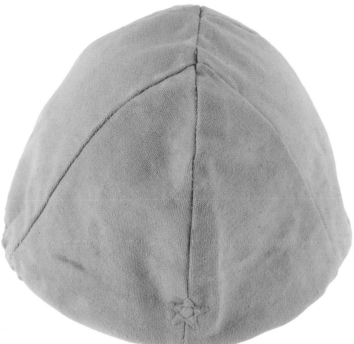

above Many Japanese helmets had a dome-shaped canvas cover over the top to provide some camouflage and some insulation.

above Another Model 90 with a metal star brazed to the front. Japanese helmets were often of poor quality and were more likely to be penetrated by bullets or fragments than those of other nations.

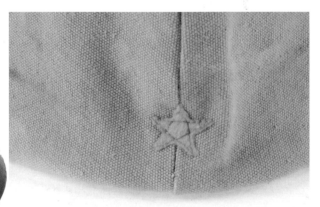

above A close-up of the canvas cover and sewn five-pointed star.

above A close-up of the rim showing characters painted on the underside to indicate ownership of the helmet.

above An interior view of a Model 90 helmet. While this example has a corroded and flaking metal shell, the leather and fabric interior seems in relatively good condition.

255

EQUIPMENT

The Japanese infantryman carried personal military equipment which was simple in design and lacked the complicated harnesses and multiplicity of straps and buckles worn in most other armies. This was, however, offset to a certain extent by the number of items which were suspended on individual shoulder straps, including water bottle, haversack, entrenching tool (when in actual combat) and, for officers, binoculars and mapcase. In the end, the weight the Japanese soldier had to carry was much the same as his foreign counterparts: about 70 pounds (32 kg) in winter or cold climates when his load included a blanket and greatcoat, although this reduced to some 56 pounds (25 kg) in summer and tropical climates. To place such loads in perspective, it should be noted that a Japanese peasant was fully capable of carrying sacks of rice weighing more than 100 pounds (45 kg).

The basic item was a brown leather waist-belt which ran through a cloth loop on the left side of the jacket for support. The belt was fastened at the front with a square, single-tongued buckle made of brass. Attached to the belt and hanging over the left buttock was a leather bayonet frog. Also attached to the belt were three ammunition pouches, likewise made of brown leather: two, containing 30 rounds of rifle ammunition apiece, were on the front of the belt, with a 60-round pouch at the back, for a total of 120 rounds. The rear pouch was attached to the belt by loops, so that it could easily be pulled to the front, when required.

above This close-up shows the wooden version of the water bottle and the waxed fabric map case. The Japanese never developed a true load-carrying harness system but instead had individual items on their own straps over the wearer's shoulder.

left Ammunition pouches were usually brown leather and strapped to the belt. This is a large version for use by cavalry soldiers and still contains cardboard packs of rifle cartridges.

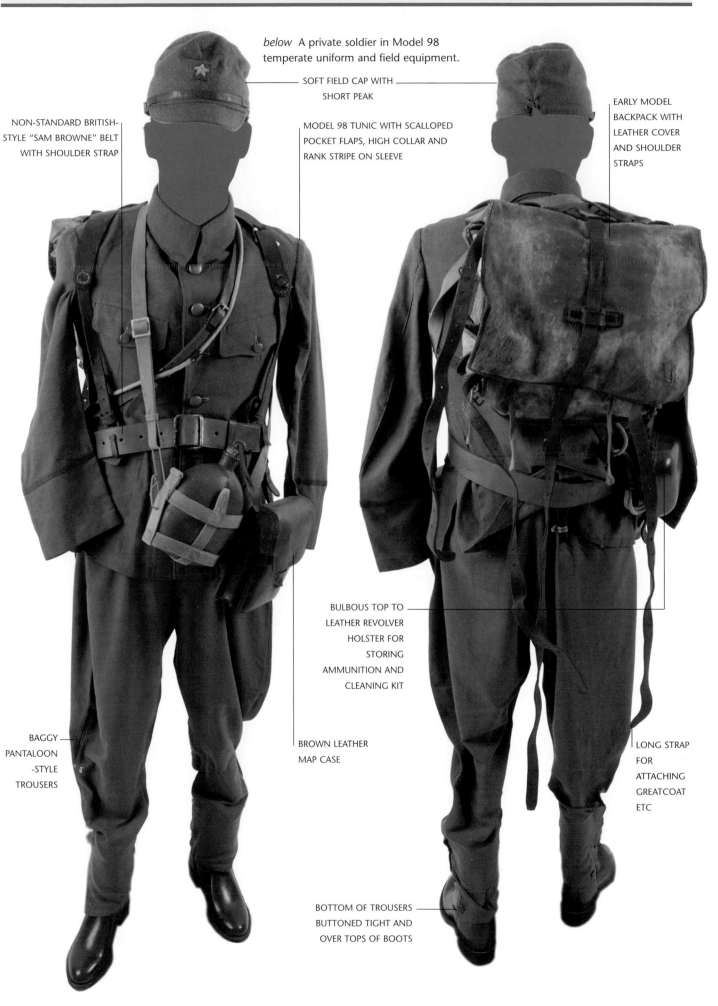

below A private soldier in Model 98 temperate uniform and field equipment.

SOFT FIELD CAP WITH SHORT PEAK

NON-STANDARD BRITISH-STYLE "SAM BROWNE" BELT WITH SHOULDER STRAP

MODEL 98 TUNIC WITH SCALLOPED POCKET FLAPS, HIGH COLLAR AND RANK STRIPE ON SLEEVE

EARLY MODEL BACKPACK WITH LEATHER COVER AND SHOULDER STRAPS

BAGGY PANTALOON-STYLE TROUSERS

BULBOUS TOP TO LEATHER REVOLVER HOLSTER FOR STORING AMMUNITION AND CLEANING KIT

BROWN LEATHER MAP CASE

LONG STRAP FOR ATTACHING GREATCOAT ETC

BOTTOM OF TROUSERS BUTTONED TIGHT AND OVER TOPS OF BOOTS

257

AMMUNITION POUCH

left Large ammunition pouch for the 7.7 mm *Arisaka* rifle. This pouch was often attached to the rear of the belt while two similar, but smaller, ones were attached to the front.

below The 1940 Model 0 backpack was made from woven canvas and had wide canvas shoulder straps. Canvas stood up to the humidity of tropical conditions much better than leather.

BACKPACK

The backpack was originally made of hide, with the hair outside, but as the war progressed was increasingly made of canvas. This pack, which was not particularly large, was mounted on a lightweight wooden frame, measuring 12 in (305 mm) wide by 11 in (279 mm) long and 4.25 in (108 mm) deep, and was secured by two leather straps running over the wearer's shoulders and hooked to the waist belt. Contents of the backpack normally comprised: two day's iron rations; change of underclothing; housewife (needles, threads, buttons, etc); bottle of oil for the feet; very minor personal effects.

When carried, the greatcoat and blanket were rolled up in the shelter square and fitted around the top and sides of the backpack by straps. Also strapped to the outside of the backpack were a mess-tin, a shovel or pick, and a pair of boots.

ENTRENCHING TOOLS

All soldiers in an infantry battalion below the rank of corporal, except for Numbers 1 and 2 on light machine guns, carried an entrenching tool. Most were shovels, normally carried dismantled, with the blade in a canvas cover which, together with the short handle, was strapped to the left side of the backpack. Prior to combat these were assembled, and then suspended by a cord over the left shoulder so that the blade offered bullet-proof protection to the abdomen, an idea practiced in no other army. About 20 per cent of the soldiers carried a pickaxe,

above Large backpack with leather cover and straps. Other equipment such as greatcoat, blanket or rain cape could be strapped to the backpack.

CANVAS POUCH

LAMP CASING

FUEL ELEMENT

SHOVEL

above As the war progressed and Japan went on to the defensive, the army dug extensive tunnel and cave complexes, especially on the pacific islands. Tunnel lamps such as those provided light inside these fortifications. Shown here are a fuel element, lamp casing and canvas pouch.

with a 14-inch (356 mm) head and 18-inch (457 mm) handle, strapped across the top of the pack. In infantry machine gun and gun platoons a small number of men carried axes instead of entrenching tools.

above Using mainly simple entrenching tools and shovels such as this, Japanese soldiers on the defense were able to prepare strong and well-camouflaged fortifications which were very difficult to assault.

259

SHELTER TENT

The shelter tent outfit was carried by all ranks except officers and warrant officers, and consisted of a rectangular sheet of waterproof canvas, two pegs and two sections of pole, each 18 inches (457 mm) long; total weight was about 1.25 pounds (0.57 kg). The sheet had eyelets and cords spaced along the periphery enabling them to be connected together to make multi-occupant tents for three men (two sections), six men (four sections) or eleven men (eight sections). The latter was the most usual arrangement, as it enabled the three spare sections to be used by officers and warrant officers. Straw was used as bedding. The ground sheet could also be worn as a waterproof cape.

right A Private First Class wearing a heavy wool tunic with rank badges on the collar but none on the cuffs. Note the dark brown leather belt and shoulder straps. Materials and colors varied, especially as shortages took hold, as witnessed by the variation in tone between the tunic and his field cap.

GAS MASKS

Like most World War II armies, the Japanese had a well-developed offensive gas capability but never used it. They also had a defensive capability and had a number of small units trained in decontamination duties. In the early part of the war front-line soldiers were issued with individual respirators consisting of a complete face mask made of rubber with a separate filtration unit, the two being linked

above A fabric backpack with numerous ties to hold other items. Japanese equipment made extensive use of ties rather than straps with buckles, especially as metals became scarce.

right Rubber gas mask with canvas straps and filter in front, alongside its canvas carrying case.

by a flexible hose. As the war progressed it became fairly certain that Japan's enemies would not use gas, so the decontamination units were disbanded and the men redeployed as infantry, while respirators were no longer carried.

COOKING AND RATIONS

There was no such thing in the Japanese infantry as a field kitchen and no such personnel as battalion/company cooks; instead, every man carried his own rations and either did his own cooking, or, perhaps, collectively in a very small group of 2–3 men within his squad. Rice was provided by the army quartermasters and carried in a cloth tube, with a day's supply cooked each morning and carried in the haversack. Small food packs were issued, but these were generally considered to be "iron rations". Fresh rations were also issued, but wherever possible soldiers found local food supplies, such as fish or game they caught themselves, or meat, fruit or vegetable taken from hapless locals. The Japanese Army never supplied facilities such as the canteens enjoyed by American and British troops where additional food and drinks, together with minor luxury items, could be purchased.

left A metal water bottle of 1905 Russo-Japanese vintage in a canvas webbing holder. As with most armies, obsolete equipment often remained in use, partly owing to shortages of modern items and partly owing to old soldiers holding on to them or young soldiers taking their fathers' equipment to war.

above Metal mess tins with pan and lid. Alongside is a set of personal chopsticks in a wooden case. Centralized cooking was uncommon in the field, and soldiers normally prepared their own meals in small groups within their squad or unit.

above An array of water bottles, from left to right: two uncovered bare metal officer's versions with metal cups; an officer's fabric-covered bottle in carrier, an enlisted man's bottle with bakelite outer cover and canvas holder; and a late-war enlisted man's version.

below and right Binoculars were an important observation tool for leaders and reconnaissance troops. There were never enough issue ones and many officers bought their own, hence the wide variation in design and size.

below A somewhat battered pair of officer's binoculars which has seen hard use. Japanese optical devices were not made to the same standard as German designs, but as with so much Japanese equipment, they were good enough.

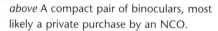

above A compact pair of binoculars, most likely a private purchase by an NCO.

right Yet another design for use by an NCO, again showing evidence of service use.

above A pair of military identity discs and their cords. Japanese soldiers were expected to sacrifice their lives for the Emperor without hesitation or question.

right Padded mittens for winter use. The lack of a separate trigger finger meant they could not be worn in combat, no matter how cold conditions were.

MISCELLANEOUS ITEMS

Mosquito nets were issued, but unlike US and British types these did not cover the whole body, only either the head or hands. Once contracted, the Japanese soldier had no treatment for malaria and losses in sickness were heavy, particularly in Malaya and Burma.

All ranks on active service wore a brass oval identity disk with writing on one side only, giving the wearer's name and arm for officers, and name, unit and individual number for enlisted ranks.

Cleaning kit for the soldier's rifle was obviously very important. The kit itself consisted of a two-piece metal rod with a screw-on wire brush for cleaning the barrel, a toothbrush-like tool with wire "bristles" and a canvas holder, all of which were carried in the backpack. A small bottle of rifle oil was secured to one end of the rear ammunition pouch by straps.

above Cavalry remained in service throughout the war, especially for internal security roles and in the wide open spaces of China. This is a fine example of a military saddle, complete with saddlebags, stirrups and water bucket for the horse.

Personal equipment also included a metal canteen, containing several plates, which could also be used for cooking. Every soldier also carried a water bottle, which was somewhat larger than those carried by US or British soldiers, and was carried on a sling, which enabled it to be drunk from or refilled while on the march without removing his belt.

above Three designs of muzzle cap for the Arisaka rifle, which could be clipped on to protect the interior of the muzzle from dirt and moisture when the rifle was not in use.

below A cleaning pull-through for an Arisaka rifle. The tubular elements are screwed together to make a long shaft and the spiral brush is screwed on to the end.

PERSONAL ITEMS

As with army-issued equipment, the Japanese soldier was frugal in his personal requisites. These almost invariably included a pair of slippers, which were either rush sandals, or tabi, rubber-soled sandals in which the upper separated the big toe from the rest of the foot.

Virtually all also carried a personal small patriotic banner, a "Rising Sun" flag covered with exhortations from family, neighbors and friends to be brave in battle, to conquer the enemy and, if necessary, to show the spirit of seppuku; none ever included a hope for a safe return.

The great majority of Japanese soldiers also wore a separate item, but with a similar purpose, known as a Sennimbari (belt of one thousand stitches), a sash about 3 inches (76 mm) wide which was worn around the waist under the uniform and tied at the back with cords. These were made by family

left Tabi boots were lightweight black rubber-soled canvas shoes with a distinctive separate toe. Normally worn with white cotton split-toed socks, they were intended for wear in barracks and when on fatigue duty. They were also worn as light boots on combat operations or if the wearer's leather boots had disintegrated.

above A pair of heavy woollen socks also intended for wearing with *Tabi* boots.

below A neat wood and bamboo parasol intended to provide shade for a senior officer.

above The Japanese Army was not noted for providing much in the way of field comforts for officers or soldiers. But here is a rare specimen of a canvas and metal camp chair for a senior officer, complete with storage bag.

members, friends, neighbors, or by members of the Japanese Patriotic Women's Association, the latter standing on the streets asking passers-by to add one stitch each until one thousand had done so. Messages on the belt included slogans such as "Everlasting success in war" and they were supposed to bring the wearer not only courage and good fortune, but also immunity from enemy fire

In general, the Japanese soldier's expectations were much lower than those of western soldiers. He was trained from an early age to live frugally and in the main brought up outside the cities and used to carrying heavy weights and to traveling on foot. The army-issued clothing and personal equipment were, therefore, simple and practical and fully met the soldiers' needs. The simplicity of the badges of rank on the collar was also very striking, although it is apparent from the introduction of cuff badges in 1944 that even Japanese officers felt a need for something more.

right A simple but serviceable folding razor, typical of those used by soldiers in most armies.

left The Japanese soldier traveled light so personal items had to be small and portable, such as this finely printed prayer book.

right Communications with home were erratic and often non-existent. Even so, many optimistic soldiers carried writing paper and pens such as this one.

above Soldiers around the world found tobacco to be an easily carried solace in the front line. Shown here is a metal cigarette case plus cigarettes, matches and cigarette packet.

INFANTRY WEAPONS

There is a widely held view that Japanese infantry weapons were poorly designed and manufactured, and not very effective in combat. The reality was that they were designed for what the Japanese General Staff wanted them to do, which was to engage the enemy as closely as possible in firefights where the Japanese infantry would always be pressing ahead and keeping the enemy off-balance. Thus, there was heavy emphasis on light and medium machine guns, mortars and grenades, although there was a serious weakness in anti-tank weapons.

The Japanese never developed a semi-automatic rifle to match the US Army's M1 Garand, nor did they place particular emphasis on sub-machine guns, but if they placed their faith in the elderly *Arisaka* series of bolt-action rifles that was no different from the Germans and the British who used the equally old *Mauser Gewehr* 98 and Lee-Enfield designs throughout the war, as well. One "self-inflicted wound" was the decision to change the standard caliber from the lightweight 6.5 mm (0.256 in) to the heavier and much more powerful 7.7 mm (0.303 in). This caused complications in production, training and in logistics.

RIFLES

The Japanese infantry went through World War II armed with very old-fashioned, bolt-action rifles, supplemented, in some cases, by weapons captured from the Americans, British and Dutch in the advances across South-east Asia. The Japanese weapons, however, were rugged and reliable, and greatly liked by the soldiers.

ARISAKA MEIJI 38 6.5MM RIFLE

Service entry: *Meiji* 38 (1905)
Origin: Imperial arsenals, Japan
Caliber: 6.5 x 50 mm
Weight (empty): 9 lb (4.08 kg)
Length overall: 50.25 in (1.276 m)
Barrel length: 31.4 in (0.798 m); 4-groove rifling; right-hand twist
Muzzle velocity: 2,400 ft/sec (732 m/s)
Feed: fixed vertical box magazine, loaded by five-round charger.
Backsight: Ramped V, graduated for 400–2,400 m
Foresight: blade, mounted on muzzle.

When they fought the Chinese in 1894 the Japanese discovered that the rifles they were using were markedly inferior to their enemy's German-supplied Mannlicher Gewehr 88 and a committee was formed to put things right. This was headed by Colonel Arisaka Nariake and the lessons were fully analysed before going on to develop a new weapon, which entered service as the *Meiji* 29th Year (1896) rifle. This was developed further into the 30th Year, 35th Year and then the definitive *Meiji* 38th year rifles, all of which also bore the name *Arisaka* in tribute to the designer.

The *Meiji* 38th year rifle so suited Japanese requirements that it remained in continuous production from 1907 to 1944, during which time well over three million were produced. This weapon was long and heavy, making it difficult to handle in jungle conditions, and the 6.5 mm (0.256 in) round did not have the same range or stopping power as the British 0.303 in or US 0.30 in rounds. Nevertheless, it was greatly liked by Japanese infantrymen who considered it very reliable and they certainly put it to good use in their campaigns against the Allies and the Chinese.

The *Meiji* 38th year rifle had a bolt action with a Mauser-type internal five-round magazine. Both the rifle and the carbine (see below) took the *Meiji* 30 bayonet. The light round and small caliber resulted in a soft recoil and

above The first 6.5 mm rifle to enter widespread Japanese service was the Type 30 *Arisaka*. The basic design was robust and effective, although the rifle was rather long, especially when the long sword bayonet was fitted.

minimal muzzle flash. Ammunition was loaded in a five-round clip. As issued, the rifle was fitted with a semi-circular, sheet metal cover, which moved with the bolt and was intended to prevent dirt entering the mechanism. It could be detached if required and most Japanese combat troops did so permanently, as it slowed down the operation of the bolt and made a characteristic noise. A cleaning rod was carried in a housing beneath the barrel, but the other necessary items such as the brush and the eye for the cleaning cloth were carried in the soldier's pack, and the oil bottle was strapped to his rear ammunition pouch.

The *Meiji* 38th Year Rifle "Short" version was reduced in overall length to 44.5 in and barrel length to 25.5 in, which cut the weight to 8.5 lb (3.86 kg). Some of these *Meiji* 38 Shorts were issued to infantry, particularly later in the war, but most went to soldiers of supporting arms and logistic services. Both long and short versions could be fitted with grenade launchers, which were of two types: cup and spigot.

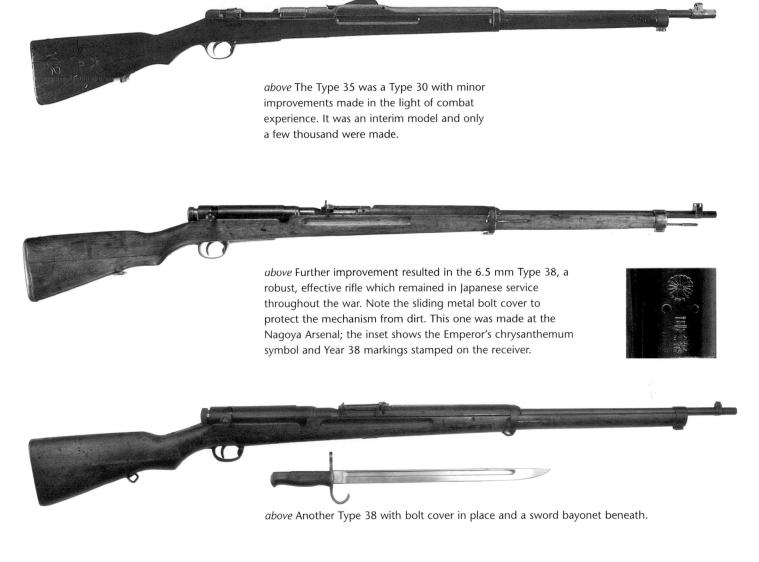

above The Type 35 was a Type 30 with minor improvements made in the light of combat experience. It was an interim model and only a few thousand were made.

above Further improvement resulted in the 6.5 mm Type 38, a robust, effective rifle which remained in Japanese service throughout the war. Note the sliding metal bolt cover to protect the mechanism from dirt. This one was made at the Nagoya Arsenal; the inset shows the Emperor's chrysanthemum symbol and Year 38 markings stamped on the receiver.

above Another Type 38 with bolt cover in place and a sword bayonet beneath.

above: A late-war Type 38 without the bolt cover but with a leather sling and an associated bayonet in its metal scabbard.

right Imperial Chrysanthemum and Type 38 characters engraved on the receiver.

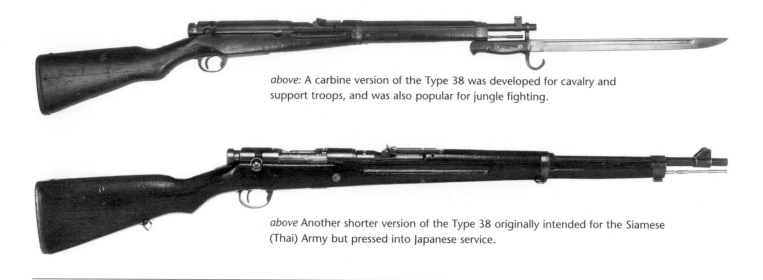

above: A carbine version of the Type 38 was developed for cavalry and support troops, and was also popular for jungle fighting.

above Another shorter version of the Type 38 originally intended for the Siamese (Thai) Army but pressed into Japanese service.

ARISAKA MEIJI 44 CAVALRY CARBINE

Service entry: Meiji 44 (1911)

Length (overall): 38.25 in (0.972 m)

Weight: 8.8 lb (4 kg)

Barrel: 18.5 in (470 mm); 4-groove rifling; right-hand twist

Caliber: 6.5 mm

Operation: bolt action

Feed: 5-round integral magazine

Muzzle velocity: 2,250 ft/sec (686 m/s)

The *Meiji* 44th Year Cavalry Carbine was accepted for service in 1911 and actually reached the army in 1912, replacing the *Meiji* 38th year Carbine (Model 1905) and remained in production until 1942. It was essentially similar to the *Meiji* 38 rifle, with the same bolt action, but, most unusually for a weapon intended for horsed cavalry, it was fitted with a permanently attached bayonet, which folded below the barrel. Even more surprising is that in successive modifications even longer bayonets were fitted.

Although originally intended for the cavalry, the carbine was popular with infantry involved in jungle warfare, since its shorter length made it easier to handle. The permanently attached bayonet also meant there was one less item hanging from the long-suffering infantryman's belt, although its weight made the weapon muzzle heavy and difficult to fire accurately.

above The Type 44 carbine was a light, handy weapon which retained the robust, reliable *Arisaka* mechanism.

above Another Type 44 carbine. The shorter barrel further reduced the range and power of the already marginal 6.5 mm round. Note the permanently fixed folding bayonet under the barrel.

ARISAKA MEIJI 38 SNIPER RIFLE

above A 6.5 mm Type 38 sniper rifle with the standard 2.5x Tokia scope mounted on the left side of the receiver.

Service entry: *Meiji* 38 (1905)
Length (gun): 50.25 in (1.28 m)
Weight (gun plus sight): 10.6 lb (4.81 kg)
Barrel: 31.5 in (0.8 m); 4-groove rifling; right-hand twist
Caliber: 6.5 mm
Operation: bolt-action
Feed: 5-round internal magazine
Muzzle velocity: 2,400 ft/sec (732 m/s)

This was the first rifle specialized sniper rifle to enter service with the Imperial Japanese Army. It was the outcome of a development program which had lasted more than ten years, but despite that length of time, the result was only a *Meiji* 38th Year rifle with an added telescopic sight, and even that was mounted so low above the action that the bolt lever had to be lengthened and angled downwards, while the sight itself was offset to the left so that the firer could still operate the bolt and use the

ammunition charger. The 2.5x magnification sight had a rubber eyepiece but was difficult to use, not least because it was offset. A steel-wire bipod was fitted to help the sniper hold the rifle steady in the aim. Approximately 35,000 were produced, some of which were subsequently modified by cutting 7.8 in (198 mm) off the barrel. This was not a successful weapon and was soon replaced by the 7.7 mm *Meiji* 99th Year Sniper's Rifle, a similar modification of the standard infantry Type 99 rifle.

above A selection of leather carrying cases for sniper scopes, complete with leather or canvas straps. These would be carried over the shoulder of the sniper.

right Japanese snipers were highly-trained, dedicated and prepared to sacrifice their own lives. These metal 'crampon' units were fitted over the wearer's boots so that the spikes enabled him to climb a tree and wait, perhaps for days, to get a clear shot, even when he had no chance of escape afterwards.

ARISAKA TYPE 99 7.7 MM RIFLE

Service Entry: Jimmu 2599 (1939)
Length (gun): 44.0 in (1.18 m)
Weight (gun): 8.25 lb (3.74 kg)
Barrel: 27.25 in (692 mm); 4-groove
Rifling: right-hand twist
Caliber: 7.7 mm
Operation: bolt-action
Feed: 5-round internal magazine
Muzzle velocity: 2,390 ft/sec (728 m/s)

Experience in the Sino-Japanese war in the 1930s showed that the standard Japanese 6.5 x 50 mm round was inferior to the 7.9 mm round used by the Chinese armies; as a result, a new 7.7 x 58 mm round was quickly developed. Various prototype rifles were trialed in 1938–1940 at the end of which a new rifle, the Type 99, was accepted for service. This was 5 inches shorter than the *Meiji* 38, fitted with a forward-folding monopod and fired the new, heavier round, but otherwise was iden-

tical in construction and operation. It was issued in some numbers, but never completely replaced the *Meiji* 38, even in front-line infantry units.

By 1943 the war was not going well and material shortages were beginning to bite hard so a revised Type 99 was put into production which featured lower grade steel in the barrel and receiver, as well as deletion of items such as the sliding bolt cover and sling swivels.

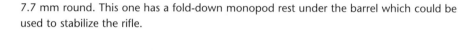

above The Type 99 was shorter and lighter than the Type 38 and fired a more effective 7.7 mm round. This one has a fold-down monopod rest under the barrel which could be used to stabilize the rifle.

above Early Type 99s were made with longer barrels, such as the one shown here.

above Another long-barreled Type 99 with the sliding bolt cover removed.

above As with the Type 38, the Type 99 was used as a sniper rifle. This view shows the scope bracket on the left side of the receiver and the separate 2.5x scope and carrier.

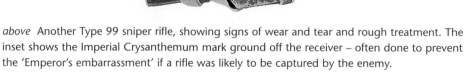

above Another Type 99 sniper rifle, showing signs of wear and tear and rough treatment. The inset shows the Imperial Crysanthemum mark ground off the receiver – often done to prevent the 'Emperor's embarrassment' if a rifle was likely to be captured by the enemy.

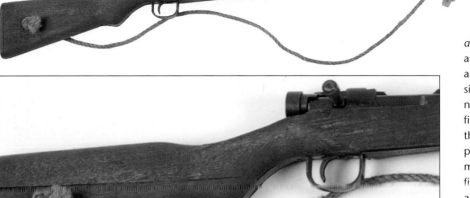

above Japan was always short of raw materials and industrial resources, which only got worse as the war progressed. Weapons were simplified as improvisation became a necessity. This "last ditch" rifle is typical of the final production of the Type 99, assembled as the Allies closed on Japan. Crudely made from poor quality material, it had a simplified mechanism and sights, and in this case was fitted with a simple piece of rope rather than a strap. Such weapons were handed out to local defense volunteers and "home guard" units. But Japan's collapse in the face of the atom bomb meant that the final battle for the homeland never took place.

above Another Type 99 with long barrel and leather sling

ARISAKA 7.7 MM TYPE 2 PARACHUTIST RIFLE

Service Entry: Jimmu 2602 (1942)
Length (gun): 45.3 in (1.15 m)
Weight (gun): 8.9 lb (4.04 kg)
Barrel: 25.4 in (645 mm); 4 groove rifling; right-hand twist.
Caliber: 7.7 mm
Feed: 5-round integral magazine
Muzzle velocity: 2,368 ft/sec (722 m/s)

Many facets of the Japanese military machine were extremely inefficient and ineffective, and it comes as no surprise that when a paratroop force was formed there were no sub-machine guns or similar lightweight weapons with which to arm them. The Type 99 rifle was far too long to be carried in an aircraft, but of greater importance was the need to provide the soldier with a weapon that was immediately available to him in the first minutes after he had landed. The army came up with a unique solution in which the rifle was split into two sections, each of which was carried in a bag attached to the parachutist and then assembled within seconds.

The first attempt was the Parachutist Rifle Type 0, which consisted of a Type 99 rifle divided into two parts at a point about one-third along the barrel from the receiver. The inner end of each half was fitted with a heavy metal section, which incorporated the barrel and an interrupted screw thread. This was not a success.

The next attempt was the Type 2, again a two-piece rifle, but this time with a wedge above the front of the receiver which had to be inserted into a receptacle above the barrel. The rifle was also fitted with a wire monopod. Although trials were reasonably successful, only a few were produced, probably because by late 1942 the Japanese Army no longer had a significant operational requirement for paratroops.

The Type 1 Parachutist Rifle was developed as a fall-back in case the Types 0 and 2 failed and was a *Meiji* 38th Year carbine with a folding butt; it never served with paratroop units and the few that were manufactured were pressed into service with normal infantry in the desperate final months of the war.

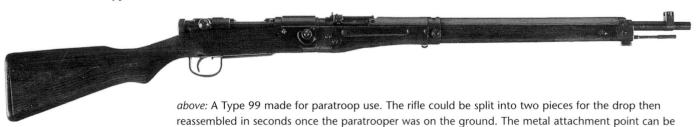

above: A Type 99 made for paratroop use. The rifle could be split into two pieces for the drop then reassembled in seconds once the paratrooper was on the ground. The metal attachment point can be seen in front of the trigger group, just under the sight.

PISTOLS AND REVOLVERS

Official pistols or revolvers were issued to cavalrymen, tank crews and soldiers with support roles, such as drivers, clerks and storemen, but overall distribution of such weapons was on nothing like the same scale as in the German Army. Officers in the Japanese Army were required to arm themselves at their own expense with a pistol and a sword, both of which were carried in combat. Not surprisingly, they selected their own designs and up to late 1941, where handguns were concerned, they frequently tended to prefer foreign models.

MEIJI 26TH YEAR 9 MM REVOLVER

above The Meiji 26th Year revolver took elements from Smith and Wesson, Nagant and other designs to make a competent, if uninspired, revolver.

right A 26th Year revolver shown open for loading, along with some 9 mm ammunition. The leather holster had a bulbous top to cover the separate pouch for spare ammunition.

Service Entry: Meiji 26 (1893)
Type: six-round revolver
Origin: Koishikawa
Caliber: 9 x 22 mm
Weight (empty): 31 oz (0.88 kg)
Barrel length: 4.72 in (120 mm); 6-groove rifling; left-hand twist
Feed: six-round cylinder; trigger-operated advance
Muzzle velocity: 640 ft/sec (195 m/s)
Backsight: V
Foresight: blade, mounted on muzzle.

The Meiji 26th year revolver (Model 1893) was produced at a time when Japan was still in the process of emerging from centuries of seclusion. The design was the outcome of a detailed study of Western ideas, the major influence being the Smith & Wesson No 3, of which a number had been purchased in the 1880s, although certain features from European designers, such as Galand (Belgium) and Nagant (Russia) can also be detected. It was heavy, not very well made, double-action only and required a very strong pull on the trigger, but was manufactured in vast numbers. It was officially superseded in the 1930s, but many remained in service throughout World War II. Early models had the fittings for a butt attachment and some of these may also have been in use in 1941–45.

NAMBU TAISHO 4TH YEAR 8 MM AUTOMATIC PISTOL TYPE A

above The Taisho 4th Year pistol bore a superficial resemblance to the German Luger but used very different design principles. Note the knurled cocking handle at the rear and the grip safety under the trigger guard.

below The insets show a serial number and manufacturer's marks stamped on the frame of this Taisho 14.

Service Entry: Taisho 4 (1915)
Type: Semi-automatic pistol
Origin: Kashikawa Arsenal
Caliber: 8 x 21 mm Nambu
Weight (empty): 31 oz (0.88 kg)
Barrel length: 4.72 in (120 mm); 6-groove rifling; right -hand twist
Feed: 8-round box magazine in butt
Muzzle velocity: 1,100 ft/sec (335 m/s)
Backsight: V
Foresight: blade, mounted on muzzle.

The recoil-operated Taisho 4th year was the first semi-automatic pistol to enter service with the Japanese Army, the outcome of a development program which started in 1909. It had a tapered barrel and a well-raked butt, and when fired the barrel, bolt and receiver recoiled together for about 0.2 in (5 mm) at which point the bolt was unlocked and continued to the rear until hitting the buffer, when it was driven forward again by two return springs. It was cocked using a cylindrical knob, knurled to provide a grip, and the ejection port was on top of the receiver, throwing the used cartridge cases vertically upwards – an unusual arrangement. It had a grip safety. When used in

the Manchurian winter in 1937/38, it was found that the trigger guard prevented the use of gloves, so a modified version was introduced with an enlarged guard. When the Baby Nambu was introduced (see below) this weapon was nicknamed "Papa Nambu."

A later, improved model was introduced in 1925 as the Taisho 14th Year pistol, using the same round. It was recoil-operated and had no slide, the bolt moving inside the barrel extension. The safety lever was on the left side, directly above the trigger. A metal loop on the rear of the receiver provided an attachment for a lanyard.

above Combat experience caused the Taisho 4th Year to be redesigned to become the 14th Year pistol. The 14th Year (or Taisho 14) was also modified to be easier and cheaper to make. It worked in the same way as the earlier pistol but had a separate safety catch instead of the grip safety and was of simplified construction.

above Another view of the same Taisho 14. Early models had a smaller trigger guard, but after winter combat in Manchuria most were built with the larger trigger guard shown here, which allowed the gun to be used when wearing protective gloves. Note also the simplified groove pattern on the grips rather than the diamond pattern on the 4th Year pistol.

above Another variation of a Taisho 14th year pistol, with a three-ribbed cocking handle at the back instead of the usual knurled one.

right: As materials became scarcer and industrial facilities were bombed, Japanese weapons of all kinds had components replaced with cheaper, poorer-quality items. Here, this 14th Year pistol has grips crudely made from inferior wood with no grooving or pattern to help the user keep a firm hold.

above Another 14th Year pistol with smooth wood grips. When the 14th Year was first introduced, users found it difficult to change magazines, especially when the gun was dirty or if they had wet hands. Not long after production started, a butt-mounted magazine release spring was fitted to all pistols. The metal catch can be seen here at the front of the grip, near the bottom of the gun.

Nambu Taisho 4th Year 7 mm Automatic Pistol Type B

above The 4th Year Type B "Baby Nambu" was an attempt to make a smaller pistol which was easier to handle and carry. Firing a relatively low-powered 7 mm cartridge, the "Baby Nambu" was marginal as a military weapon, although reasonably popular for self-defense. This one has no magazine fitted, hence the cut-out under the butt.

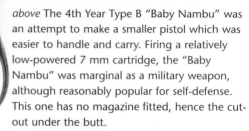

Service Entry: 1930s
Type: semi-automatic pistol
Origin: Koshikawa Arsenal
Caliber: 7 x 20 mm Nambu
Weight (empty): 21 oz (0.6 kg)
Barrel length: 3.27 in (83 mm); 6-groove rifling; right -hand twist
Feed: 7-round box magazine in butt
Muzzle velocity: 1,000 ft/sec (305 m/s)
Backsight: V
Foresight: blade, mounted on muzzle.

The Nambu Type A was intended for sale to officers, but failed to attract much interest, mainly because of its size and weight. As a result, the designers at Koshikawa Arsenal reduced the design by approximately 25 per cent to produce a weapon which immediately became known in the Japanese Army as the "Baby Nambu." Despite this, pre-war officers continued to prefer Western designs until the war closed supply routes. About 6,000 Baby Nambus were manufactured in total and they proved very popular with US servicemen as souvenirs.

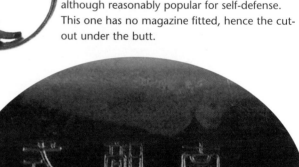

above Another Type B "Baby Nambu", this time with a magazine in place. All Nambu 4th and 14th Year pistols followed similar principles, with the barrel and receiver made as a single piece, with an internal bolt locking the cartridge in place.

SWORDS AND BAYONETS

Many armies retained swords as part of their full dress and ceremonial uniforms throughout World War II (some do so to this day) but the Japanese Army was the only one in which swords were routinely carried in battle and not infrequently used to behead wounded or prisoners. When the Imperial Japanese Army was formed on modern lines in the 1870s a military sword for officers was introduced, based on European designs, but a resurgence in nationalist fervor in the 1930s led to the shin gunto, a type of sword which represented a reversion to a traditional samurai design, of which there were three models.

SHIN GUNTO TYPE 94

The Type 94 (1934) Officers Sword was based on the katana (long sword) carried by samurai in the 12th century. The blade could vary in quality from traditional hand-made to modern machine-produced, but always featured a finely honed cutting edge. The hilt (tsuka) was longer than on Western swords because it was always used with two hands, covered with skin from a ray fish, and covered with leather lacing, which was designed to enable the decoration to be seen. The scabbard was made of wood and usually covered in brown leather (or, in cheaper cases, painted brown) and had two suspension rings, one of which was worn only in full dress uniform.

Above A mass-produced NCO's *Katana* and scabbard; factory-made and manufactured at the Kokura Arsenal just before or during the war. It has a factory serial (65557) stamped on the blade and the Imperial Crysanthemum on the crossguard. The handle is an alloy casting patterned to simulate the binding of traditional hand-made swords.

above Another factory-made sword with a metal handle and metal scabbard.

SHIN GUNTO TYPE 95

This was issued to NCOs and was a cheaper version of the officers' sword, with a single suspension ring and painted scabbard and hilt.

SHIN GUNTO TYPE 98

Introduced in 1938, this was a cheaper, simpler officer's sword with a number of minor changes from the Type 94, the most obvious of which was deletion of the second suspension ring. It was always better than the NCOs sword, but like that weapon the quality reduced as the war progressed; nevertheless, it remained in production until August 1945.

right A British Commonwealth soldier being marched off into captivity. The Japanese officer has his sword in his hand but still in its scabbard, which is probably a a relief for the prisoner.

above A close-up of the handle of a mass-produced sword. Visible is the cast metal pattern designed to simulate the sharkskin and binding found on traditional swords. The metal clip on the handguard holds the sword securely in the scabbard.

below This officer's sword is an extremely high-quality item, hand-made by a swordsmith in the 1800s. It will have been a family heirloom and passed from father to son, being rehilted as necessary. The blade is hand forged, in a complex process of heating and folding to produce a tempered blade and cutting edge of exceptional strength and sharpness. The hilt is covered in white sharkskin over which the binding forms the decorative pattern.
Note also the leather and metal scabbard, complete with a leather cover for the hilt.

MODEL 30 INFANTRY BAYONET

Service entry: Meiji 30 (1897)
Type: infantry bayonet
Weight: 14–15 oz (400–430 g)
Length, overall: 20 in (mm)
Blade: length – 16 in (406 mm): width – 0.75 in (19 mm)

left The bayonet and rifle combination was often taller than the man who carried it.

Japanese infantry were great believers in the value of the bayonet, so much so that riflemen and machine gunners usually had their bayonets fixed in battle, even when not engaged in actual hand-to-hand combat. Training in bayonet fighting was frequent and rigorous, and there were well-authenticated reports that prisoners captured in China were sometimes used as living targets.

The bayonets carried by Japanese infantrymen were designated Type 30. These were attached to the weapon by means of a hole in one side of the quillon (crosspiece) which fitted over the muzzle, and a slide with spring-loaded retaining clip on the end of the pommel, which fitted onto a boss beneath the barrel. As several million were produced over a period of 48 years by large number of manufacturers, there were numerous minor variations in design. In general, there were some 18 identifiable patterns, which fell into three major groups:

- Pattern 1. Hooked quillon. Curved pommel. Fullered blade.
- Pattern 2. Straight quillon. Curved pommel. Fullered blade.
- Pattern 3. Straight quillon. Straight-edged pommel. No fullers.

In Pattern A the lower side of the quillon (as fitted to the weapon) ended in a sharp curve, which was intended to hook over and trap the blade of the opponent's bayonet, following which a firm twist would break his blade. This sounds like one of those ideas which are fine in theory but useless in practice, and later production models did not have this feature. The fuller was a longitudinal recess along each side of the blade, which had the same effect as an "I-beam" and simply stiffened the blade to prevent flexing, but added to the production costs. The pommel was the handle and in common with most bayonets in most armies was usually curved to fit the shape of the hand. Pattern 3, which was introduced late in the war was greatly simplified to make production cheaper and easier by eliminating curved edges and fullers.

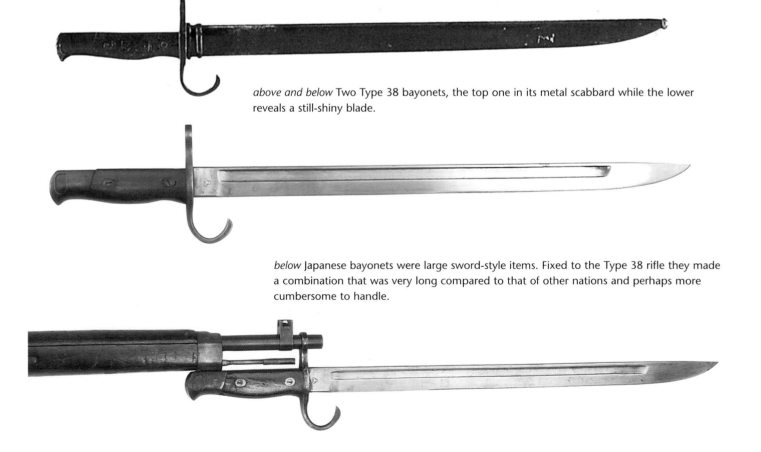

above and below Two Type 38 bayonets, the top one in its metal scabbard while the lower reveals a still-shiny blade.

below Japanese bayonets were large sword-style items. Fixed to the Type 38 rifle they made a combination that was very long compared to that of other nations and perhaps more cumbersome to handle.

GRENADES

Grenades assumed a greater tactical importance to the Japanese Army and their opponents in the Pacific and South-East Asia campaigns than almost anywhere else in World War Two. This was in part because Japanese tactical doctrine stressed close-quarter combat, but also because they highly effective weapons in night attacks and other short-range engagements, especially in jungle terrain.

above and right Rifle grenades were not as common in the Japanese Army as in others, but they were sometimes used with the Type 38 and Type 99 rifles. The top image shows a barrel attachment with a grenade in place. The middle image shows the barrel attachment on its own with its fixing clamp open, while the lower image shows the crudely-made grenade.

TYPE 91 GRENADE

Service Entry: Jimmu 2591 (1931)
Type: Fragmentation
Delivery: hand thrown or grenade launcher
Length, overall: 4.95 in (126 mm)
Length of grenade element:
3.75 in (95 mm)
Diameter: 1.97 in (50 mm)
Weight: 18.8 oz (0.53 kg)
Fuze: 8–9 seconds

The Type 91 grenade had a cast-iron, cylindrical body, marked with deep serrations to maxiize the fragmentation effect. There were two methods of delivery: thrown by hand, or launched from a Taisho 10 (1921) or Type 89

above Two Type 91 grenades showing different patterns of serrated outer cover.

(1929) grenade launcher. There was a screw-threaded recess at either end, one for a small cylinder containing the firing-pin assembly, the other for another small cylinder containing propellant for use with the grenade launcher. The firing-pin assembly included a U-shaped metal safety-pin, which had a short length of cord permanently attached.

The throwing procedure when used as a hand grenade was unusual. First the small cylinder containing propellant was unscrewed and discarded, since it had no function in this mode. The thrower then took the grenade in one hand with the fuze downward, grasped the cord on the safety pin, pulled it clear and then struck the firing-pin cover firmly against some convenient hard object, such as a stone or, more usually, his own steel helmet. The firing-pin then struck the percussion cap, which started the fuze train and the grenade had to be thrown at once, since the fuze could sometimes burn too quickly, an unnerving thought for all except those using the grenade for seppuku.

When fired from a grenade launcher the procedure was different, the start being that the second small cylinder containing propellant was not

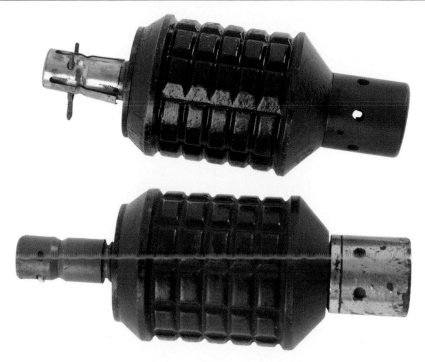

above Another pair of Type 91 grenades. The short, fat cylinder at one end contained propellant for use with a grenade launcher, while the thin cylinder at the other contained the fuze mechanism. One of these grenades still has the safety pin and wire attached.

unscrewed. The safety pin was first removed from the firing-pin assembly, as before, but the whole grenade was then dropped down the launcher tube, propellant assembly first, where it rested until the trigger arm was pulled and the

firing pin in the base of the tube struck the percussion cap, thus activating the propellant. The acceleration of the grenade out of the tube caused the grenade to arm itself, but the fuze time remained the same, 8–9 seconds.

TYPE 97 GRENADE

Service entry: Jimmu 2597 (1937)
Remainder: As for Type 91 grenade

The Type 97 grenade was identical in all respects, including dimensions and weight to the Type 91, except that it was

for hand throwing only. Thus, there was no second recess and no propellant assembly.

above A row of Type 98 grenades with a variety of safety pins and retaining cords.

TYPE 99 (KISKA)

Service entry: Jimmu 2599 (1939)
Type: Fragmentation
Delivery: hand thrown
Length, overall: 3.5 in (89 mm)
Diameter: 1.6 in (41 mm)
Weight: 10 oz (0.28 kg)
Fuze: 4–5 seconds

The Type 99 (1939) hand-grenade was initially known to the US forces s as the "Kiska" model since it was first encountered during the occupation on that island in 1943. This grenade, which was for hand-throwing only, was smaller than both Types 91 and 97. It was cylindrical in shape and the outside was not serrated; there were two protruding rims at either end. The firing-pin assembly screwed into the top of the grenade and contained the firing pin, which, like the earlier grenades, was released by a U-shaped safety pin and activated by hitting the cap against a hard object such as a helmet. Fuze burning time was 4–5 seconds, which encouraged throwers to get rid of it quickly. Unusually, when burning the fuze train emitted sparks which could be seen in flight, thus giving the enemy notice (admittedly very brief) of its impending arrival.

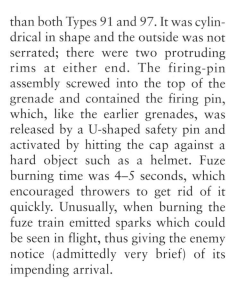

left A small canvas bag for storing Type 99 grenades and fuzes

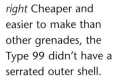

right Cheaper and easier to make than other grenades, the Type 99 didn't have a serrated outer shell.

HIGH-EXPLOSIVE STICK GRENADE

Service entry: not known
Type: Fragmentation/blast
Delivery: hand thrown only
Length, overall: 7.9 in (201 mm)
Diameter of grenade body: 2 in (51 mm)
Weight (grenade): 1 lb 4 oz (0.57 kg)
Fuze: 4–5 seconds

above and right A rare Japanese stick grenade. The handle was much shorter than the German models and contained a pull cord and ring which was slipped over the user's finger to ignite the fuze as the grenade was thrown.

The stick grenade consisted of a flat-topped metal canister which was screwed to a hollow wooden throwing handle. It depended on blast rather than fragmentation which, in combination with its method of throwing, made it of more use as an offensive weapon. Although this weapon looked very similar to the German type the method of activation was different. The screw cap was removed from the end of the handle, which released a ring attached to a pull cord. The ring was then placed over a finger of the throwing hand and when the grenade was thrown the ring and cord remained in the hand, thus igniting the friction primer. This grenade could easily be made into a booby-trap, in combination with a trip-wire. It could be differentiated from the incendiary stick grenade in two ways: it was rather smaller and the canister had a flat end. There was also an incendiary variant with a white phosphorous warhead.

below As well as last-ditch rifles the Japanese devised last-ditch grenades for defense of the homeland. These crude devices are made from clay, with explosive inside and a simple lit fuze. Their effectiveness was marginal.

MORTARS AND GRENADE DISCHARGERS

Grenade-launchers and mortars were widely used by Japanese infantry, enabling company and battalion commanders to bring down a heavy volume of fire quickly and accurately.

The Japanese only occasionally bought-in foreign expertise in weapon design, one example being the Stokes-Brandt 81 mm mortar, which was sold all around the world in the mid/late-1930s because it was by far the best on the market. In their own mortar designs, the Japanese introduced some unusual ideas, such as the variable-volume chamber for altering the range and the recoil system on the 90 mm mortar, but overall their mortar designs were not particularly outstanding.

In one area, they did cause the Americans a serious problem, although this was quite unintentional. This concerned the Types 10 and 89 grenade launchers which had small curved baseplates and when these were first encountered early in the Pacific War someone assumed that the firer must adopt a kneeling position and then rest this plate on his thigh. They were accordingly given the name "knee mortars," and pictures were issued of marines with such mortars ready to fire. Unfortunately, this proved to be a complete misunderstanding and led to at least one US serviceman suffering a broken thigh-bone when testing this supposed "capability."

above Infantrymen move forward during street-fighting in Malaya. The nearest figure, lying on the road, is carrying a Type 89 Grenade Discharger.

V50 MM TYPE 89 GRENADE DISCHARGER

Service entry: Jimmu 2589 (1929)
Type: Grenade launcher
Length, overall: 24 in (610 mm)
Length, barrel: 10 in (254 mm); rifled
Caliber: 50 mm
Weight, launcher: 10.3 lb (4.76 kg)
Maximum Range: Model 89 shell –
770 yd; Model 91 grenade – 175 yd

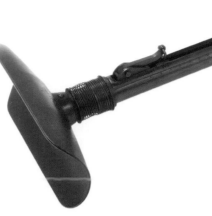

above and right: Two views of the Type 89 and the curved baseplate which gave rise to the misconceived nickname "knee mortar."

The Type 89 grenade-launcher came into service in 1929 and although it resembled the earlier Type 10 visually, it was, in fact, a completely new design. The barrel was 50 mm caliber and rifled, and held at 45 degrees for firing. Range variations were achieved in a novel manner, where a knob was used to adjust the position of the trigger housing within the leg, thus increasing/decreasing the position of the firing-pin within the barrel. This, in its turn, adjusted the distance travelled by the projectile while in the barrel and the range it would achieve.

Fired from either the kneeling or prone position, the Type 89 used a variety of ammunition. The Type 89 high-explosive shell weighed 28 oz (0.79 kg) and contained 5 oz (0.14 kg) of explosive which was detonated by an impact fuze and had a range of 130–770 yd. The weapon also fired the Type 91 HE grenade. The Type 89 shell was relatively accurate as it took on the rifling

in the barrel, but the Type 91 grenade did not and was, therefore, somewhat inaccurate as it was unstable in flight. Fuzes in both cases operated by setback on launch. There was also an incendiary grenade and various illuminating and smoke shells.

above Another Type 89, with a canvas carry sleeve around the leg. Note that the trigger mechanism has been slid closer to the barrel to give reduced range. The projectile is the Type 89 high-explosive shell.

Infantry Mortars				
Type	**Barrel**	**Weight**	**Range**	**Notes**
50 mm Type 10	9.5 in (241 mm)	5.3 lb (2.4 kg)	65–175 yd	Lightweight hand-held. Used variable gas pressure for range.
50 mm Type 89	10 in (254 mm)	10.3 lb (4.76 kg)	65–770 yd	Lightweight hand-held. Known by allies as "knee" mortar.
50 mm Type 98	25 in (635 mm)	48 lb (21.77 kg)		10 lb (4.54 kg) stick-mounted projectile
70 mm Taisho 11		134 lb (60.8 kg) incl baseplate	800–1,600 yd	
81 mm Type 97	49.5 in (1.26 m)	137 lb (62 kg) incl baseplate and bipod	200–3,000 yd	Based on French Stokes-Brandt design
81 mm Type 99	25.25 (641 mm)	52 lb (23.6 kg)	200–3,280 yd	Shorter and lighter Type 97
90 mm Type 94	50 in (1.27 m)	340 lb (154 kg)	4,140 yd	Heavy and complex recoil system
90 mm Type 97	52 in (1.32 m)	233 lb (106 kg)	610–4,140 yd	Simplified Type 97 with no recoil system

SUPPORT WEAPONS

In many ways Japanese support weapons were not the equal of British or American design, but on the whole they worked well enough for the conditions in which they fought. Anti-tank weapons were a particular weakness, which became apparent once the army came up against US and British M3 Lee and M4 Shermans, or Russian T-34s.

The main infantry anti-tank weapon was a 20mm anti-tank rifle, a heavy beast normally moved by four men. Semi-automatic and gas-cooled it fired both armor-piercing and explosive rounds, it was a large weapons which provided minimal anti-armor capability.

The army also had larger 37 mm and 47 mm anti-tank guns largely copied from foreign designs.

Japanese soldiers did make extensive use of infantry-manned light artillery, and each regiment had some under direct control, intended to give close support fire in both attack and defense, which, most importantly, was under the direct command of the infantry. These guns were necessarily light and easily manhandled on the battlefield, and proved remarkably successful. The most common was the 70 mm Type 92 battalion howitzer, but there were also heavier weapons such as the older 75 mm *Meiji* Type 41.

above A Type 94 37 mm anti-tank gun with its high shield and archaic spoked wheels. As with those of other nations, guns of this caliber were soon rendered obsolescent as armor increased in thickness.

right and below Metal case and periscope for use by an artillery forward observer

below Heavy artillery is outside the scope of this book, although the infantry often depended on its support and on forward observers to plan and bring down fire on targets. This figure belongs to an artillery observer unit and on his back is the case for a viewing periscope.

above and right The optical head for a stereoscopic artillery periscope and the unit mounted on its tripod. Stereoscopic vision allowed the observer to estimate the range to a target and help him plot it on his map. The observation team would then need to communicate the target and the results of fire to the artillery command post, either by radio or field telephone.

70 MM TYPE 92 BATTALION HOWITZER

Service entry: Jimmu 2592 (1932)
Length, barrel: 25 in (625 mm) rifled
Caliber: 70 mm
Weight: 468 lb (212 kg)
Elevation; -10 to +50 degrees
Ammunition: HE, incendiary, smoke
Muzzle velocity: 650 ft/sec (198 m/s)
Range: 1,500 yd effective; 3,000 yd maximum
Rate of fire: 10 rounds per minute

Every combat infantry battalion had two of these neat and useful little guns, which were known as *dai-tai ho* (battalion artillery). They could be either horse-drawn or pulled by manpower, and could also be broken down into pieces and carried by either men or animals, this mobility enabling the crews to take up fire positions on hillsides where their enemy did not expect artillery.

One of its most important recognition characteristics was its barrel which was just 25 in (635 mm) or 9 calibers long, very short by any standard, but made to look even shorter by the very long trail legs. The wheels were normally steel discs with steel rims and eight prominent holes to reduce weight, although it was also seen with wooden, spoked wheels. There was a removable gun shield to protect the crew.

The official crew consisted of no less than ten men, although it could easily be operated with five, three of whom were ammunition numbers. It was used for both direct and indirect fire, using high-explosive, shrapnel and smoke shells, all of which had stubby cartridge cases, just 3 in (76 mm) long. When horse-drawn, there was a two-wheel caisson, which carried first-line ammunition, accessories and tools.

The high-explosive shell weighed 8 lb 5 oz (3.77 kg) and was 9 in (229 mm) long giving it a very short travel down the bore and resulting in a low muzzle velocity (650 ft/sec – 198 m/s), the subsonic speed giving the enemy a chance to hear the incoming round and (perhaps) take cover.

above Moving a Type 92 battalion howitzer into position. Light and well balanced, it could be easily moved by two or three men.

left The Type 92 was a compact source of firepower under the control of the infantry. It could be moved intact or broken down into separate man-or mule-portable loads.

above An American soldier demonstrates a captured Japanese flamethrower. During the island battles Japanese soldiers tended to be the recipients of flamethrower attacks rather than the instigators.

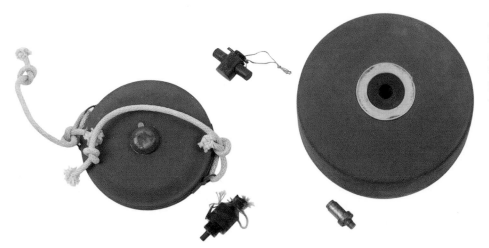

below An array of mines. On the left is the Type 93 anti-tank mine, in the centre is the Type 3 general purpose land mine and on the right is the Type 99 magnetic anti-tank mine. The long item is a bar-type mine, usually used against tanks, but in this case it is anti-personnel item.

PARATROOPERS

right Japanese parachute units only made a few operational drops such as this one, and eventually became used as elite ground-based infantry in a similar way to Germany's *Fallschirmjager*.

As noted earlier, the Japanese had little use for special forces and the like, believing that their line infantry were tough and dedicated enough to carry out all the tasks that might be allocated to them. Even their use of paratroopers was half-hearted, with the first training schools not being set up until 1941.

In general, Japanese Army paratroops wore standard field uniform, with only minimal specialized items, which included a two-piece coverall, the tunic reaching halfway to the knees and a pair of reinforced trousers. The paratroopers' helmet was hemispherical in shape, with built-in earflaps and a securing arrangement which was modeled on that employed in traditional samurai helmets. Paratroopers were also issued with brown leather gloves.

The army issued qualified parachutists with badges, which consisted of an embroidered design on a brown cloth backing. The design was a golden kite perched on a spear, both in golden thread, and the remainder of the design — a stylized parachute and star — in scarlet.

The paratroopers originally carried everything with them in their normal pack or a chest pack, but later in the war a special canvas bag was developed, two of which were attached to the wearer's outer leg/thigh. These were used to carry the take-down weapons and ammunition.

The navy also formed paratroop units, based on two of their Special Naval Landing Force units. They took part in operations in south east Asia in 1941 and 1942.

WEAPONS

The Japanese Army did not develop any weapons specifically for use by paratroopers. Most carried pistols, and many used sub-machine guns. The only modified weapons were the parachutist versions of the Type 99 rifle (described earlier) in which the weapon was split where the barrel met the body, giving two sections which were roughly equal in weight and bulk. There was also a parachutists' version of the Type 99 7.7mm light machine gun with a detachable butt, folding pistol grip, revised trigger group and a new, more efficient gas-piston.

ORGANIZATION

There is a curious feature of the Japanese *Taishin* (raiding) organization in that the designations gave an exaggerated impression of the size of the unit. Thus, the basic unit was a *Taishin Rentai* which translates as "raiding regiment," but was in effect a battalion-sized unit. It had approximately 700–800 officers/men in three rifle companies, a heavy weapons company, and a headquarters and signal unit, and was commanded by a lieutenant-

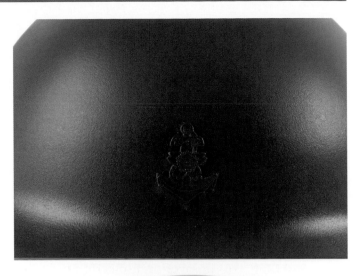

above and right: This unusual helmet with a 'peaked' brim is the Model 92, worn by paratroops before it was replaced by a rimless one. This helmet was actually worn by Special Naval Landing Force paratroops, hence the anchor badge soldered on to the front.

colonel or major.

Similarly, the next higher formation, *Taishin Dan* (raiding brigade), was the equivalent of a regiment, consisting of a headquarters and two *Taishin Rentai* with a total strength of about 1,450 and commanded by a colonel or lieutenant-colonel.

The highest command echelon was the *Taishin Shudan* (raiding group) which was commanded by a major-general. This comprised a transport aircraft brigade, a raiding brigade, two glider infantry regiments, a raiding machinegun company, a raiding signal company, and a raiding engineer company. The total was about 5,600 men.

above A crysanthemum-shaped plate above a ventilation hole in the Model 92 helmet, and below, an interior view of the leather and straps.

OPERATIONS

Despite the size of the airborne units and the time spent in training them, paratroopers were remarkably little used. The first major drop, and the largest ever undertaken by Japanese paratroopers, was at Palembang in Sumatra (February 14–16, 1942) which was conducted by a regiment. The operation was mounted at short notice and, despite many Japanese errors, was successful, although the enemy troops were a mix of Dutch logistics personnel, and British RAF aircrew and ground mechanics recently evacuated from Singapore. The Japanese quickly identified and corrected their mistakes and the next operation at Koepang, on the island of Timor.

(February 21–22, 1942) went more smoothly. Some 350 men were dropped on each of two days and the drop was noteworthy as the paratroopers held their SMGs as they jumped and the fired them during the descent. Later operations, including an attempt in 1944 to capture five airfields on Leyte were complete failures.

NAVAL INFANTRY

The Imperial Japanese Navy (IJN) decided that it needed infantry soldiers under its own command, so formed permanent naval infantry units 1920s. These were known as "Special Naval Landing Forces" (SNLF [*Kaigun Rikusentai*]) and by December 1941 there were twelve such units, with a total of some 12,000 men. These SNLFs were, however, independent of each other and there was no over-arching command and support structure to enable them to come together to form a single body equivalent to the US Marine Corps or the British Royal Marines.

SNLFs

Internal organization, weapons and equipment were generally on army lines, but size varied according to mission and ranged from about 800 to about 1,500 men. A typical organization was two rifle companies plus one heavy weapons company.

A rifle company consisted of four Rifle Platoons, each of three squads (13 men) plus a fire support squad (13 men armed with 50 mm Grenade Dischargers). The company also included a Machine gun Platoon of four squads, each with two tripod-mounted medium machine guns. The company was commanded by a Commander of the Imperial Japanese Navy, with a small headquarters. Each SNLF also had its own Heavy Weapons Company, which normally comprised two 75 mm guns, two 75 mm pack-howitzers, as in an army battalion, but with the addition of four 3 inch (76.2

below Special Naval Landing Force soldiers storm ashore from light boats on the Malayan coast. The picture also gives an idea of how awkward the long 6.5 mm Type 38 *Arisaka* could be.

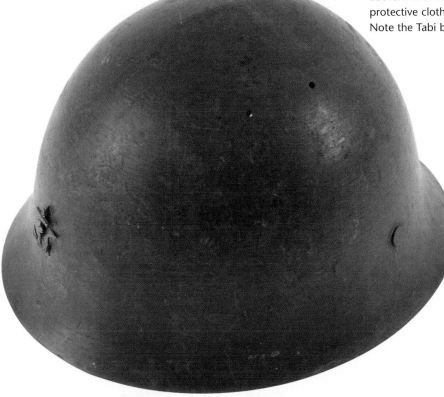

above: Naval infantry posing with senior officers, most wearing protective clothing and carrying weapons for martial arts sparring. Note the Tabi boots and high puttees with crossed tapes.

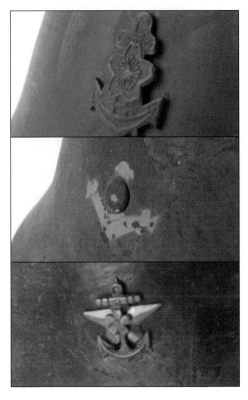

above and right A Model 90 helmet with the anchor badge of the Special Naval Landing Force. The insets show other, similar helmets with different versions of the badge.

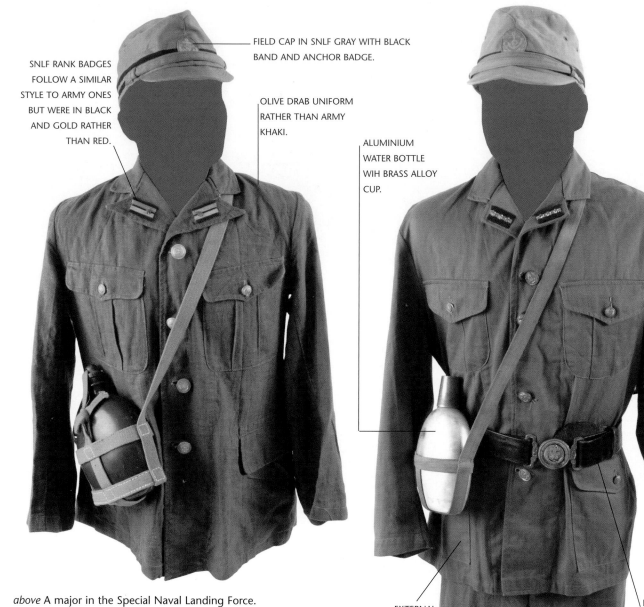

SNLF RANK BADGES FOLLOW A SIMILAR STYLE TO ARMY ONES BUT WERE IN BLACK AND GOLD RATHER THAN RED.

FIELD CAP IN SNLF GRAY WITH BLACK BAND AND ANCHOR BADGE.

OLIVE DRAB UNIFORM RATHER THAN ARMY KHAKI.

ALUMINIUM WATER BOTTLE WIH BRASS ALLOY CUP.

EXTERNAL LOWER POCKETS ON THIS TUNIC. COMPARE TO HIDDEN STYLE ON TUNIC TO LEFT.

BLACK LEATHER BELT WITH SNLF BUCKLE

above A major in the Special Naval Landing Force.

mm) naval guns on wheeled carriages. The Heavy Weapons Company also included two rifle platoons for defense of its fire positions and forward controllers. If the mission required it, the company could be reinforced by 81 mm mortars and 47 mm anti-tank guns.

UNIFORM

On field operations naval infantry troops wore a combat uniform general similar to that of the army, but colored olive drab rather than khaki and with black leather boots rather than brown. These boots were worn with either long black leather

above right An SNLF lieutenant in full uniform and with aluminum water bottle.

above Naval infantry marching ashore unopposed, wearing tropical uniform and sun helmets

above Rear view of the uniform tunic and cap of the major on the previous page

above A neat leather pouch clipped to the belt for carrying folding spectacles.

leggings or long woolen puttees, secured at the top by a tape. They wore the same helmet as the army but with a naval anchor badge, rather than a star. The ranks were as for the Imperial Japanese Navy as were the badges, which were worn on the right sleeve. The only special badge was for naval parachutists, which consisted of an embroidered naval anchor with crossed open parachutes topped by the imperial chrysanthemum, on circular cloth backing. In winter, the backing was dark blue with the design in red; in summer dress the backing was in white with the design in black,

OPERATIONS

The amphibious SNLFs first saw action in Shanghai in 1932, followed by minor operations elsewhere in China and Manchukuo until December 19412 when they carried out landings in the Philippines, the Dutch East Indies and Wake Island. These operations were against coastal targets and were intended to support shipborne operations, although several were intended to secure forward operating bases for IJN seaplanes. By mid-1942 Japan's strategic role had switched from offense to defense, particularly of the many captured Pacific islands.

ITALY

Italian soldiers had already been fighting for six years in Ethiopia and in Spain before World War II broke out.

The country was led into this war having very few natural resources and a poor industrial base, so that, despite Mussolini's grandiose speeches and bluster, the armed forces were grossly under-resourced, generally poorly equipped and usually short of vehicles, fuel, modern weapons and ammunition.

Nevertheless, some 4.5 million Italian fighting men fought doggedly and bravely throughout all their campaigns: in Italy, Africa, Greece, the Balkans and in Russia. But they paid a heavy price for one man's dreams of glory: some 78,000 were killed and 120,000 wounded, while several hundred thousand also served two or more years as prisoners-of-war.

ITALY

One of Britain's greatest World War II generals, Field Marshal Sir William Slim, once remarked that there are "no bad soldiers, only bad officers", and if the Italian infantry emerged from World War II with a poorer reputation than it deserved then the blame lies with the higher leadership rather than with the soldiers themselves. Those who doubt Italians' capability to undertake courageous and determined actions need look no further than the history of the navy's special forces unit, 10th MAS, which carried out some of the most daring raids of the war, using two-man torpedoes and high-speed motor-boats to attack British warships in the Mediterranean. Unfortunately for the Italians, there was no equivalent in the Royal Army.

The Italians had long had dreams of an empire to match those of other European powers, but the territories that were acquired, principally along the North African coast and in the Horn of Africa, were separated from Italy by British-dominated seas, making reinforcement and supply in war difficult

above Small metal shields were popular badges on Italian uniforms. This one shows that the wearer was or had been a member of the Fascist Youth.

above Officer's caps such this were usually of high quality. Later versions copied the German style.

above A Model 1928 sun helmet. The crest indicates it was worn by soldier in the colonial 158th Regiment.

above A metal shield of the 24th "Gran Sasso" Division.

above Infantry on parade with steel helmets, ammunition pouches in front of their tunics and rolled greatcoats around their shoulders.

if not impossible. To add to their problems, the war plans made by the government and general staff – and the resulting training and exercises – were based on a war in mountainous European terrain. Units were thus ill-prepared for the campaigns they actually had to fight in Ethiopia, North Africa and Russia. Finally, Italy had very few natural resources and a poor industrial base, so that, despite Mussolini's grandiose speeches and bluster, the armed forces were grossly under-resourced and poorly equipped, and throughout the war the

infantry was always short of vehicles, fuel, modern weapons and ammunition.

During World War II some 4.5 million Italians served in their country's armed forces, of whom approximately 78,000 were killed and 120,000 wounded. Several hundred thousand also served two or more years as prisoners-of-war. It was all a very heavy price to pay for one man's dreams of glory.

THE ITALIAN ARMY

At the outbreak of World War II the Italian leader Benito Mussolini assumed direct personal control of the armed forces, of which the army was by far the largest component. It consisted of some two million men in 3 armored divisions, 3 cavalry divisions and 69 infantry divisions of varying types.

There were four types of foot infantry division, composed as follows:

• **Standard infantry division** (*divisione fanteria*). The standard division was known as a "binary" division as it was built around two infantry regiments (each of three infantry battalions), plus one two-battalion CCNN legion (the CCNN was the military arm of the fascist "blackshirt" militia). There were 48 infantry divisions in total, although 9 of them were designated Infantry Division (Mountain) and retained the same basic organization but with extra manpower and transport animals.

• **Alpine division** (*divisione alpina*). The five Alpine divisions were made up of men from the mountainous regions of northern Italy and comprised two Alpine infantry regiments together with an Alpine artillery regiment and support and logistic troops, all also from the same regions. The infantry regiments often operated independently, in which case they were given a "slice" of artillery and support units, leaving the divisional headquarters to serve in coordinating and administrative roles.

• **Blackshirt division** (*divisione milizia*) – two CCNN Legions, each of three battalions. When mobilization took place, an artillery regiment,

above Dressed for temperate conditions this soldier has a steel helmet, gray woolen tunic, leather belt and ammunition pouches, and a canvas bag over his shoulder.

left Alpini mountain troops were regarded as elite forces. The men shown here wear the alpine cap with feather.

above The *Bustina* was a comfortable, serviceable cap with side flaps that could be turned down in cold weather. This one bears the single star of a 2nd lieutenant.

right Early-war uniforms often had arm-of-service patches on the collar. This uniform belonged to an artillery officer, while the blue and black breast ribbon indicates he fought in the Ethiopian campaign.

engineer battalion, antitank company, together with logistic support units were provided from Royal Army (i.e., non-blackshirt) resources.

• **Libyan division** (*divisione libica*) – two Libyan regiments (each of three battalions)

All of these had an artillery regiment, composed of guns which were either horse-drawn (Libyan divisions), carried on pack horses/mules (mountain/Alpine divisions) or towed by trucks, motorized tractors or automobiles.

above Many badges and awards commemorated Italy's cooperation with Nazi Germany. This one was awarded to Italian soldiers who completed training in Germany.

right The Italian Model 1933 steel helmet gave good cover to the side of the head and neck. Most were painted gray-green (like this one) until 1940, when a darker green color was introduced.

below This interior view of the Model 1933 helmet reveals well-preserved leather insides and chin strap.

There were also two types of motorized division:

• The Motorized division (*divisione motorizzata*) had two infantry regiments, each with two truck-mobile infantry battalions, plus a Bersaglieri regiment (two battalions mounted in trucks, one on motor-cycle), plus one towed artillery regiment. In this division the trucks were an integral part of the units they supported.

• A Transportable division (*divisione auto-trasportabile*) was essentially a standard infantry division (two infantry regiments, each of three battalions) which could be moved by trucks when the situation required it. It was, however, a curious hybrid, halfway between an infantry and a motorized division, because although the infantry was mounted in trucks, these were operated by units controlled by corps headquarters and were frequently taken away for logistic and other tasks. There were some differences between transportable divisions deployed in Europe and those deployed to Africa (*Divisione Autotrasportabile AS*): the Europe-based divisions had no CCNN legion and tended to retain their animals for resupply should the trucks not be available, while the North African divisions had added light tank and anti-tank battalions.

For completeness, the other two types of division should be mentioned:

• Armored division (*divisione corazzata*) which comprised one tank regiment (medium or light

above Fabric sleeve patches were often worn on uniform tunics. This one is of the 8th "Po" Motorized Division.

above A patch from the Frontier troops in the XIII sector.

above A patch from the 26th "Assietta" Infantry Division.

left A spotter team on the frontier. Note the short tunic and leather gaiters instead of puttees on the nearest man.

above Italian firearms were usually serviceable if not outstanding. The most successful were probably the range of light automatic pistols produced by Beretta, such as the Model 1934 shown here.

left Collar "flame" worn by Fascist Militia troops on a lightweight tropical jacket.

tanks), one *Bersaglieri* regiment (two infantry battalions mounted in trucks and one motorcycle battalion), plus one towed artillery regiment.

- "Rapid" division (*divisione celere*) comprising two mounted cavalry regiments, one *Bersaglieri* regiment (thee truck-mounted battalions) and one light tank battalion. Plus one towed artillery regiment.

As with many contemporary Fascist statistics, the numbers of divisions told nothing like the full story. Only 19 divisions were at full strength; 34 were at about 75 per cent; and the remaining 22 at 60 per cent strength or less. The infantry divisions were also short of equipment and transport, while in almost every case their weapons were simply not up to international standards.

right Another Model 1933 helmet in the late-war green color. Many helmets had a regimental or unit badge painted on the front. This example sports the badge of the Marine Infantry.

above Interior view showing intact fixings. Compare with the one shown on page 310.

THE ITALIAN INFANTRY

Under the Fascist regime all Italian boys were given state-sponsored training aimed at preparing them for their compulsory military service. This started at about the age of six when they joined the "Children-of-the-She-Wolf" (*Figli della Lupa*) organization, graduating to the "Fascist Youth of the Lictors" (GIL) at the age of eight, in which they served until reaching the age of 21. These organizations provided training in various activities, but particularly in military subjects such as military discipline, foot and arms drill, map-reading and national history. All this was supposed to ensure a disciplined, physically fit and mentally prepared body of young people who would adapt quickly to military life when they were conscripted. Conscription lasted 18 months, starting in the year in which they reached their 20th birthday. On joining the army the conscript was allocated to a specialization and the general policy was that the brightest and most mentally alert went to corps such as engineers, communications, armor and artillery and then logistics and maintenance, with those that were left being placed in the infantry. This was not a recipe for high-quality front-line combat units.

left NCO's tunic worn by a corporal-major. It is made from inferior material to officers' types but is still a reasonably comfortable and effective garment.

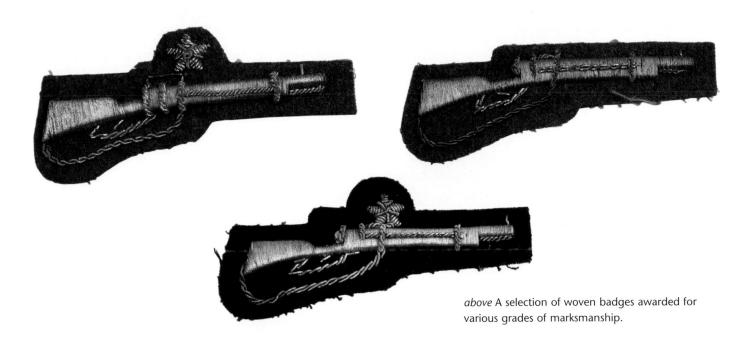

above A selection of woven badges awarded for various grades of marksmanship.

CARABINIERI

The *Carabinieri* have always considered themselves to be a fourth arm of the state, co-equal with the army, navy and air force, and since, under certain conditions, they also acted as infantry, they need to be mentioned here. The *Carabinieri* (the word translates as "carrying a carbine") was formed in the Kingdom of Piedmont-Sardinia in 1814 and was based on the French Napoleonic Gendarmerie. In peacetime they were a combined military and civil police force, but in war they served under the direct control of the Minister of War as military police, when their missions included the usual range of military police duties, such as maintaining military law and order in the Italian armed forces, traffic control, convoy escorts, moving prisoners-of-war to the rear and setting up and guarding prisoner-of-war camps. In addition, they were responsible for security duties in base areas and on the lines-of-communication, as well as guarding vital points such as railroad stations. They also had specific duties in conducting the yearly conscription process and in ensuring that when mobilization was ordered it was achieved quickly and efficiently. In contrast, they also had responsibilities in the civil sphere, serving as police in cities, towns and villages on normal police duties. They also provided guards of honor and guards at vulnerable points such as harbors and railroads. In addition to this, in an emergency they were required to form combat infantry units up to battalion in size, where their duties normally included liaison and reconnaissance, but could include combat.

below Ammunition pouch and white belt worn by Carabinieri. Note the embossed metal "bursting bomb" badge on both.

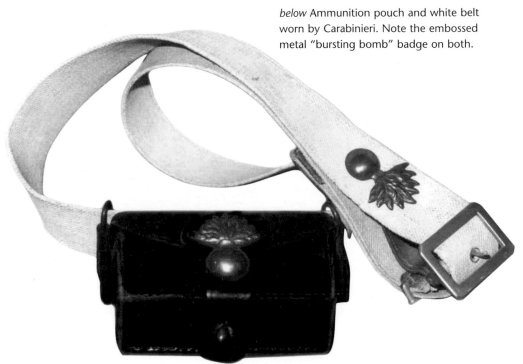

BERSAGLIERI

The word *Bersaglieri* translates into English as "sharpshooter" and the corps, which was founded in 1836, was part of the Italian infantry. All officers and soldiers were required to be very fit, to be skilled marksmen, and to possess a high level of individual initiative; they were thus equivalent to the British "light infantry" and the French "*chas-*" *seurs.*" At all times they moved running at the double (even when in barracks), and were instantly recognizable by their wide-brimmed hats with a large plume of capercaillie feathers on the right side. During World War II there were twelve regiments, each of three battalions, with one such regiment in each armored and mechanized division. They were well trained, superbly fit and invariably fought hard.

above The *Bersaglieri* wore versions of this "flaming bomb" badge on *Bustina* and sun helmet headgear.

above and below Black headgear with patent leather brim worn by *Bersaglieri* with their dress uniform. The plume of black feathers was a distinct identifier of this elite light infantry force.

above A *Bersaglieri* motorcycle reconnaissance patrol in north Africa. They are wearing tropical uniform and the Model 1928 sun helmet,

COLONIAL TROOPS

Following their colonial conquests the Italians were quick to start raising native troops who were then engaged in helping to maintain Italian rule in their own territory, or in imposing it in some other Italian colonial possession. The Italians formed units of colonial infantry wherever possible, always from volunteers. The usual procedure was to have Italian officers, a mix of Italian and indigenous NCOs and all-indigenous enlisted men. Such units were armed, equipped and trained for colonial police actions, and thus ill-equipped and poorly trained for modern warfare.

- **Albania**. Following its occupation of the country in 1939 the Italians formed the Fascist Albanian Militia, an all-infantry force. There were four battalions, known as legions. They never served outside Albania and were disbanded in 1943.
- **Italian East Africa**. A total of seven groups (equivalent to weak battalions) were formed in Ethiopia and Eritrea. All were defeated and captured during the Allied advance in 1941.
- **Libya**. Originally separate units were formed for Tripolitania and Cyrenaica, but these were amalgamated into the *Regio Corpo Truppe Coloniali*

above Uniform belt worn by colonial Fascist Militia recruited in Albania.

opposite The Italians recruited extensively in their colonial territories, both from the native population and from Italian nationals who were living there. This sergeant is issuing items of uniform and personal equipment to a new recruit in Tunisia.

above A rather splendid wire-braided badge which would be worn on the service cap by mountain-trained Frontier Troops.

della Libia (Royal Corps of Libyan Troops) in 1935. At the outbreak of war in 1940, this corps was some 28,000 strong and formed into two infantry divisions – 1st Libyan *Sibelle* Division and 2nd Libyan *Pescatori* Division, which were some 8,000 strong, compared to 13,000 for a metropolitan infantry division. Both these divisions were wiped out in the desert campaign of 1940–41 and were only partially reformed after this disaster. Among the more noteworthy elements were the six Saharan companies (*Compagnia Sahariana*), which were not only fully motorized, but also included two or three Caproni Ca-309 Ghibli twin-engined reconnaissance aircraft. Each company had 20 vehicles and two or three machine gun platoons, with a total of eight heavy machine guns and two 47 mm anti-tank guns.

OTHER MILITIAS

Mussolini was very keen on forming militias, where professional groups could be employed in wartime to protect their own services, but while dressed in uniform and subject to military discipline. The significance here was that by doing so, he did not have to employ infantry to provide guards and escorts. One such was the Railway Militia, founded in 1923, which provided railway police in peacetime, but in war they were embodied as a military force responsible for the protection of the railway system. Other similar forces were the Port Militia, Post and Telegraph Militia, Forest Militia, Highway Militia and the Frontier Militia. Typically, these militias consisted of a national HQ in Rome, which was functionally responsible to the relevant civil ministry; for example, the Highway Militia was responsible to the Ministry of Public Works. There were also two functional militias, one responsible for fixed anti-aircraft artillery, searchlights and observers, the other for coastal defense artillery.

RANKS

above Fabric sleeve badge for a lieutenant-colonel.

above Late-war black rank badges were smaller than the earlier gold

left Compare the black badge with this gold braid set of sergeant-major's stripes.

There were more graduations in the rank structure in the Royal Army than in most comparable foreign armies and the insignia appeared in a wide variety of places: on the head-dress, shoulder straps, high on the sleeve, on the cuff and on the chest in various types of protective clothing. There were also discriminations in certain grades between those in command or staff appointments. The Italians divided their officer grades into:

- **General grade.** There was no rank of brigadier-general.
- **Superior grade.** Equivalent to US Army field grade.
- **Junior grade.** As in the US Army, except that captains and lieutenants who had held those ranks for twelve years were graded 1st Captain and 1st Lieutenant, respectively.

There were three grades of warrant officer, but only two grades of NCO: sergeant-major (who was not a warrant officer) and sergeant. Corporal-major and corporal were not considered to be non-commissioned officers, but higher grades of private, with corporal-major equivalent to the US Army's Private First-Class.

All uniforms included an indication of the wearer's status and rank. For officers and warrant officers these included a peaked service cap with rank indicated on the cap band, rank badges on either the shoulder or the cuff (but not both at the same time). Also, officers' pantaloons had two stripes, and were made from cloth of far superior quality to those worn by NCOs and enlisted men. For the latter, rank was indicated by chevrons worn on the upper left arm.

ITALIAN ARMY INFANTRY RANK BADGES

NCOs

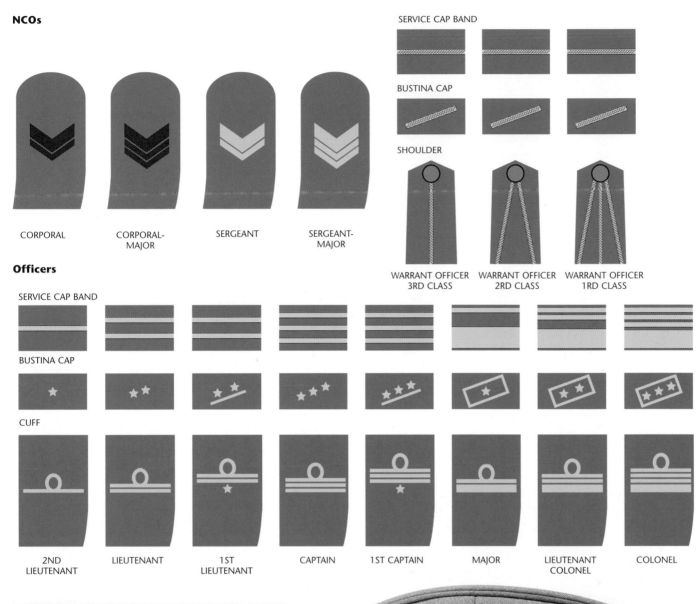

CORPORAL

CORPORAL-MAJOR

SERGEANT

SERGEANT-MAJOR

SERVICE CAP BAND

BUSTINA CAP

SHOULDER

WARRANT OFFICER 3RD CLASS

WARRANT OFFICER 2RD CLASS

WARRANT OFFICER 1RD CLASS

Officers

SERVICE CAP BAND

BUSTINA CAP

CUFF

2ND LIEUTENANT

LIEUTENANT

1ST LIEUTENANT

CAPTAIN

1ST CAPTAIN

MAJOR

LIEUTENANT COLONEL

COLONEL

above and right Rank was also shown by the gold braid on the capband of the uniform service cap. The cap to the left belonged to a captain while the inset shows the markings of a lieutenant-colonel.

ORGANIZATION

above Italian infantry moving forward under cover of smoke in north Africa.

above and right Cloth cap badges for the 91st Infantry Regiment on the left and the 2nd *"Sforzesca"* Regiment on the right.

As explained earlier, there were several different types of infantry division, and even within those divisions the organization was adjusted as the war continued. However, the start point was the 1940 infantry division, which was commanded by a lieutenant-general and consisted, at least on paper, of just under 13,000 all ranks.

THE INFANTRY DIVISION

The combat element of the division comprised two infantry regiments (commanded by a colonel) and a CCNN Legion, with fire support from an artillery regiment, a mortar battalion and an anti-tank company.

There was also an engineer battalion, with one engineer company and a telecommunications company (there was no separate signal corps). The logistical support and most of the prime motive power depended upon horses and a standard division in 1940 on mainland Europe included some 3,500 horses, ponies or mules, and just 130 motor vehicles.

THE INFANTRY REGIMENT

The infantry regiment was composed of three battalions, each of three rifle companies and a heavy weapons company, the latter being armed with eight heavy machine guns and eighteen 45 mm light mortars.

The regiment also included a mortar company (six 81 mm mortars) and an infantry gun company (four 65 mm guns).

CCNN LEGION

The CCNN legion was composed of two battalions (each of three companies) and a heavy weapons company of twelve heavy machine guns and eighteen 45 mm mortars.

DIVISIONAL ARTILLERY

Artillery support appeared adequate in numbers of guns, but the weapons themselves were elderly designs, and all were either towed by horses or carried by pack-horses/mules, while the shells were of World War I design and effectiveness. The major components of the artillery regiment were three battalions, each of three batteries, each with four weapons. One battalion was equipped with twelve 100 mm Skoda Model 1914 howitzers, the second with twelve 75 mm Model 1912 field guns, and the third with twelve 75 mm Skoda Model 1918 pack-howitzers. The regiment also included an anti-aircraft battery armed with eight 20 mm Breda Model 35 cannon, which were very effective in 1939–40 against aircraft flying at low speed and height, but thereafter of little use. In addition to this, there was an anti-tank battery, armed with eight 47 mm Model 1937 anti-tank guns.

LIBYAN INFANTRY DIVISION

There were two Libyan infantry divisions in 1940: 1st Libyan *Sibelle* Division and 2nd Libyan *Pescatori* Division. The fighting strength of both was concentrated in two infantry regiments and, as with

above A captain of artillery in a coastal artillery command post.

the metropolitan divisions, each infantry regiment had three battalions, each of three rifle companies plus a heavy weapons company, although in this case there were no 45 mm mortars. Nor, it should be noted, were there any CCNN legions allocated to these divisions, despite the fact that the "binary" organization had already been proved to be unsatisfactory.

The artillery regiment included only two battalions, each with twelve 77 mm guns, and two anti-aircraft companies, each with eight 20 mm cannon. There was also a company with eight 47 mm anti-tank guns, together with engineers, communications and logistics elements, all under regimental command.

There were also two companies on camels (*Meharisti*). All these companies were employed mainly on policing duties, such as keeping an eye on nomadic tribes, guarding wells and road junctions, and escorting caravans. The corps also provided a battalion of paratroops as well as their own artillery, engineers and logistic support. The corps was formally disbanded in January 1943.

UNIFORMS

above Infantryman in dark gray uniform and Bustina.

below This lieutenant's dress tunic has the green collar "flames" of the Alpini mountain troops.

As in other areas such as weapons, so, too, with clothing and equipment, the Italian government and high command failed to look after its infantrymen properly. A few items were acceptable, such as the comfortable sahariana shirt, the well-designed Model 1933 steel helmet and the smart and adaptable bustina cap, but in the vast majority of cases the design was bad and the quality of the finished product poor. Indeed, with his Model 1891 rifle and Model 1907 ammunition pouches, the World War II infantryman was armed and equipped almost identically to his predecessor of 1914.

In general, officers' parade and barracks uniforms were well designed, well cut, made of excellent material, and smart. On parade they wore the same steel helmet as their men, but off parade they wore a high-crowned, peaked service cap, usually (and, in particular, with the younger officers) worn at a rakish angle. In contrast, NCOs' and enlisted men's parade and barracks uniforms were made of a coarse material and poorly tailored and by no means smart.

The national authorities were simply not

above Cloth cap badge of the 13th Artillery Regiment.

above The crossed halberds indicate the badge of a sapper unit, in this case the 10th Regiment.

above Tunic belonging to a warrant officer of the 13th Cavalry Regiment with the pre-war style of all-black collar.

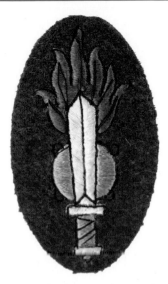

above Arm badge worn by assault engineer troops.

above Cap badge of an Alpine artillery unit.

above Cockade cap badge of the 66th Infantry Regiment.

above Another sapper regiment cap badge, this time in black thread rather than gold.

prepared for war on such a scale, on so many fronts, in such different forms of terrain, and in climates varying from the scorching heat of the Sahara to the desperate cold of a Russian winter. There were reasonable, although still inadequate, preparations for uniforms and equipment for the desert and temperate European conditions, but the Italian soldiers who went east suffered probably more even than the Germans.

As in Germany and Japan, Italian industry proved unable to cope with increasingly severe shortages of manpower and raw materials. As a result, the army's uniforms dimished in quality as the war progressed, increasingly being badly made out of poor-quality materials.

above A broad-bladed fighting knife that some soldiers carried, either on the belt or in the tunic.

left The hilt has *"Opera Balilla"* engraved on it: the name of an Italian fascist youth organization.

above and below Another fighting knife and, below, its metal scabbard.

ARMS OF SERVICE

Like other armies, the Royal Army was divided into a number of arms and services, each of which had its own cap-badge. Within the infantry, there were different badges for line infantry, grenadiers, *Alpini* and *Bersaglieri,* and at the center of each of these badges was a small circle which bore the number of the specific regiment. Others with their own badges included cavalry, artillery, engineers (which included the telecommunications and motor transport troops) and the logistic services such as quartermaster, supply, medical, veterinarian and chaplains. The militias also had their own badges, all of which incorporated the fasci, the emblem from which the fascist movement took its name.

In addition to the cap-badges, collar patches also gave a great deal of further information about the wearer. In the case of the infantry these patches were rectangular in shape and used combinations of background color, and vertical and horizontal stripes (also in various colors) to denote the specific regiment or division. A further series of patches had one or two vertical tails, or three for cavalry. Known as *flamme,* these came in a wide variety of colors and could be on their own or superimposed upon divisional signs. To give just one example (among many hundred), a single-tailed gray *flamme* mounted on a red rectangle with horizontal black and yellow stripes denoted the supply company of 31st Calabria Infantry Division. There were also metal or woven shields worn on the upper arm to denote a particular division or, for the CCNN, zone.

Five-pointed stars, made of a yellow metal, were also worn, usually on the collar patches, or even on the collar without a patch, as, for example, on greatcoats and tropical jackets. This was purely decorative and symbolized Italy's unity.

CLOTHING

TEMPERATE CLIMATE

The basic pattern of clothing for temperate climates worn by all ranks of the infantry in both the Royal Army and CCNN was introduced in 1933 and remained in use until 1945, except for some simplification in 1940 to meet wartime conditions. This consisted of a jacket with open collar, worn over a shirt and tie, and pantaloons which secured below the knee. These items, plus the puttees, stockings and gloves that went with them were of a unique color – gray with a slightly greenish tinge – although there was a minor difference between officers/warrant officers and NCOs/enlisted men, but this was due more to the much better quality of the material than to the use of different dyes.

The jacket had four pockets and full skirt, with an open collar. The collar was lined with a gray-green material. The shirt and tie were also gray-green, although some regiments wore red or blue ties, while the Carabinieri sometimes wore black ties and the CCNN, in conformance with their title, wore black shirts and ties.

In all but a few cases, both officers and enlisted men wore pantaloons which were broadly cut in the leg and which were secured with laces or buttons just below the knee. Pre-war, officers' and warrant officers' pantaloons were made of the same superior material as their jackets and had two parallel, vertical stripes, each 0.8 inches (20 mm)

above A tunic bearing the badges of a sergeant-major of artillery. The material is relatively coarse and the cut not as fine as an officers' style garment.

above This tunic has the badges of a sergeant in the 37 Infantry Division *"Modena"*. Made in gabardine twill, it is of a quality normally worn by officers.

above Rear view of a soldier in temperate uniform, showing crossed straps, water bottle and canvas badge.

wide, either side of the outside seam. Once the war had started officers and warrant officers were ordered to wear pantaloons of the same material as their men and without the stripes, although the previous style could be "worn out." After the first winter in Russia a new type of pantaloon, with thick lining was developed but there were never enough to outfit everyone who should have had them.

A greatcoat, introduced in 1934, was single-breasted and cut on generous lines so that it could be worn over the basic uniform and could also be worn with a fleece liner. Unfortunately, because it was single-breasted, it was not as warm as a double-breasted

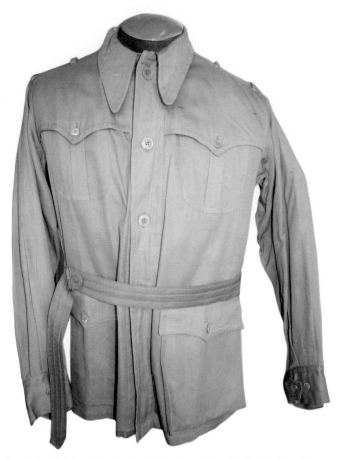

above The lightweight tropical Saharina shirt with its fabric belt proved to be a popular and practical item in Africa and other hot weather theaters.

above Baggy pantaloon-style trousers worn by an officer.

above A privately-purchased officer's uniform shirt made from silk. Note the unusual double pockets.

design would have been. The NCOs and enlisted men's greatcoat was made of a coarse material but that for officers and warrant officers was made of finer material and of double-breasted design. NCOs and enlisted men in Alpine, *Bersaglieri* and CCNN units were also issued with a distinctive cloak in a coarse gray material

Other clothing items included gray or gray-green pullovers, which were issued to all enlisted men, while officers bought their own (or had them knitted for them). The authorities seem to have been very relaxed about the styles, which extended from V-neck to rollneck. Knitted gloves in the usual gray-green wool were issued, as well as a larger mitten with felt inserts, both of which had separate thumb and forefinger. Paratroopers had their own design of black leather gauntlets. Officers and warrant officers usually wore brown leather gloves (black for CCNN) except in combat, where they wore the same woollen gloves as their troops.

above The standard gray leather belt which was worn outside the uniform tunic.

BELT

The NCOs and soldiers' belts were a cloth pattern worn in barracks and a leather belt dyed gray-green for field use. Officers wore the same, but were also frequently to be seen in a wide leather belt with leather strap over the right shoulder only, which was closely modeled on the British "Sam Browne," except that the false buckle was fixed in position and the belt secured by means of a stud. When necessary, a leather pistol holster was worn on the left side of the belt.

right When the Italian Army fought in north Africa most soldiers wore a version of the Saharina tunic shirt. This is an officer's variant, with shoulderboards and the standard fabric belt.

TROPICAL CLIMATES

A new uniform was developed in 1935 for the campaign in Ethiopia, which then remained in use, with only minor variations, until 1945. This was made of a cool and hard-wearing khaki-colored linen, and consisted of a jacket and pantaloons cut on the same style as the temperate uniform. Initially the trousers tucked into the top of the boots, but once the Eritrean campaign had ended these were replaced by the traditional pantaloons, albeit in the same khaki material.

A particularly popular item was the sahariana, a bush jacket style with large patch pockets below the waist, but with the breast pockets formed from

329

a continuous strip of material which ran around the entire upper section of the garment. Its success was such that it was even adopted by as many German officers and soldiers as could get their hands on one.

NATIVE TROOPS

The Italians formed units of indigenous troops in their North and East African territories who were armed and equipped in the same way as Italian troops, but wore uniforms more suited to their own climate and traditions. Libyan troops wore a white jacket with closed collar, white turban and khaki-colored, ankle-length pantaloons. Rank badges were small, red and worn on the right sleeve, while a multi-colored sash worn around the wait indicated the particular unit. In East Africa, the troops wore a knee-length white tunic, white pantaloons and a red tarboosh (fez) hat, with a tassel whose color indicated the unit. They also wore puttees, but often without boots. The badges of rank were very large, red in color, and worn on the left sleeve.

above A sand-colored Saharina shirt as worn by a lieutenant in a colonial Fascist Militia unit. On the breast is the ribbon for the Ethiopian campaign medal.

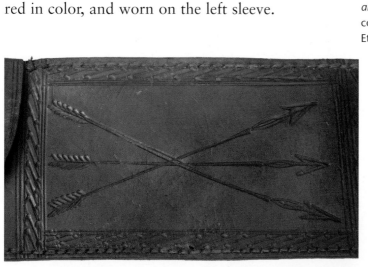

below A finely tooled leather belt with scabbard and dagger as worn by Somali colonial troops.

above and above left Detail of the markings include the words *"REGIO TRUPPE"* and *"CORPO COLONIALE"*.

HEADGEAR

STEEL HELMET

The Italian Royal Army probably had more varieties of headgear than any other army, one of the most recognizable being the Model 1933 steel helmet. This was of a distinctive shape, particularly when seen from the side, and had a rather higher front profile than most other types and a rim without a crimped edging. It was pierced by three hollow rivets which provided ventilation as well as anchoring the liner, and was secured with a leather chinstrap, gray-green for the Royal Army and black for the CCNN. As manufactured, the helmet was gray-green in color, but in Russia it was painted white in winter or covered with a specially-made white cloth, while in North Africa it was painted a sandy color. In 1942 a camouflaged helmet cover was issued to all. A feature copied by no other army was that the *Alpini* and *Bersaglieri* wore their traditional feathers attached to their steel helmets in special holders. There was also a special helmet for paratroopers which was virtually hemispherical in shape.

The steel helmet was worn by all ranks, both officers and enlisted, on formal parades.

above and below A well-preserved Model 1933 helmet, the outside view showing two of the three liner-anchor and ventilation rivets. The interior view shows the adjustable leather liner and chin strap.

SERVICE CAP

Until 1933 Royal Army officers in European stations wore a kepi but this was then replaced by a much more modern peaked service cap with a fairly low crown, although increasing contact with Germany led to a higher, more German-style crown in about 1939. The cap was made of a high-quality gray-green material with a black leather peak and chinstrap. The wearer's rank was indicated on the cap-band; various combinations of gold stripes from warrant officer to colonel and a combination of an elaborate braid pattern and stripes, both in silver, for generals. There was a tropical version of the service cap which was of the same design, but the

left and below An officer's cap from a Fascist Militia unit. Some wearers removed the interior stiffening of their caps to give the floppy, rather rakish look seen here. The interior view (below) shows the leather band and lining.

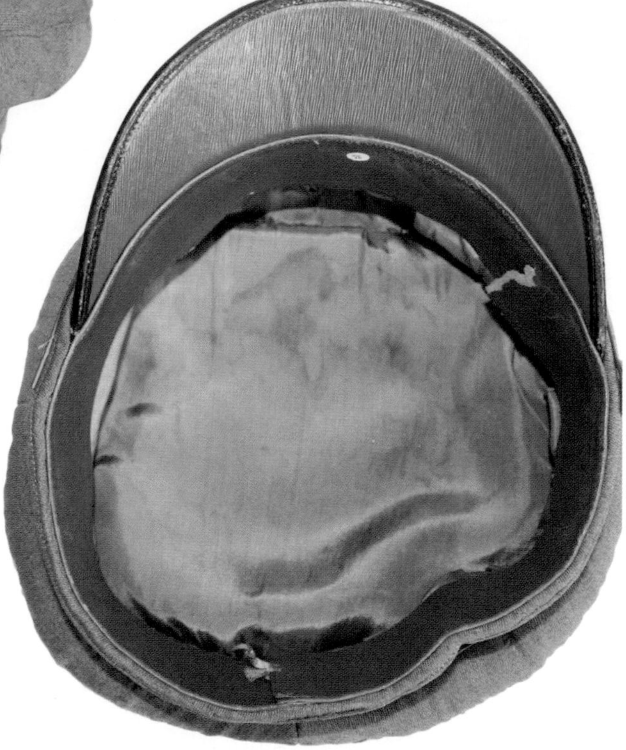

material was lighter in weight and in a variety of colors, ranging from a pale green to sandy khaki, while the chin-strap and peak were of brown leather. The rank bands were the same as for the European cap but were on a khaki rather than red band.

Prominent badges at the front of the cap indicated either the wearer's rank or his arm-of-service/regiment. For general officers, the badge consisted of a crown of Savoy (the royal house) surmounting an eagle with outstretched wings, which was embroidered in silver wire (brigade and divisional commanders) or gold wire (corps commanders and above), and was on a red felt backing if in a command appointment, or a gray-green felt backing if in a General Staff appointment. For colonels and below, the badge indicated the wearer's arm-of-service and, in many cases, his regi-

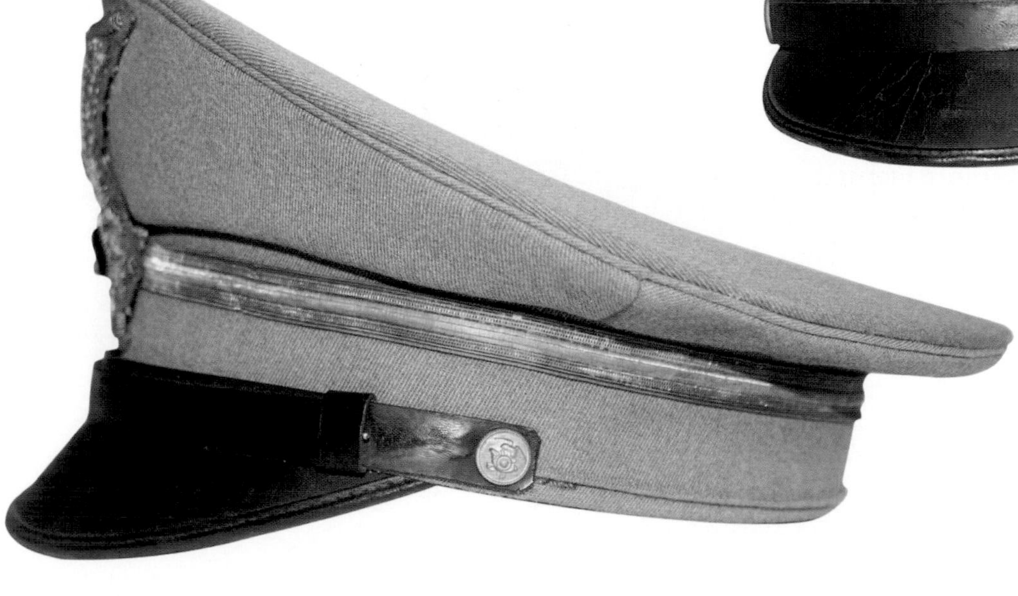

above and left The design of the service cap changed as the war progressed, with a new *"Imperiale"* version being introduced. Based on German style, this had a leather peak which was angled more downward than the earlier design, along with a higher crown that rose vertically above the peak.

left Another cap in the high-peaked *"Imperiale"* style: this one has the crossed-lances badge of the 6th Lancers.

ment, as well. The line infantry badge, for example, consisted of a crown of Savoy surmounting crossed rifles and, where they crossed, a small circle inset with the number of the regiment.

BUSTINA SIDE-CAP

The *Bustina* ("envelope") was a lightweight and practical cap for wear by all ranks in both barracks and field. Introduced in 1934, it appeared in several versions, but in all cases those for officers were made of better quality material. At the front was a curved visor which was normally turned up, making an excellent setting for a cap-badge in its face. This visor could also be turned down, and as originally made it had no stiffening, resulting in a somewhat floppy appearance

right Another view of the same cap, showing the vertical profile and the braid around the capband denoting the rank of 2nd lieutenant.

above A high-quality *Bustina* cap sporting the badges of a major-general.

when lowered. In 1942, however, the visor was given some in-built stiffening and this problem was overcome. There was also a large soft cloth flap at the rear, normally secured across the top of the wearer's head, but which could be lowered to protect the wearer's neck and ears and secured under the chin. Small rank badges were worn on the front left side of the *bustina*, just visible between the folded-up visor and ear/neck flap. The *bustina* was made in various materials, including cloth for temperate wear and cotton twill for the tropics, and with different lining, ranging from silk for officers through red cotton in the tropics to wool for wear in Russia. Another version, introduced in 1942, had a permanently-lowered visor, while retaining the ear and neck cover; this was clearly based on the German *Feldmütze*, but had not come into wide-scale use by the time of the Armistice.

above An enlisted man's *Bustina*, made to the same design as that of an officer but from inferior material.

above Another *Bustina* with the side flaps down. They could be fixed under the chin in severe conditions.

above The side flaps of the *Bustina* could be folded down in poor weather.

below Interior view of a Model 1928 sun helmet showing interior stiffening and how the canvas cover wraps around inside.

SUN HELMET

A British-style pith helmet was commonly worn in Italy's African possessions, right through to the end of the war. The standard helmet was made of cork with a khaki-colored cotton outer cover, narrow pugri of the same material as the cover, green cotton inner liner and an adjustable, chin-strap made of leather. Ventilation was by means of a metal boss with several holes at the top and two mesh-covered holes on either side of the crown. A cap-badge was normally worn at the front, and *Alpini* and *Bersaglieri* also wore their customary plumes. Up to June 1940, officers tended to purchase their helmets privately from sources in India or Aden and there were many minor variations in shape and style.

ALPINE CAP

Alpini troops wore a gray-green mountaineer's cap with a wide rim, turned up at the back, with a bird's feather on the left – crow for NCOs and enlisted men, eagle for company and field grade officers, and goose for generals. This type of hat was much sought-after and was also worn by frontier and finance guards, as well as some of the Fascist Militias.

above The sun helmet may have provided protection from the sun but it gave none against bullets or shell splinters.

right A finely-decorated Alpini hat showing the raked profile and feather mounted on the side.

above Another view of the Alpini hat, showing the rather fine embroidered badge of the 3rd Mountain Artillery Regiment.

right A simple, unadorned enlisted man's Alpini hat with no badge and with the feather missing.

335

FEZ

The most curious headgear worn by some Italian infantry was the fez, or tarboosh, which was adopted by the Bersaglieri after fighting alongside French Army *Zouaves* (North African infantry) in the Crimean War. The *Bersaglieri* version was made of soft red felt in a pointed design, rather than the hard, truncated cone worn by the *Waffen-SS*, for example, with a blue woollen tassel hanging from a long blue cord, while the Fascist Militia (Blackshirts) wore an all-black version. A seemingly archaic, even foreign, form of head-dress for an Italian, the fez was, nevertheless, a source of great pride to those entitled to wear it.

BALACLAVA HELMET

Two types of woollen balaclava helmet were issued to Alpini troops: gray-green for normal winter use and white for snow conditions.

right Colorful cloth fez with blue tassle as worn by some *Bersaglieri* in Africa.

above and left Some Italian units also wore this serviceable beret. This simple design gave great scope to the wearer to determine the final shape of the beret on his head.

above Woolen balaclava as worn by Alpini troops and others.

below and right "Chetnik"-style forage cap worn by some units and by partisan groups.

FOOTWEAR

NCOs and enlisted men wore black leather ankle boots with front lacing and hobnails in a prescribed pattern on the sole. These could be worn with woollen puttees, which were wrapped around the leg from the ankle upwards and secured just below the knee by a cloth tape. Alternatively, soldiers often wore long gray-green stockings together with ankle socks which were turned over the top of the boot.

Officers wore knee-length black riding boots up to 1940, after which they usually wore ankle boots with either knee-length woollen stockings or separate leather leggings. Where leather leggings were worn by infantrymen, they were always black.

The Italian Royal Army socks and stockings were unusual in being made without a toe section, but with an integral strip which went between the large and fourth toe to prevent them slipping back inside the boot. A separate piece of cloth was then placed over the toes for protection and to absorb any sweat. Quite how this originated is not known but even officers, who had to buy their own outfits, bought this type of sock/stocking, rather than the conventional type with an integral toe covering.

left A gray-green fabric puttee which was wrapped around the ankle above the short boot, and into which the trousers were tucked.

right A pair of puttees still in their original wrapping.

above Soldier's short ankle boots with puttees tightly wrapped around the top. Italian soldiers used to say that after wearing these puttees the hair would never again grow on your legs.

right Cavalry officer's black leather boots with spurs fixed to the heel.

PERSONAL FIELD EQUIPMENT

The unfortunate Italian infantryman was sent into battle throughout World War II wearing equipment whose design dated back to the turn of the century.

Unlike other nations he had no harness system on which to attach pouches and haversacks. Instead he wore an M1891 waist belt over his tunic, which was threaded through two loops at the back of his two M1907 cartridge pouches. A suspender strap was clipped to the back of one pouch, passed around the neck and then clipped to the other pouch. The strap was sometimes crossed at the front, so that it passed from left pouch, across right shoulder, around the back of the neck and then down to be clipped to the right pouch. It was intended to support the weight of the pouches and ammunition, but it was inherently uncomfortable and it seems quite extraordinary that it was never improved upon.

Belt, pouches and strap were made of green leather for metropolitan troops, black leather for colonial troops and white canvas for *Alpini*. These pouches were used for clips of rifle ammunition, but separate, larger pouches were issued for the M1938 MAB sub-machine gun.

above Reverse view of the belt holster for a Beretta pistol.

above Leather pouches for 6.5 mm Carcano ammunition. A pair of these pouches was usually worn on the belt in front, with another strap passing around the wearer's neck. Other configurations included being mounted on a belt over the wearer's shoulder.

above Two double ammunition pouches on a shoulder belt as worn by cavalry troops.

above Beretta's Model 1934 automatic pistol fired a 9 mm round and was a handy, light design, popular with the Italian Army and others.

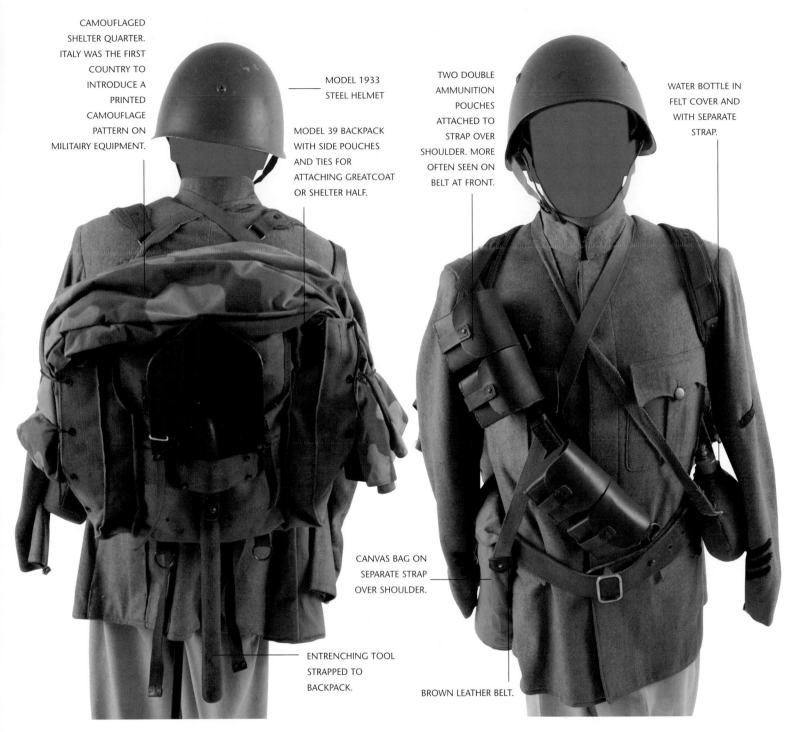

CAMOUFLAGED SHELTER QUARTER. ITALY WAS THE FIRST COUNTRY TO INTRODUCE A PRINTED CAMOUFLAGE PATTERN ON MILITAIRY EQUIPMENT.

MODEL 1933 STEEL HELMET

MODEL 39 BACKPACK WITH SIDE POUCHES AND TIES FOR ATTACHING GREATCOAT OR SHELTER HALF.

TWO DOUBLE AMMUNITION POUCHES ATTACHED TO STRAP OVER SHOULDER. MORE OFTEN SEEN ON BELT AT FRONT.

WATER BOTTLE IN FELT COVER AND WITH SEPARATE STRAP.

CANVAS BAG ON SEPARATE STRAP OVER SHOULDER.

ENTRENCHING TOOL STRAPPED TO BACKPACK.

BROWN LEATHER BELT.

above and above right Front and rear views of an NCO in temperate uniform and carrying an array of field equipment.

PACKS

A variety of packs was issued, each with its own single or double shoulder straps because there was no harness for them to be attached to, as, for example, in the British or German systems. A small knapsack, the Model 1939, contained two partitions to form three pockets, and had straps on the outside to enable a rolled greatcoat, rolled blanket, or shelter-quarter (or a combination of them) to be carried. A larger and more satisfactory mountaineering-style rucksack was issued to *Alpini* and CCNN. A small haversack with a single shoulder strap, similar to the German *Brotbeutel,* was used to carry the day's rations, mess tins, water bottle, field dressing and further supplies of ammunition. Another small sack was used exclusively for used clothing awaiting laundering.

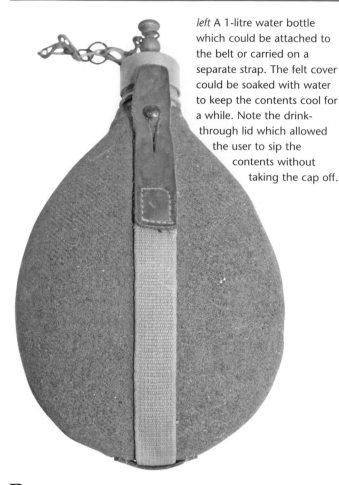

left A 1-litre water bottle which could be attached to the belt or carried on a separate strap. The felt cover could be soaked with water to keep the contents cool for a while. Note the drink-through lid which allowed the user to sip the contents without taking the cap off.

RESPIRATORS

Although they did not employ chemical weapons in World War I, the Italians did use gas in Ethiopia in 1935–36 and had the capability to do so again during 1940–43. To counter enemy use of gas, troops were issued with a respirator, which was either the Model 1933 with separate face-mask and filter joined by a rubber hose, or the Model 1935, in which the cylindrical filter screwed directly into the bottom of the mask. These were carried in a canvas carrier suspended from a single sling. There was no form of protective cloak.

EATING EQUIPMENT.

Every soldier carried a kidney-shaped, two-piece mess-tin, which contained a separate drinking cup; all were made of aluminum and had wire handles. The assembled mess tin was carried in its own canvas cover with a single carrying strap. Various patterns of water-bottle were also issued, all with single carrying-straps. This bottle had an unusual feature; a simple valve in the stopper, which enabled the water to be sipped rather than gulped, thus reducing the rate of consumption. As with many other armies of this period, the water-bottle was frequently contained in a woollen cover, which, when wet, was supposed to cool the contents. The soldier was also issued with a fork and spoon, but used his bayonet as a knife.

SHELTER QUARTER

Each man carried a Model 1929 shelter-quarter together with three aluminum tent-pole sections and three metal pegs. These shelter-quarters and poles could be used on their own or joined in various combinations to make larger capacity tents for up to a maximum of 20 men. The shelter quarter could also be worn as a poncho or ground-sheet. The material was in one of two camouflage patterns, basically green-brown for European use, and khaki for desert use.

PERSONAL IDENTIFICATION

In line with international conventions, Italian soldiers wore a metal identity disc which was secured by a metal chain and hung around the neck. It was stamped with two, duplicated sets of information so that when he died in combat it could be split, one half staying with the corpse, the other sent to his regimental depot with other personal effects. This personal information included full name, regimental number, religion, home town, recruiting depot, and year of birth.

right A gleaming set of mess tins. As with those of many other nations the lid doubled as a cooking pan and eating tray.

left Another water bottle with felt cover and drink-through lid. This one is strapped into a metal carrier which doubles as a cooking pan.

left Aluminum water bottle without the felt cover but with the carrying strap attached to buckles fixed to the outside of the bottle.

above Identity tag for a soldier, showing his name, number, date of birth (1921) and place of birth.

above Paper bag in which the identity tag was stored, with the soldier's name and date of birth on the outside.

Virtually all World War II armies also issued their NCOs and soldiers with a pocket-size book in which were recorded all the significant events in his military career. In the Italian case this was the Libretto Personale, which not only covered details such as name, place and date of birth, religion and physical features, but also events such as conscription, marksmanship, and clothing and equipment issues. It was not, however, the pay-book, which was a separate item.

OTHER ITEMS

Other items of personal equipment included entrenching tools, usually carried in a frog which also held the bayonet, and, for officers, map-cases and binoculars, which were carried in leather cases

right Individual field dressing which would be carried in the soldier's uniform or pouches. Italian medical support was reasonably effective and comprehensive, only breaking down when supplies and resources dried up.

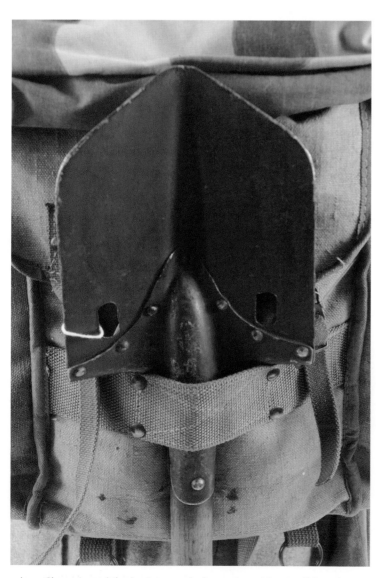

above Close view of the business end of an entrenching tool/shovel, strapped to a Model 39 backpack.

above Italian industry found it difficult to produce enough modern weapons and equipment, but it did manage to provide comfort goods for the soldiers, such as this pack of prophylactics, complete with quality control marks.

left Communication at close ranges was always a problem before the widespread use of lightweight radios. This pistol could be used by an officer or NCO to fire colored flares or illumination for night actions.

right More peaceful personal equipment included this sewing and repair kit.

right Contents of the sewing kit. Life in the front line took a heavy toll of clothing and equipment, and running repairs were often needed.

right The leather frog for this Carcano bayonet would usually be fitted to the belt. Some Italian rifles had permanently fixed folding bayonets under the barrel.

INFANTRY WEAPONS

above A typical uncamouflaged and unprotected defensive position in open terrain in north Africa. The riflemen have Carcano short rifles while the machine gun is a Breda Model 37. Note that both sun helmets and soft fezzes are being worn.

The officers and men of the Italian infantry had many problems to put up with, but one of the most avoidable was the antiquity and inadequacy of the great majority of their weapons. Their rifle had been designed in 1891 and their one-and-only light machine gun was generally acknowledged to have been one of the worst of its type in any contemporary army. Two areas were given very low priority – mortars and anti-tank guns – and this is reflected in the poor equipment in the hands of the troops. That the infantry should have been about one-third of the way through re-equipping with a new caliber of small-arms ammunition just as war broke out was sheer bad luck, rather than bad planning, but the decision to abandon the new caliber and revert to the old caused endless complications at unit level. This overall neglect is the more inexcusable in that Mussolini was desperately keen to strut around on the world stage and sent his army on military adventures in Abyssinia, Spain, France, Yugoslavia, Albania, Greece, Libya and the Soviet Union – the very least he could have done for them in return was to ensure that they were properly armed.

RIFLES

All rifles and carbines used by the Italian infantry in World War II were based on an 1891 design which was the work of Salvatore Carcano, Chief Inspector of the *Reale Fabrica d'Armi* at Turin, in cooperation with a Colonel Paravacino. This was closely based on the Mauser bolt system, the predominant mechanism in the last decades of the 19th century, but with some significant developments, one of which was "progressive rifling" in which the degree of twist increased towards the muzzle. The loading system was a developed version of the *Mannlicher*, in which an en bloc clip, containing six rounds, was inserted into the fixed magazine from above; the clip was then held securely as a spring-loaded lever, known as the "ejector," forced the rounds up each time the bolt was drawn to the rear and an empty cartridge case ejected. Only when the last round had been loaded was the clip released to fall through a hole in the base of the magazine. Among the Carcano modifications was the ability to load the clip either way up, whereas in the original there was only one way.

The ammunition around which this weapon was designed was the 6.5x 52 mm (.256 in) Carcano round which sufficed for World War II, but by the late 1920s was beginning to appear too light; indeed, it was demonstrably ineffective when used in Italy's Abyssinian campaign in 1936–38. As a result, a heavier round was developed with a caliber of 7.35 mm (0.289 in), although this was still lighter than the then current international standards, which were: USA – 0.30 in (7.62 mm); UK – 0.303 in (7.69 mm); German – 7.92 mm (0.312in); USSR – 7.62mm (0.30 in). Rather than develop new weapons to take full advantage of the new round, the army carried out a redesign of the Model 1891, which appeared in 1938, but, following difficulties with the new cartridge, production reverted to the 6.5 mm round. It was not bad planning that led to Italy rearming with a new small-arms caliber in the first years of a new war, it was just bad luck – but the result was the same: disruption and confusion.

CARCANO MODEL 1891 LONG RIFLE

above The Model 1891 and sword bayonet served from 1891 to 1945.

Type: bolt-action, single-shot rifle
Origin: Real Fabrica, Brescia; Fabbrica Nazionale d'Armi, Terni
Caliber: 6.5 mm
Weight (empty): 8 lb 6 oz (3.8 kg)
Length, overall: 49.5 in (1.26 m)

Barrel length: 30.7 in (0.78 m); four-groove rifling; right-hand twist
Ammunition: 6.5 x 52 mm Mannlicher-Carcano
Magazine: 6-round fixed box; loaded by charger
Muzzle velocity: 2,400 ft/sec (732 m/s)

The Fucile di Fanteria Modello 1891 (Infantry Rifle, Model 1891) was developed by Salvatore Carcano at the Italian State Arsenal in Turin and adopted for service in 1891. It was then in constant production, with minor modifications, from 1892 to 1945 and equipped the Italian Army in World Wars I and II, as well as in numerous colonial conflicts. It was adopted by a few other countries, including Bulgaria, which was still using it during World War II. It had a Mauser-type bolt action handle which protruded at right-angles to the receiver and a Mannlicher-pattern fixed magazine, which was loaded by means of a six-round clip inserted in guides and then pushed down with the thumb. The original cartridge was the 6.5 x 22 mm Carcano rimless, which was developed specially for this rifle, one of the earliest rimless cartridges to be adopted by any country.

The Carcano Model 1891 (it is incorrect to designate it the "Mannlicher–Carcano") was a reliable weapon and various versions were produced. Curiously, no sniper version was ever developed, although prototype weapons with telescopic sights were produced in very small numbers in both World Wars. Following the problems over converting to the 7.35 mm round, the old 6.5 mm version was put back into production, but this included the minor changes introduced in the 7.35 mm weapon.

CARCANO MODEL 1891 CAVALRY CARBINE / M1891TS SPECIAL TROOPS CARBINE

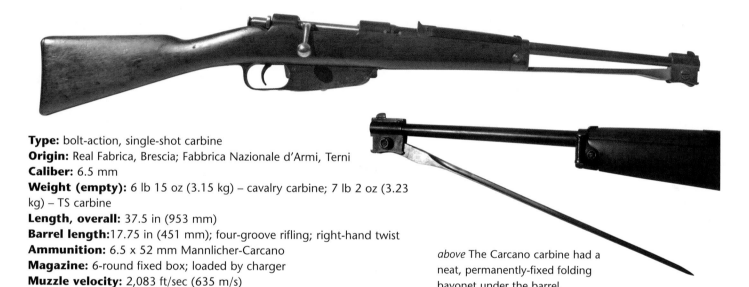

Type: bolt-action, single-shot carbine
Origin: Real Fabrica, Brescia; Fabbrica Nazionale d'Armi, Terni
Caliber: 6.5 mm
Weight (empty): 6 lb 15 oz (3.15 kg) – cavalry carbine; 7 lb 2 oz (3.23 kg) – TS carbine
Length, overall: 37.5 in (953 mm)
Barrel length: 17.75 in (451 mm); four-groove rifling; right-hand twist
Ammunition: 6.5 x 52 mm Mannlicher-Carcano
Magazine: 6-round fixed box; loaded by charger
Muzzle velocity: 2,083 ft/sec (635 m/s)

above The Carcano carbine had a neat, permanently-fixed folding bayonet under the barrel.

The *Moschetto da Cavalleria Modello* 1891 was a shorter, lighter version of the Model 1891 rifle for the cavalry , but some undoubtedly found their way into infantry hands. The action was identical but the barrel was greatly reduced in length and the stock was cut back in order to accommodate the permanently fitted bayonet, which folded back under the barrel. The result was a short, light and effective weapon.

The *Moschetto per Truppe Speciali Modello* 1891 (Carbine for Special Troops, or

Model 1891TS) differed from the cavalry carbine only in having a full-length stock and fittings on the nose-cap for the detachable bayonet as on the full-length rifle. It was slightly heavier than the carbine.

A new version of the carbine was developed in the 1930s to take the new 7.35 mm round. These were the Model 1891/38TS and the Model 1891/38

Para, but both were superseded by more 6.5 mm versions on the failure of the 7.35 mm cartridge.

above Butt and sling mount for the cavalry carbine.

above This carbine has a ramped rear sight in front of the breech. Note the distinctive fixed box magazine typical of all Italian Carcano rifles.

CARCANO MODEL 1938 SHORT RIFLE

above A 7.35 mm short rifle with the bayonet fixed. The leather and metal scabbard is still covering the blade.

above The short rifle was built for the 7.35 mm cartridge but many were converted to 6.5 mm.

Type: bolt-action, single-shot rifle
Origin: Fabbrica Nazionale d'Armi, Terni
Caliber: 7.35 mm
Weight (empty): 8 lb 2 oz (3.69 kg)
Length, overall: 40.16 in (1.020 m)
Barrel length: 22.13 in (562 mm);
four-groove rifling; right-hand twist
Ammunition: 7.35 x 51 mm Carcano
Magazine: 6-round fixed box; loaded by charger
Muzzle velocity: 2,477 ft/sec (751 m/s)

Fucile Corto Modello 1891/38 (short rifle, model 1891/1938). In the 1930s the Italian Army decided to switch from the underpowered 6.5 mm round to a new and much more effective 7.35 x 55 mm round. They also decided to achieve the conversion as simply and cheaply and as quickly as possible by redesigning the well-tried Model 1891 rifle and carbine to accommodate the new caliber. The result was the Model 1938 Rifle, which was shorter and lighter than the Model 1891, and the Model 1938 Carbine. These retained the action, magazine and most of the features of the earlier versions, but with a new barrel, which apart from being larger caliber also did away with the progressive rifling, which had achieved little. A further change was that the ramped rear sight was replaced by a fixed rear sight set to 300 m (330 yd).

The new weapons were put into production in 1938 and many reached troops, but production problems with the 7.35 mm cartridge, plus the realization that changing calibers at the start of a new war was not a good idea, caused the program to be halted in 1940 and the 6.5 mm versions to be reinstated in the weapons factories. The result was chaotic, with both 6.5 mm and 7.35 mm versions being in use on all fronts for many months. Units on the Russian front armed with the 7.35 mm version sent them home in 1942 and replaced them with the 6.5 mm version, but other fronts retained both versions until the war's end. It must have been a quartermaster's nightmare.

Some troops in North Africa had their rifles bored out to accept the German 7.92 mm round. This eased ammunition supply, but the weapon had considerable recoil, although nothing like as much as an 8 mm variant which was tested in prototype form in 1941.

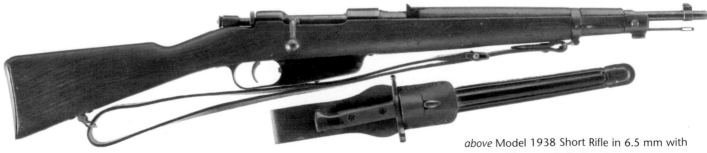

above Model 1938 Short Rifle in 6.5 mm with sling and bayonet in leather frog.

REVOLVERS AND PISTOLS

One model of revolver and two models of automatics were used by the Italian Army in World War II. In general, those NCOs and enlisted men who were in machine gun and infantry gun detachments were armed with the revolver, while officers carried one of the two types of self-loading pistol. Only the Beretta automatic was in any way outstanding.

GLISENTI MODEL 1889 SERVICE REVOLVER

Type: revolver
Origin: Societa Siderurgica Glisenti, Turin
Caliber: 10.4 mm
Weight (empty): 2 lb 2 oz (0.96 kg)
Length, overall: 9.25 in (235 mm)
Barrel length: 4.53 in (115 mm); six-groove rifling; right-hand twist
Ammunition: 10.4 x 20 mm R Italian Ordnance
Magazine: 6-round cylinder
Muzzle velocity: 836 ft/sec (255 m/s)

above A typical late nineteenth-century military revolver, the Model 1889 was solid, reliable and popular.

The *Pistola a rotazione Modello* 1889 (Revolver Model 1889) was the most important revolver to enter service with the Royal Army and remained in production until well into the 1930s. It was produced in several large and many small factories and workshops, resulting in minor, but unimportant, differences. The design was derived from an earlier weapon produced by Chamelot-Delvigne which had been adopted by the French Army in 1871, and was considered to be both reliable and comfortable to hold and fire. There were originally two models: that for officers and NCOs having a round barrel and a trigger guard, while that for enlisted men had a hexagonal barrel and a folding trigger without a guard. This seems a very odd distinction and the latter version was phased out of production in 1914. An unusual feature of both types was that the cylinder did not swing out for loading/unloading so that empty cases had to be removed one at a time using a built-in spring-loaded, ejecting rod. This was sometimes known as the "Bodeo" revolver.

There were many variations including the Model 1889 Light, which was 8.2 inches (208 mm) long, with round barrel, normal trigger and guard, and weighing slightly less, but still using the large 10.4 mm (0.41 inch) bullet. These revolvers were popular and were still being carried by numerous Italian officers and soldiers during World War II, particularly in the colonial units, but eventually the supply of ammunition gave out.

GLISENTI MODEL 1910 SERVICE AUTOMATIC PISTOL

Type: automatic pistol
Origin: Societa Siderurgica Glisenti, Turin
Caliber: 9 mm
Weight (empty): 1 lb 13 oz (0.82 kg)
Length, overall: 8.2 in (208 mm)
Barrel length: 3.9 in (99 mm); six-groove rifling; right-hand twist
Ammunition: 9 x 19 mm Glisenti
Magazine: 7-round box
Muzzle velocity: 1,050 ft/sec (320 m/s)

above The original 7.65 mm pistol had been designed and manufactured by Glisenti although they sold the patents to Brescia before the 9 mm military version was sold. The first army version was known as the Model 1910 and used a 9 mm cartridge that was less powerful than the 9 mm Parabellum.

above The external finish of the Model 1910 was clean, with a grip safety under the trigger. It had a relatively fragile mechanism, however, hence the use of a relatively low-powered round. But it was a reliable enough weapon and remained in service long after it was declared obsolete.

The *Pistola automatica Glisenti Modello* 1910 entered service in 1911 and, although designed by Glisenti, was produced by both that company and Brixia of Brescia. The two types were identical in appearance and operation, but had some minor differences in details. In appearance, the weapon resembled the Luger, but any likeness to the famous German pistol was purely superficial. It operated on the recoil principle and it fired a 9 x 19 mm Glisenti bullet, an Italian round which was less powerful than the 9 mm Parabellum. The well-angled butt held the magazine and seven rounds

The Model 1910 was issued to officers from 1911 to 1935, after which it was replaced by the Beretta, but it remained in production until 1943 and continued to be carried by at least some officers up to the end of the war.

right The later Model 1912 had a few improvements, including the removal of the grip safety, but was in most ways identical to the earlier weapon. Both variants had no separate cocking lever; instead the long trigger pull cocked the hammer before releasing it to fire the round. The small knurled nut in front of the trigger was unscrewed to remove the side plate and give access to the mechanism. The one shown here is in excellent condition and has the Italian imperial eagle molded on the plastic grips.

BERETTA MODEL 1934 SELF-LOADING PISTOL

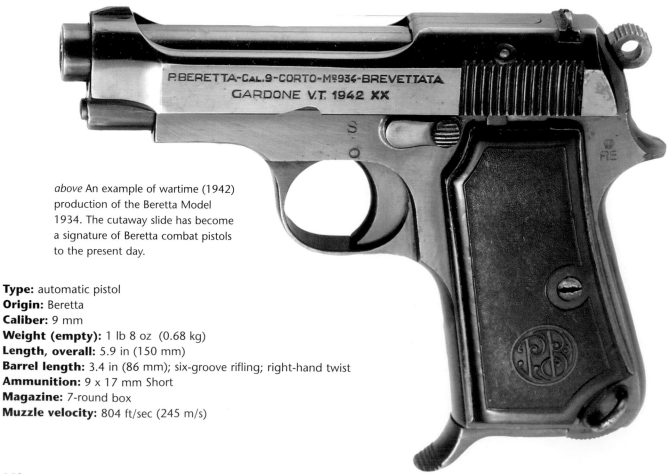

above An example of wartime (1942) production of the Beretta Model 1934. The cutaway slide has become a signature of Beretta combat pistols to the present day.

Type: automatic pistol
Origin: Beretta
Caliber: 9 mm
Weight (empty): 1 lb 8 oz (0.68 kg)
Length, overall: 5.9 in (150 mm)
Barrel length: 3.4 in (86 mm); six-groove rifling; right-hand twist
Ammunition: 9 x 17 mm Short
Magazine: 7-round box
Muzzle velocity: 804 ft/sec (245 m/s)

above The Model 1934 was also produced in 7.65 mm for the Italian Navy and Air Force.

above A pre-war (1936) example of the Model 1934 in 9 mm. The pistol was quite small and many had magazines with the spur at the bottom to extend the length of the grip.

above This well-preserved Model 1934 was made in 1943.

above A 1942-vintage pistol which saw service and was captured as a souvenir by an Allied soldier in Italy.

Beretta produced its first automatic pistol design in 1915 and then continued to develop it until eventually receiving official acceptance as the *Pistola automatica, Modello* 1934. A blowback weapon, it was well-designed and manufactured to Beretta's usually high standards. It had an external hammer, fixed barrel and recoiling breech slide, which was kept closed at the moment of firing by its own inertia reinforced by pressure from the return spring. It did, however, require a short cartridge case and while it could also fire 0.38 in as used in the US Army's Colt it could not fire 9 mm Parabellum. The Model 1934 was carried by most Italian Army officers, and a version in 7.65 mm caliber was produced for the Italian Navy and Air Force.

SUB-MACHINE GUNS

Italy was the first country to field a sub-machine gun (SMG), in the shape of the Villar Perosa Model 1915, a twin-barreled, 9 mm weapon which was designed as an infantry support machine gun, and initially produced without a stock. Two separate companies saw its potential and took one barrel and action from the Villar Perosa, added a stock and produced a sub-machine gun. The first of these was the Beretta Model 1918, designed by Tuillio Marengoni, and in February of that year it became the first true SMG in the world to enter service, beating the Austrian Bergmann by a matter of weeks. The second of these designs, developed by the Villar Perosa company itself and designated the OVP, followed in 1920. Both the Model 1918 and OVP were produced and both remained in service in small numbers during World War II.

BERETTA MODEL 1938A SUB-MACHINE GUN

above A late model Beretta 1938A with compensator slots on the muzzle and fitted with a tiny 10-round magazine.

above This Model 1938A has a large 40-round magazine and leather sling. The unusual twin trigger mechanism is a feature of Beretta sub-machine guns.

Type: sub-machine gun
Origin: Beretta
Caliber: 9 mm
Weight (empty): 9 lb 4 oz (4.2 kg)
Length, overall: 37.25 in (946 mm)
Barrel length: 12.4 in (315 mm); six-groove rifling; right-hand twist
Ammunition: 9 mm Parabellum
Magazine: 10/20/40-round box
Muzzle velocity: 1,378 ft/sec (420 m/s)
Cyclic rate: 600 rounds per minute

For many years the most talented engineer working at Beretta was Tullio Marengoni. One of his best designs was this *Moschetto automatica, Beretta, Modello* 38A sub-machine gun, also known as the MAB, which was very popular with any army, including the Allies, that could get its hands on it. It was chambered for 9 mm Parabellum and the early versions were manufactured to peacetime standards, which meant that they were very well-built and extremely reliable, although rather expensive. It worked on simple blowback and had two triggers: front for single rounds; rear for full automatic. The rear trigger was fitted with a locking device to prevent accidental selection of automatic fire. The first production model had a permanently fitted, folding bayonet, oval cooling slots and a single hole compensator. The second model differed only in having round cooling slots in the barrel jacket. The third model, which was the most common, had no bayonet and a new compensator consisting of four transverse slots, and remained in production throughout the war.

BERETTA MODEL 1938/42 SUB-MACHINE GUN

Type: sub-machine gun
Origin: Beretta
Caliber: 9 mm
Weight (empty): 7 lb 3 oz (3.26 kg)
Length, overall: 31.5 in (800 mm)
Barrel length: 8.4 in (213 mm); six-groove rifling; right-hand twist
Ammunition: 9 mm Parabellum
Magazine: 10/20/40-round box
Muzzle velocity: 1,250 ft/sec (381 m/s)
Cyclic rate: 550 rounds per minute

The *Moschetto automatica, Beretta, Modello* 38/42 sub-machine gun, also designed by Marengoni, was, essentially, a much simplified and cheaper version of the Model 38A, optimized for mass production, for example, by using stamped steel rather than forged parts. It also differed from the Model 38A in having a shorter stock and a fixed (instead of ramped) rear sight, while the slotted barrel jacket was simply omitted altogether and the compensator reduced to two transverse slots. To aid in cooling the barrel had shallow longitudinal flutes, but these were found to contribute little and were later omitted. Compared to the Model 38 there were also some minor internal changes, all aimed towards cheaper and quicker production.

above The Model 1938/42 was effectively a value-engineered Model 1938A designed to be much cheaper and simpler to produce.

below Elite forces such as these *Alpini* preferred sub-machine guns as easier to carry in rough terrain and more effective than rifles in close combat.

LIGHT MACHINE GUNS

BREDA 6.5MM MACHINE GUN, MODEL 1930

Type: light machine gun
Origin: Breda
Caliber: 6.5 mm
Weight (empty): 22 lb 12 oz (10.32 kg)
Length, overall: 48.5 in (1.232 m)
Barrel length: 20.5 in (521 mm); four-Groove rifling: right-hand twist
Ammunition: 6.5 x 52 mm Carcano
Magazine: 20-round box
Muzzle velocity: 2,065 ft/sec (629 m/s)
Cyclic rate: 500 rounds per minute

The Breda company produced one of the first post-World War I light machine guns (LMG) for any army, which entered service as the Modello 1924. A number were produced, followed by several thousand of the improved Modello 1928. This led to the 6.5 mm

Fucile Mitragliatore Breda Modello 1930, which was the standard light machine gun for the Italian infantry throughout World War II.

The Model 1930 was an air-cooled weapon, using recoil operation with delayed blowback. It had a bipod which hinged at the forward end of the barrel cradle, but whose legs were unadjustable, making it difficult to aim for long ranges. The barrel was easily changed, usually after about 250 rounds had been fired, being held by a small knob wrapped around with insulating tape, but there was no carrying handle to be used when on the move. The gun incorporated a cartridge-case lubricator, which, like all such devices, caused more problems than it solved, particularly in the sand and dust of the North African

desert.

One of the most unusual features was the box magazine, which was situated at 90 degrees to the gun on the right-hand side, and was permanently fixed to the gun by a forward hinge. When empty, the magazine was released and swung forward to be reloaded using a 20-round charger. This meant that if the magazine was damaged – it was only made of thin steel plate and stood proud of the right side of the gun in a most vulnerable position – then the whole gun was out of action.

As part of the program for changing to the new round, the 7.35 mm Model 1938 was introduced, but virtually the only change was a new barrel. The Model 1930 and the Model 38 were among the worst LMGs of the war.

below It may look sleek and elegant but the Breda Model 1930 was awkward to carry, unreliable and prone to stoppages.

above The Model 1930 may have been a poor design but it was what the Italian soldier had to fight with.

MEDIUM MACHINE GUNS

FIAT-REVELLI 6.5MM MEDIUM MACHINE GUN, MODEL 1914

Type: medium machine gun
Origin: Fiat
Caliber: 6.5 mm
Weight (empty): 37 lb 8 oz (17.01 kg)
Length, overall: 46.5 in (1.181 m)
Barrel length: 25.75 in (654 mm);
four-groove rifling; right-hand twist
Ammunition: 6.5 x 52 mm Carcano
Magazine: 50/100-round strip feed
Muzzle velocity: 2,100 ft/sec (640 m/s)
Cyclic rate: 400 rounds per minute

The *Mitragliatrice Fiat, Modello* 14 was first tested in 1908 but was not accepted for service until 1914, when the Italian Army rushed to prepare for the war which had broken out in the rest of Europe. A water-cooled weapon, it bore a superficial resemblance to the British Vickers and German Maxim machine guns, but internally it was quite different. It employed a delayed blow-back action in which the barrel and bolt recoiled a short distance locked together by a swinging wedge, which then opened, allowing the bolt to continue to the rear under the impetus of the gases. There was a magazine on the left of the gun, holding the rounds in 10

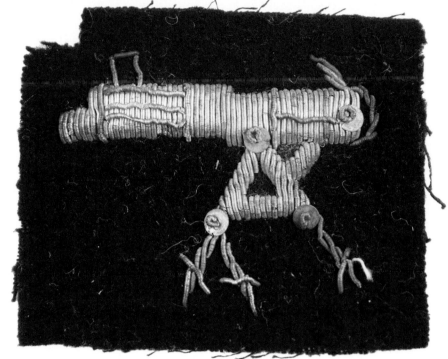

above Fabric badge worn by members of the machine gun corps.

columns of five (later ten) rounds each. The complexity of such an arrangement, coupled with the oil lubricator and the inevitable dust, led to frequent jamming. The weapon was mounted on a sturdy tripod. Despite its shortcomings, the Model 1914 served throughout both World Wars.

BREDA 8MM MEDIUM MACHINE GUN MODEL 1937

Type: medium machine gun
Origin: Societa Italiana Costruzioni Meccaniche Ernesto Breda, Brescia
Caliber: 8 mm
Weight (empty): 42 lb 8 oz (22 kg)
Length, overall: 50.0 in (1.270 m)
Barrel length: 25.0 in (635 mm); four-Groove rifling: right-hand twist
Ammunition: 8 x 59 mm Breda
Magazine: 20-round strip feed
Muzzle velocity: 2,600 ft/sec (792 m/s)
Cyclic rate: 450 rounds per minute

left Even though the Breda Model 1937 used an unusual strip feed and oil lubrication system it turned out to be an effective weapon which served well in all theaters.

The Mitragliatrice Breda Modello 1937 was a tripod-mounted, air-cooled, gas-operated medium machine gun, using a gas piston and a vertical sliding lock to lock the breech. The feed system consisted of a 20-round metal strip and during the loading process each cartridge case was lubricated by an oil pump, a system which was inherently unreliable due to the oil picking up dirt and dust and passing it into the action where a buildup quickly caused a stoppage. This problem was common to all oil-lubricated machine guns, but this particular weapon had an added complication in that the empty cartridge cases were replaced in the strip after extraction and when the last round had been fired the clip was ejected. The theory was that this enabled the empty cases to be recycled and re-used. Despite all these complications the Model 37 was well thought-of and considered one of the more reliable Italian machine guns.

The Model 1938 was used by the Portuguese Army as the M938. A modified version with a 24-round box magazine was used in Italian tanks as the Breda Model 1938. A number of these weapons were later converted for infantry use, mounted on a tripod, but retaining the box, as opposed to the strip feed system.

above A machine gun team and spotter behind a hastily-built stone and earth wall, typical of those used where the terrain was too rocky to dig.

above Ammunition strip for a Breda 37 with some rounds in place. The mechanism would carefully place empty cartridge cases back in the strip as it passed through the breech.

HAND GRENADES

The Italian infantry used three types of hand grenade, all very similar to each other, all using TNT. as the explosive, and all accepted for service in 1935. Allied soldiers considered them very light and possessing poor fragmentation characteristics, although the blast was effective enough. Each of the three types was fitted with an "all-ways" fuze designed to detonate them regardless of the angle at which they hit the ground. These fuzes sometimes failed to work, but then proved all too effective when the grenade was picked up by an unsuspecting Allied soldier or a local civilian. The Italian color coding for grenades was:

Live (high explosive)	Dull red (known to British troops as "red devils")
Practice (small charge)	White with 0.5 in (12.7 mm) red band around middle
Instruction (inert)	Unpainted or painted black

SRCM HAND GRENADE MODEL 1935 / MODEL 1938

Weight: 7 oz (200 g)
Weight of explosive: 1.5 oz (40 g)
Overall length: 3.1 in (79 mm)
Maximum diameter: 2.5 in (63.5 mm)

Bomba a mano SRCM (Hand Grenade, *Societa Romana Costruczioni Meccaniche*)consisted of an internal aluminum cylinder surrounded by an outer casing made of thin sheet metal, which was made in two halves and screwed together. The outside canister had a flat top and slightly convex bottom. The internal cylinder contained the explosive and a twisted metal cord was wrapped around the outside which fragmented on the explosive being detonated. The top and part of the side were covered by a large safety cap, held in place by a metal strip, to which was attached a rubber tab. In action, the grenade was held in the right hand, the rubber tab pulled away by the left hand, and the grenade then thrown in the usual manner. The safety cap detached itself in flight, pulling out the safety bar so that on impact a shutter moved to one side, allowing the striker to fire the detonator. A fail-safe mechanism was supposed to ensure that the grenade would only explode if it hit an object with sufficient force; i.e., having been thrown, as opposed to being unintentionally dropped. This was the most successful of the three, being adopted by the German Army as *Handgranate 328*; it also remained in production until well after the end of the war.

OTO HAND GRENADE MODEL 1935

Weight: 7.4 oz (210 g)
Weight of explosive: 2.5 oz (70 g)
Overall length: 3.4 in (86 mm)
Maximum diameter: 2.1 in (53 mm)

The *Bomba a mano, OTO Modello 1935* was the simplest of the three, consisting of a cylindrical outer container, inside which was an aluminum container for the detonator and TNT. The outer can had a flat bottom and cone-shaped top, the latter enclosing a small number of lead pellets, which were intended to improve the anti-personnel effects. This was considered to be the most dangerous of the three types if found unexploded on the ground.

above An array of Italian hand grenades in the red color which denoted high explosive. They all have wire or pellet fragmentation sleeves inside their smooth metal outer shells.

BREDA HAND GRENADE MODEL 1935

Weight: 7 oz (200 g)
Weight of explosive: 2.1 oz (60 g)
Overall length: 3.8 in (97 mm)
Maximum diameter: 2.1 in (53 mm)

This was generally similar to the OTO. type, except that the lead shot was contained in a small lead ball. The arming mechanism was very simple and involved the safety cap separating from the grenade immediately after throwing and pulling out a metal safety rod. Unfortunately there was some friction, which was not always overcome, meaning that the grenade did not explode on hitting the ground – but might well do so when picked up!

BAYONETS

The Italian infantry was equipped with bayonets for rifles and carbines. The Model 1891 bayonet was 16.3 inches (414 mm) long and intended for use with the Carcano rifle. There were three major sub-types — Models 1891, 1891/97 and 1891/97/15 — as well as many minor variations. The basic design consisted of wooden grips, steel pommel, crossguard, and a single-edged, fullered blade. There were two scabbards, one made of thin steel, the other of heavy leather.

A new bayonet was introduced for the MAB38A sub-machine gun and M1891/38 rifle, both of which were carried at all times on the weapon. Again, there were various sub-types, but all used the muzzle ring as the top of crossguard quillon.

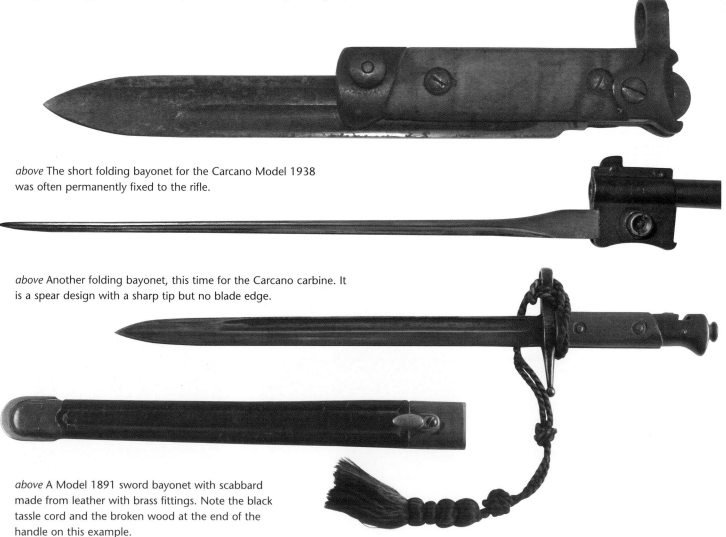

above The short folding bayonet for the Carcano Model 1938 was often permanently fixed to the rifle.

above Another folding bayonet, this time for the Carcano carbine. It is a spear design with a sharp tip but no blade edge.

above A Model 1891 sword bayonet with scabbard made from leather with brass fittings. Note the black tassle cord and the broken wood at the end of the handle on this example.

FLAMETHROWERS

above and below Flamethrower teams in action. While the flamethrower could be devastating, both physically and in terms of morale, it was also a risky business for the operator. One flame would pinpoint his location for the enemy, who would treat him as a priority target.

FLAMETHROWER MODELS 1935/1940

Weight: 22.0 lb (9.98 kg) empty; 56.2 lb (25.49 kg) action
Liquid capacity: 51 pints (29 litres)
Flame: 20 seconds constant or 25–30 one-second bursts.
Target area: approx 38 x 16 yd (35 x 14.6 m)
Working pressure: 20 atmospheres
Maximum range: 27 ft (8.23 m)

The Lanciaflamme Spalleggiabile Modello 1935 was a man-portable flamethrower. It was widely used in the Second Italo–Abyssinian War (1935–41) and some 1,500 were in service in 1940. The apparatus consisted of two cylinders, each divided into two with nitrogen propellant in the upper half and fuel in the lower. There was a short hose from the cylinders to the barrel, which was held by the operator and used to direct the fire; it also contained the ignition device. The apparatus was very heavy and required a two-man crew. The only significant differences between the Models 1935 and 1940 was that the former had flint ignition, the latter a much improved electrical ignition system.

MORTARS

The Italian Army had two standard mortars: the 81 mm Model 1935 and the 45 mm Brixia Model 1935. The 81mm mortar was of conventional Stokes–Brandt design with a good range, but let down by poor terminal effects of the bombs. The 45 mm was of an unusual and somewhat complicated design but was again let down by the poor fragmentation of its bombs.

BRIXIA 45 MM MORTAR MODEL 35

below Brixia 45 mm mortar and bomb. Fitted with an elaborate mount, complete with padded cushion, this was a much heavier and more complex device than the light mortars used by other nations.

Caliber: 45 mm
Barrel length: 10.3 in (262 mm)
Weight: 34 lb (15.42 kg) including mounting
Maximum range: 586 yd (535 m) ports closed; 352 yd (322 m) ports open
Bomb weight: 16 oz (0.45 kg)
Rate of fire: 25–30 rpm (max); 10 rpm (practical)
Elevation: +10 to +90 degrees
Traverse: 20 degrees
Crew: 2
Magazine: 10 rounds

The Mortaio d'assalto Brixia, Modello 35 fired a 45 mm (1.77 in) round, which was marginally smaller than the British 2 in (51 mm) mortar bombs, but the Italian weapon was much more complicated and much heavier. The mortar could only be fired from the folding tripod mount in which the tube was mounted between the two front legs and there was a padded rest on the rear leg, on which the mortarman could either rest his chest, or sit, depending on the tactical situation. There was only one charge, but the tube was fitted with two ports which could be closed for maximum range or opened to achieve a "reduced charge" effect. The tube could also be elevated using a handwheel on the left side of the mount and the lowest limit of 10 degrees meant that the weapon could be used as a gun, rather than as a high-register mortar.

Unusually for a small caliber mortar it was loaded through the breech by the Number 2. The bomb was loaded manually, but the charge was fed automatically from a ten-round magazine. There was only one bomb which had a steel body and aluminum tail and was reckoned to have a very limited terminal effect.

81MM MORTAR MODEL 35

Caliber: 81 mm (3.20 in)
Barrel length: 46 in (1.168 m)
Weight: barrel – 47 lb (21.32 kg); bipod – 42 lb (19.05 kg); baseplate – 46 lb (20.87 kg); complete –135 lb (61.24 kg)
Maximum range: 1,640 yd (1500 m) heavy bomb; 4,430 yd (4050 m) light bomb
Bomb weight: heavy bomb – 15 lb (6.8 kg); light bomb – 7 lb 4 oz (3.29 kg)
Rate of fire: 18 rpm (practical)
Elevation: +40 to +90 degrees
Traverse: 8 degrees
Muzzle velocity: 515 ft/sec (157 m/s)
Crew: 4

The *Mortiao da 81mm Modello* 1935 was the licence-built Italian version of the widely-used Stokes–Brandt mortar. It consisted of a smooth-bore tube with a fixed striker, a baseplate and a bipod, which included the sights and elevating gear. The bomb was placed in the muzzle and allowed to fall under its own weight until it hit the striker, which fired the charges and launched it towards the target. Most other 81 mm bombs, including those of the German and US armies, could be fired from the Model 35, but not the British 3 inch, although this was due to the needle nose clip fouling the striker housing and thus preventing a clean strike, rather than to an incompatibility in calibers.

This was the largest caliber mortar used by the Italian Army and was to be found in the mortar company of a standard infantry regiment (6 mortars) and of a mountain infantry battalion (4 mortars), while a battalion in North Africa had 9.

right and above Light mortar teams in action. Note how the crew in the lower picture have their regimental crest painted on the front of their helmets.

ANTI-TANK WEAPONS

There can be no doubt that the high command of the Italian Army seriously neglected the development of anti-tank guns and projectiles, possibly because they judged the capabilities of enemy tanks by their own very inadequate fighting vehicles. They were not alone in the 1930s in seeing the answer to be a 20 mm semi-automatic rifle, but once this had been proved to be not up to the job, they should have reacted more rapidly. Thus, the Italian infantry had no real answer to the thick armor of British infantry tanks such as the Matilda, Churchill or US medium tanks such as the M4 Sherman, while the outstanding protection of Soviet tanks (for example, the T-34) was totally out of their reach.

SOLOTHURN 20 MM ANTI-TANK RIFLE

above The Solothurn 20 mm anti-tank rifle was a massive beast, almost impossible for one man to carry.

below A propaganda photograph showing a *Bersaglieri* team in the western desert with a Solothurn 20 mm. The rifle could be fired from its own bipod or, as here, from a more elaborate tripod which better absorbed the recoil.

P. N. F. - Federazione dei Fasci di Combattimento di Napoli

UFFICIO STAMPA E PROPAGANDA

A.S. - Postazione anticarro tenuta da reparti di bersaglieri.

Type: self-loading rifle
Origin: Solothurn
Caliber: 20 mm
Weight (empty): 99 lb 3 oz (45 kg)
Length, overall: 5 ft 9 in (1.75 m)
Barrel length: 35 in (890 mm); four-groove rifling; right-hand twist
Ammunition: 20 x 105 mm B Short Solothurn
Magazine: 10-round box
Muzzle velocity: 2,500 ft/sec (762 m/s)
Penetration: 1.4 in (35.6 mm) at 300 yd (274 m)

As with many other armies, in the late 1930s the Italians placed their trust in a large caliber rifle to deal with enemy tanks, in this case the massive Fucile anticarro Solothurn da 20 mm. It was known in its country-of-origin, Switzerland, as the S18/100 and was made by Solothurn, a company 100 per cent owned by the German arms giant, Rheinmetall. It was mounted on a conventional bipod with a monopod under the butt, and also had a hydro-pneumatic shock absorber above the barrel, the curved magazine was on the left side of the weapon and was intended to accommodate ten rounds, although users normally loaded with only eight. Heavy and with a very powerful recoil, this was at the very limits of what one man could handle, but it was certainly deployed in North Africa, although whether it was taken to Russia is doubtful.

47/32 ANTI-TANK GUN MODEL 37

Type: anti-tank gun
Origin: made in Italy under licence from Böhler, Austria
Caliber: 47 mm
Weight: 695 lb (315 kg) traveling order; 612 lb (278 kg) in action
Length, overall: 5 ft 6 in (1.68 m)
Barrel length: 60 in (1.524 m)
Elevation: -15 to +56 degrees
Traverse: 62 degrees
Range: HE – 7,600 yd (6950 m)
Shell weight: AP – 3.2 lb (1.45 kg); HE – 5.3 lb (2.4 kg)
Ammunition: AP; HEAT; HE; HE-tracer; blank; grapeshot
Muzzle velocity: AP – 2,067 ft/sec (630 m/s); HE – 820 ft/sec (250 m/s)
Penetration: AP – 1.7 in (43.2 mm) at 550 yd (503 m); HEAT – 4.4 in (112 mm) at 110 yd (101 m)

The *Cannone da 47/32 Modello* 1935 was an Italian development of the Austrian Böhler gun, which was purchased by a number of armies in the 1930s as a combined infantry and anti-tank weapon. It could be fired either from its wheels or, with its wheels removed from a circular platform, which gave the weapon a stable and low-profile firing position. It could also be dismantled into five parts which could be carried by men or pack animals. The Italian version did not have a shield. It was used by infantry battalions of the Italian Army in all theaters and also used by Italian paratroop units.

In the Western Desert it was effective against British light and cruiser tanks but not against the US tanks which arrived later such as the M3 Grant and M4 Sherman, and it had very limited performance against Soviet tanks. As its effectiveness as an anti tank gun decreased it was increasingly deployed as an additional infantry gun. It served in several other armies, most notably the German army where it was designated the PaK 47.

INFANTRY GUNS

65/17 INFANTRY GUN, MODEL 1913

Type: infantry gun
Origin: Italy
Caliber: 65 mm
Weight: 1,235 lb (560 kg) in action
Barrel length: 3 ft 7 in (1.09 m)
Elevation: -10 to +20 degrees
Traverse: 8 degrees
Range: HE – 7,440 yd (6800 m)
Shell weight: 9.5 lb (4.31 kg)
Ammunition: HE; antitank; grapeshot
Rate of fire: 6–8 rounds per minute
Muzzle velocity: HE – 1,132 ft/sec (345 m/s)

The *Cannone da 65/17 Modello* 1913 was just entering service at the start of World War I and was intended as a lightweight artillery piece for use by mountain units. It served them throughout the war and when it was replaced by a new mountain gun all stocks were transferred to standard infantry battalions, with whom it then served through 1945. It was simple, very reliable and reasonably effective in its intended role as a close support weapon under infantry command. It had solid-rim wheels with steel tires, a single trail and a detachable shield.

above An abandoned 65 mm gun in a captured Italian position. Italian gunners had a well-deserved reputation amongst their enemies for staying at their guns and fighting to the end.

BLACKSHIRTS

left A silver "death's head" ring typical of those worn by a member of a Fascist militia.

above Two fighting knives with MSVN crests on the scabbards. Many elite units liked the idea of a fighting knife unique to them, although very few of them actually saw use in combat.

left A silver ring with swastika and fasces commemorating Italian - German cooperation.

The *Milizia Volontaria Per la Sicurezza Nationale*, or Voluntary Militia for National Security (usually abbreviated to MVSN) was a Fascist para-military group, founded by Mussolini himself in 1922. It was originally formed from bands of thugs known as *squadristi*, who were mainly disgruntled former soldiers, but Mussolini reorganized them into the MVSN to exert greater control and to prevent the racketeering and protection rackets being practiced by some *squadristi* leaders. The organization was widely known, quite simply, as the "Blackshirts" (*camice nere*) a term derived from the original identifying feature of their dress. This type of political strong-arm organization was adopted by Adolf Hitler in Germany with his "Brownshirts" (the SA) and copied by Oswald Mosley in the UK, whose men also wore, and were known as, Blackshirts. Mussolini himself was always the commanding general of the MVSN, although day-to-day matters were dealt with by a chief-of-staff in Rome.

The original function of the MVSN was political, providing strong-arm thugs to support Mussolini's regime and serving as the Fascists' praetorian guard, but once Mussolini was firmly established in power it rapidly assumed additional duties and became involved in police work in both the home country and the colonies, anti-aircraft defense of the homeland and some coastal defense, for which it was organized on a geographical basis into zones.

The MVSN also, however, harbored military ambitions and began to train Blackshirt units for armed combat service, this military arm being known as the CCNN (from the plural of the term *camice nere*). In line with Mussolini's penchant for harking back to the glories of the Roman army and empire, the CCNN was organized into a different set of sub-units reflecting this:

CCNN Title	Composition	Rank of commander	Army Equivalent unit	Equivalent rank
Divisione	Three (or more) *Legioni*	*Commandante*	Division	General
Legione	Three *Coorti*	*Console*	Regiment	Colonel
Coorte	Three *Centurie*	*Seniore*	Battalion	Major
Centuria	Three *Manipoli*	*Centurione*	Company	Captain
Manipolo	Three *Squadre*	*Capomanipolo*	Platoon	Lieutenant
Squadra		*Capo Squadra*	Section	Sergeant

ORGANIZATION AND RANKS OF MILITARY ARM OF THE CCNN

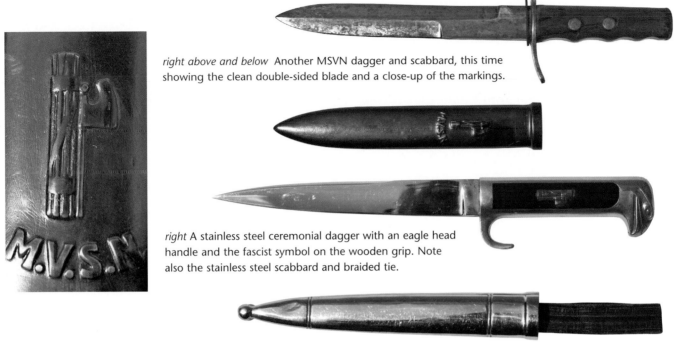

right above and below Another MSVN dagger and scabbard, this time showing the clean double-sided blade and a close-up of the markings.

right A stainless steel ceremonial dagger with an eagle head handle and the fascist symbol on the wooden grip. Note also the stainless steel scabbard and braided tie.

Seven Blackshirt divisions served in the Ethiopian campaign in 1935–36 and six divisions in the Spanish Civil War, where they suffered very heavy losses. By 1939 there was sufficient manpower (veterans from Spain plus new recruits) and equipment to form only four new divisions, which were then deployed to North Africa. But all four were still under strength, so one was disbanded in May 1940 and its men and equipment shared among the remaining three. In his usual bombastic way, Mussolini saw these units as an elite which would be used as shock troops, but the reality was that no matter how motivated and courageous the individuals, the units were poorly organized, ill-trained and short of modern equipment. As a result, when they took part in the first campaign against the British in North Africa all three divisions were surrounded and captured, one at Sidi Barrani (December 12, 1940) and the other two at Bardia (January 4, 1941).

CCNN units also took part in the campaigns in Yugoslavia, Greece and Russia.

Wartime operations had also shown the weakness of the two-regiment "binary" structure of the Royal Army's infantry division, so it was decided to add one CCNN combat legion (equivalent to a regiment, but with less manpower) to each division. Such legions were firmly under army command for operations, but the MVSN kept control of personnel management, including promotions and assignment of individuals to specific posts.

This integration of CCNN formations and units into the order-of-battle was bitterly opposed by the Army high command and they resisted stubbornly until April 1940, when Mussolini issued a direct order that Blackshirt units would immediately become part of the Army order-of-battle. Throughout the war, however, there was always tension between the Army high command, which was strongly royalist, and the CCNN which, not surprisingly, strongly supported Mussolini and the Fascists.

The CCNN bore some resemblance to the German *Waffen-SS*, wearing not only black shirts but also an entirely black uniform, but the Italian organization was never as ruthless and brutal as its German counterpart, nor did its military ambitions ever extend beyond the divisional level. And since its head, Mussolini, was also the effective head-of-state there was no Himmler to provide an alternative focus of loyalty.

PARATROOPS

Italy was the first nation in the world to develop paratroop units, but thereafter its armed forces had a rather mixed experience where these were concerned and, although a large number of men were eventually trained, only a few operations were carried out, most of which were rather inconclusive. Indeed, one of the best formations, the *Folgore* Parachute Division, achieved its greatest success while fighting in a conventional role at the Battle of Alamein.

Mussolini's Fascist movement promoted modernity in all things and great emphasis was placed on aviation, resulting in major developments in aircraft and the use of air transport. In one noteworthy incident in 1928, the airship *Italia* was on the return-leg from a flight to the North Pole when it crashed on an ice-floe and not only was the wreck located from the air but supplies were dropped from an aircraft to the survivors, one of the first ever examples of an emergency air-drop. In another example, in 1933, air force General Balbo led large formation flights of seaplanes on return flights across the South and North Atlantic oceans.

It was in this progressive atmosphere that the Italian armed forces started to organize and train paratroops, conducting the first group drop by nine soldiers with their equipment at Cinisello airfield in Italy on November 6, 1927. They jumped from a Caproni Ca-73, then the air force's standard heavy bomber, which had been hastily converted for the purpose. Training proceeded, and by 1937 there were sufficient men and aircraft for there to be a major drop during an exercise in Libya in 1937.

A parachute school was established at Castel Benito airfield in 1938 to train Libyan volunteers. The aim was to institute a full regiment of colonial troops, although a number of accidents led to a more realistic aim of manning a battalion (*1º Battaglione Fanti dell'Aria*). A second battalion was then formed from volunteers from the metropolitan army stationed in Libya (*1º Battaglione Nazionale Paracadutisti della Libia*). Both battalions fought as ground troops against the British in 1940–41 and both put up stout resistance before being overwhelmed.

There were sufficient parachute resources for the *1º Divisione Paracadutisti* (*Folgore* Division) to be formed in September 1941, composed of 185, 186 and 187 Parachute Regiments, together with supporting artillery, engineer and logistic units. It was planned that this division, in conjunction with German *Fallschirmjäger* units, would spearhead the attack on Malta (Operation C3) but when this was canceled the division went to North Africa as conventional ground infantry where it was virtually wiped out at El Alamein. There were sufficient

below An airborne trooper with a Breda 30 light machine gun.

below High laced boots as worn by paratroop soldiers.

above Airborne soldiers made extensive use of sub-machine guns such as this Beretta Model 1938/42.

right A re-enactor kitted out in the uniform and equipment of a soldier from the *Folgore* division, complete with rimless paratrooper's helmet.

survivors only to form a battalion (285th *Folgore* Battalion) and this was eventually destroyed in Tunisia in 1943. Other missions in Africa were also considered including an attack on the Suez Canal, but were canceled in the planning stage.

In mainland Italy the Division *Paracudisti Nembo* was formed, but its units were frittered away in campaigns against partisans in Yugoslavia and then in fighting the Allied landings in Sicily, before ending the war in Sardinia, all in a strictly ground-borne role.

The only major operation carried out by the army paratroops took place on April 30, 1941 when 5 Company, 2 Parachute Battalion landed on the island of Zante Cephalonia. The attack was successful, although resistance was very weak and most of the casualties were from paratroopers who fell into the sea.

CARABINIERI

The Carabinieri also raised a parachute unit, *1° Battaglione Carabinieri Paracudisti* (1st Carabinieri Parachute Battalion) in 1940, which was sent to Libya with the intention of being deployed, like the British Long-Range Desert Group, in operations behind enemy lines. This did not happen and the unit was employed on ground tasks and after suffering heavy losses the survivors were absorbed into one of the army parachute battalions.

ADRA

The Italian Air Force (*Regia Aeronautica*) also raised a special forces unit, *Ariditi Distruttori Regia Aeronautica* (ADRA) (Air Force Brave Raiders). This unit carried out various minor raids behind enemy lines in North Africa in January to April 1943. Targets were enemy lines of communication and airfields, but the unit had little effect on the Allied campaign.

WEAPONS AND EQUIPMENT

When they were established in the late 1920s the Italian Army paratroops already had a fully-developed and proven static line parachute, the *Salvatore*, which was issued to military aircrew. However, there numerous accidents and deaths, including the general commanding the paratroops, who was killed when his parachute failed to open. A new type, the Model 1939, was then developed, which proved more successful. Their main weapon was the Beretta M38A sub-machine gun.

UNIFORM

Paratroopers wore normal Italian army uniform, but with the addition of a loose-fitting, three-quarter length camouflaged smock, which was added in 1942. Protective knee pads and leather gauntlets were worn, as with the German *Fallschirmjäger*.

PARA HELMET

Paratroopers had their own pattern steel helmet, the Model 1938, which was almost hemispherical in shape and with a flat rim and a leather neck-flap. This was replaced by the Model 1941 which had a padded liner inside the front to protect the paratrooper's nose when landing.

OTHER AXIS COUNTRIES

Many other European nations entered the war on the side of Germany and Italy. Some were enthusiastic, others reluctantly drawn into conflict. All had their own objectives, whether it was to preserve their independence, reclaim lost territory or simply gain at the expense of their neighbors.

Each country was different, although there are some generalizations that can be made. Most of them had relatively poorly-equipped forces, with only a smattering of modern equipment and with outdated training and tactics. Their infantry soldiers may have fought bravely enough, especially when their homelands were at risk, but they were almost all hampered by inadequate support such as artillery, anti-tank and anti-aircraft weapons. Their battlefield transport was mainly by foot or horse, while a lack of radios and outmoded command and control systems meant they were often slow to react to events on the battlefield.

But in the end, their biggest problem was that they had chosen the wrong side to support. Most nations who supported the Axis ended the war significantly worse off than before, having suffered heavy casualties and with enemy forces overrunning their territory.

BULGARIA

Bulgaria took part in World War I on the side of Germany and Austria, and suffered accordingly when they were defeated in 1918. The country underwent a military coup in 1934, but the generals were soon brought to heel by Tsar Boris III, who established what amounted to a royal dictatorship. A rearmament program was started in 1938, but had not made much progress when war broke out in 1939. Boris declared his country to be neutral, although there was an underlying national desire to regain territory lost during the Second Balkan War in 1913 and World War I. In 1941 the country came under overwhelming pressure from Germany and, with some reluctance, joined the Axis (March 1, 1941), thus enabling German troops to transit across Balkan territory to attack Greece. One major national gain from this brief campaign was that Bulgaria was granted the territories of Greek Macedonia, Thrace and Salonika, which went a long way to easing any resistance to the war.

Boris resolutely refused to ally himself with Germany against the Soviet Union, although he did agree to declare war on both the UK and USA – a symbolic gesture on his part, although it did result in Sofia and other Bulgarian towns being bombed by both the RAF and USAAF. Boris died in September 1943 and was succeeded by his six-year old son, Simeon, with power being exercised by a regency, which was toppled in a coup on 9 September 1944. The newly-established Fatherland Front made peace with the Allies and placed its forces under Soviet operational control. Bulgaria never committed any troops to the Axis campaigns in France or the USSR, its main involvement being the provision of occupation troops to undertake anti-partisan operations in its own regained territories to ensure that the German lines-of-communication to their forces in Greece were kept open.

ORGANIZATION

The Bulgarian army was predominantly an infantry force and at its strongest in May 1944 it fielded 21 infantry divisions, two cavalry (horsed) divisions, one armored brigade and two frontier brigades.

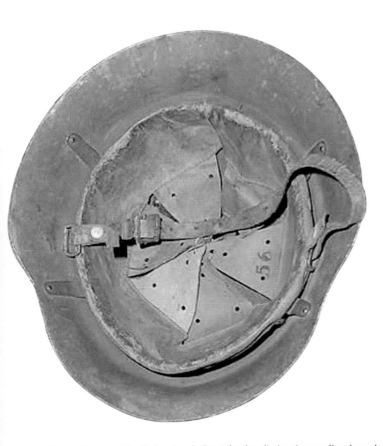

above A Luger P8 pistol made for the Bulgarian Army.

Equipment was mostly antiquated with the main personal weapon being the Model 1891 6.5 mm Carcano rifle. Only ten of the infantry divisions had any modern equipment at all, which was provided by Germany. There were serious weaknesses in artillery and anti-tank weapons, and all divisions were dependent on horse-drawn transport for logistic support.

UNIFORMS

Prior to 1941 the predominant influence on the Bulgarian army was Russian and due to the stagnation in the inter-war years, much of the uniform and personal equipment dated back to Tsarist, rather than Soviet Russia, although during the period 1941–44 some German influence began to be seen. Thus, officers rank badges were Russian-style shoulder boards, but German-style collar patches in Waffenfarbe (arms colors) began to appear.

There were three main forms of headdress. Officers wore a peaked service cap made of a khaki-colored material, which had a low, Russian-style crown with soft edges, a short, black leather peak, and a black leather chinstrap. The cap-badge, common to all officers was the national cockade, ovoid in shape, consisting of a red center and a ribbed silver outer, with a green ring in between them.

top and above The Bulgarian helmet had a distinctive outline loosely based on the French "Adrian" design.

FINLAND

left Finnish troops on parade. Their uniform was a simple gray tunic, peaked field cap and breeches tucked into their high leather boots. Weapons were mainly Moisin Nagant rifles improved with Finnish modifications.

The Baltic Grand Duchy of Finland attained its independence from Russia in 1918, becoming a republic. It was, however, in a strategically crucial position and found itself dragged, greatly against its wishes, into World War II in order to protect its national integrity.

Finland had been fighting since March 1939. At that time the USSR had sought to secure its northern flank against a possible future conflict with Germany, and when the Finns refused to comply with their wishes, the Soviets attacked in what they thought was overwhelming force, allowing a mere six weeks for the campaign. Unfortunately for the Soviets, the Finns united and fought back with tremendous courage and, in a brilliant campaign, brought the Soviet aggressors to a standstill, whereupon, both sides being completely exhausted, they signed a peace treaty in March 1940. Soviet losses have never been publicly revealed, but were probably around 250,000 dead and 4–500,000 wounded, whereas the Finns lost 25,000 dead and 43,000 wounded.

In the uneasy period that followed, Finland tried to obtain military aid from Sweden or the UK, but, when these approaches were rebuffed, turned to Nazi Germany. As a result, and even before Operation Barbarossa, German troops were allowed to move into Finnish Lapland and the Finnish armed forces began to receive German equipment.

On the German invasion of the USSR the Finns became formally allied with Germany (but not part of the Axis Pact) and advanced into Soviet territory, beginning the conflict known to Finns as the Continuation War. One result was that the United Kingdom declared war on Finland on December 6, 1941. In general, however, there was little military activity until June 1944 when the USSR launched a massive attack which took the Finns by surprise. The Finns lost territory before they were once again able to bring the Red Army to a standstill, by which time the USSR was much more interested in its advance into Germany. It therefore signed a truce with Finland, which obliged the Finns both to disarm and to expel the Germans.

The Finns now found themselves with ever-smaller forces (to meet the Soviet conditions on force reduction) while in conflict with their erstwhile ally, Germany. Most of the latter were in the north and sought to retreat into neighboring Norway, apart from trying to protect the strategically important nickel mines around Petsamo. Fighting began when the Germans made an unsuccessful attempt to invade the island of Suursaari in the Gulf of Finland and soon spread to the north, as well, with the Germans laying waste to the countryside and towns as they retreated. The Germans were finally expelled in April 1945.

ORGANIZATION

On the outbreak of fighting in 1939, the Finnish Army was small, having a tiny peacetime cadre of regular officers and NCOs, but with all Finnish males serving for either 12 or 18 months, depending on the arm of service. On completion of their regular period, they then moved to the reserve until age 60 when they were transferred to the militia. The conscription and mobilization systems were the responsibility of nine geographical military districts, each of which fielded one infantry division on mobilization.

These nine divisions were approximately 14,200 strong and comprised a headquarters, three infantry regiments, and a field artillery regiment, together with engineer, telecommunications, medical and logistic support. There was also an independent cavalry brigade, mounted on horses. Equipment was lacking in both quantity and quality, with particular shortages in artillery, mortars, medical support and supplies, motor transport and telecommunications. There were, however, two excep-

tions: the *Suomi* M1938 sub-machine gun and the *Lahti* 20mm anti-tank rifle (see below).

During the Continuation War period Finland was split into two military areas, with the Germans commanding in the north and the Finns in the south. By mid-1944 there were some 400,000 men in the army, of which 270,000 were in front-line units organised into sixteen infantry divisions: two in the north (under German command); fourteen, plus three independent brigades (two Jäger, one cavalry) in the south. There was also a recently-formed armored division.

The Finnish infantry fought with incredible bravery, showing great endurance in the face of both large numbers of well-equipped enemy and the extremes of winter. The Finns were, however, well adapted to their weather conditions – more so than either the Germans or the Russians – and this, coupled with their very detailed local knowledge, enabled them to outfight their enemies at every tactical level.

UNIFORMS

The Finnish army kept its uniforms simple and achieved a common pattern for all ranks. The normal service dress consisted of a grey jacket, with rank and arm-of-service indicated by collar patches on the stand-and-fall collar, with matching breeches tucked into knee-length, black leather boots. Officers wore a black service cap, with a black leather peak and a gold braid chinstrap, and also wore the ubiquitous Sam Browne leather belt. Greatcoats were worn by all ranks where the ranks badges were on the cuff for officers and on shoulder straps for NCOs. In winter all ranks were issued with sheepskin cap, with ear, and neck flaps and a turn-down visor, and there was also a linen snowsuit which was worn over the usual winter outfit. The steel helmet was the World War I vintage German M1915. Every Finnish officer and soldier carried

right A Finnish soldier unpacks mortar ammunition from its crate.

a personal knife, the actual design being a matter of personal choice.

Close contacts with the German army in 1941–44 resulted in the adoption not only of much German weaponry and equipment, but also of some German items of clothing and badges. The latter included the M 1935 Stahlhelm (steel helmet) and a soft cap similar to the German Feldmütze.

WEAPONS

The Finns used mostly foreign-designed, but Finnish-manufactured weapons. For example, the standard rifle was the Russian-designed *Mosin-Nagant* firing a 7.62 x 54R round, which had been manufactured and improved by the Finnish company, Valmet, for many years. The basic Finnish model was the M1924, basically the Russian M1891, but with new barrels produced in Switzerland. These were supplemented by the M1927, M1928, M1928/30 and M1939 Short Rifles, which shared a shorter barrel and slight reduction in weight, but differed in minor details. Two nationally designed weapons are, however, worthy of separate notice.

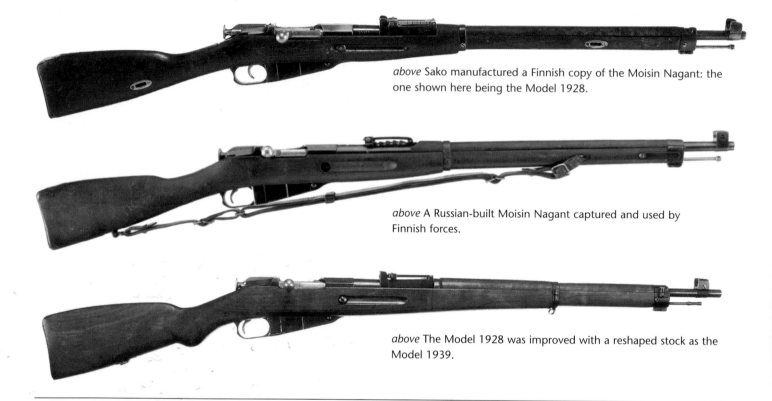

above Sako manufactured a Finnish copy of the Moisin Nagant: the one shown here being the Model 1928.

above A Russian-built Moisin Nagant captured and used by Finnish forces.

above The Model 1928 was improved with a reshaped stock as the Model 1939.

SUOMI MODEL 1931 SUB-MACHINE GUN

above The large and solid Suomi sub-machine gun, in this case with no magazine.

Type: fully automatic, blowback sub-machine gun
Origin: Finnish State Arsenal, Tikkakoski
Caliber: 9mm
Weight (empty): 10.34 lb (4.69 kg)
Length, overall: 36.02 in (916 mm)
Barrel length: 12.5 in (317 mm); six-groove rifling; right-hand twist
Ammunition: 9 mm Parabellum
Magazine: 20/5-round box, 40/71-round drum
Muzzle velocity: 1,312 ft/sec (400 m/s)
Cyclic rate: 900 rpm

Johannes Lahti was one of the select few gun designers, like John M. Browning, who seemed to get gun design just right. Lahti's first sub-machine gun design was the Model 1926, a complex and expensive weapon, chambered for the 7.65 x 21.5 mm Parabellum round, which was produced in small numbers. He took the lessons from this and incorporated them into a totally new weapon, the Model 1931. This used normal blowback operation, was perfectly orthodox in layout, and, like most pre-war weapons, was very well engineered and finished. The result was a reliable and robust weapon, which never failed, even in the harshest Arctic weather conditions. It was a little heavy, 15 pounds (6.8 kg) when carrying a fully-charged 71-round magazine, but this resulted in reduced vibration and greatly increased accuracy, delivering accurate fire out to over 300 yards (274 m). The Lahti M 1931 was adopted by a number of other armies and inspired the designers of a number of other sub-machine guns, including the German MP34, and the Soviet Army's PPD 1934G/38G and PPSh 41.

SUOMI MODEL L-39 20 MM ANTI-TANK RIFLE

Type: semi-automatic, 20 mm rifle
Origin: Finnish State Rifle Factory, Tikkakoski
Caliber: 20 mm
Weight (empty): 109 lb (49.4 kg)
Length, overall: 88.0 in (2.23 m)
Barrel length: 51.2 in (1.3 m)
Ammunition: 20 x 138B Long Solothurn
Magazine: 10-round box
Muzzle velocity: 2,625 ft/sec (800 m/s)
Cyclic rate: 30 rpm

The Finnish L-39 Lahti 20 mm was one of the best of the 20 mm anti-tank rifles produced in the late 1930s. It had a semi-automatic action and a large magazine containing ten rounds. The powerful ammunition resulted in a substantial recoil, while its size and weight – the troops dubbed it the "Elephant Gun" – made it difficult to move around the battlefield. The first few production models reached the front during Finland's "Winter War" and were very successful against the AFVs used by the Soviet Army in that campaign. In the "Continuation War" however, its 20 mm rounds were defeated by the front armor of the new T-34 and KV-1 tanks, but the weapon was so accurate that it continued to be used against vulnerable spots, or against other targets such as bunkers. It was supplied with solid, HE and phosphorous shells.

FOREIGN CONTINGENTS

The Finnish army had foreign contingents. In the original Winter War, the resistance of the Finns to Soviet aggression won much international sympathy, although not much of this was translated into actual help. One of the few examples was the formation of an international battalion from American, British and French volunteers, but, although the men had arrived in the country, they had not completed their training when the truce was signed, and the volunteers returned home. There were, however, sufficient volunteers from neighboring Estonia to form, first, a battalion, and later a full regiment, which fought for the Finns until August 1944 when most of the men returned home to defend their own homeland against the advancing Red Army.

HUNGARY

above Hungarian troops on parade wearing helmets of the German World War I pattern.

When the Austro-Hungarian Empire was broken up in the aftermath of World War I the newly-created Kingdom of Hungary was not only deprived of much territory and many people it considered its own, but the size and composition of its armed forces were also strictly limited. An added complication was that although legally a kingdom, the country as a whole refused to sanction the return of the Hapsburgs and the effective head-of-state, Vice-Admiral Miklos Horthy, was officially The Regent.

This led to a decade in which the country was surrounded by much more powerful neighbors, while the great majority of Hungarians harbored a desire to regain their "lost" territories. In the mid-1930s Horthy sought international help over both issues but the only countries to offer any assistance were Nazi Germany and Fascist Italy. These two countries went so far as to engineer the "Vienna Arbitral Award" in 1938, in which some of the territory Hungary had lost in 1920 was returned. In the following year the Hungarian army invaded

the Ruthenian part of the Czechoslovak Republic thereby not only regaining lost territory but also establishing direct contact with Poland. Then the Second Vienna Arbitration result in the return of large parts of Transylvania to Hungary. Hungary repaid these actions by taking part in the German invasion of Yugoslavia (April 1941) although there was a major degree of self-interest, because they were thus able to occupy the Bacs-Kiskun region, another of the lost territories, whose population included some 500,000 ethnic Hungarians.

Several months later Horthy was manipulated by Hitler into agreeing that the *Honvédség* (Hungarian army) should take part in Operation Barbarossa. Its "Rapid Corps" served as part of the German 17th Army, but by December it had suffered so many casualties and lost so much equipment that the remnants had to be sent back to Budapest to regroup. Despite this bad experience the Hungarians next sent their 2nd Army to Russia where it survived the early part of the 1942–43 winter only to be attacked by the Red Army on

January 12–14, 1943 when its fragile defensive positions were easily penetrated. After further heavy casualties (40,000 dead, 70,000 wounded) the remaining Hungarian troops straggled home for a second time. The Hungarian government resisted further active operations, although its troops continued to serve under German operational command in rear areas. A provisional ceasefire was negotiated with the advancing Red Army in October 1944, which resulted in the Germans removing the Hungarian government, installing a puppet regime and insisting that the army continued to support the war, but the Axis cause was hopeless.

ORGANIZATION

In 1939 the Hungarian army divided the national territory into nine geographically-based army corps areas. Each of these corps comprised three infantry divisions, each with one regular and one reserve infantry regiment. These regiments included three battalions, each of three rifle companies (each of four platoons) plus a machine gun company. Each division also included a cavalry reconnaissance troop, an artillery regiment (two battalions, each of 12 guns), a telecommunications company, and logistic units, with most of these divisional assets decentralized to the regiments. At army corps level there was a mobile infantry battalion, which was mounted either in trucks or on bicycles, an anti-aircraft battery and a telecommunications unit. Outside these corps were a number of border and mountain brigades and other smaller independent units.

UNIFORMS

The Hungarian Army wore a khaki uniform, introduced in 1923, which was the same for all ranks. The jacket had a stand-and-fall collar, with shoulder straps in the same khaki color, but with no shoulder-boards, ranks being displayed only on collar patches, which also bore the arm color (green in the case of infantry). The infantrymen wore breeches which fastened below the knee and high boots, or full-length trousers with a unique and most unusual built-in ankle fastening and ankle boots.

above Hungarian infantry conferring with German soldiers in Budapest.

Standard headdress was a sidecap with a high crown, which bore the national cockade. Rank was indicated by chevrons on the front of the cap and there was a patch on the left side of the cap in arm-of-service color. Members of the field gendarmerie also wore cockerel feathers, mounted on the left side of their cap. In the field, troops wore either the sidecap, or a German M 1935 steel helmet, or a khaki-colored cap of the same design as the German *Feldmütze*, but with the same badges and insignia as the sidecap.

The army greatcoat was double-breasted with rank and arm-of-service patches as on the jacket, but with additional rank bars on the cuffs. All ranks wore a belt to which were affixed two ammunition pouches, all in brown leather. There was no harness, the pack being carried by means of two shoulder straps. The soldiers' field equipment was standard, but they had a well-designed shelter-quarter which had special attachments to add it to the greatcoat. An unusual distinction was a small triangle worn on the left sleeve above the elbow which indicated that the wearer was a regular, as opposed to conscripted, soldier, a practice not known to have been followed in other armies.

WEAPONS

The *Honvédség* was generally poorly armed, especially the infantry. The standard infantry weapon was the 8 mm *Mannlicher* bolt-action rifle although some units did receive Mausers, which came either from German reserve stocks or from the Hungarian arms factories making them for the Wehrmacht under contract. For light machine guns, Hungarian units were armed with German-supplied MG 42 or Czech-manufactured ZB 37 light machine guns. The standard heavy machine gun however, was the much older, water-cooled, *Schwarzlose* M1907. In 1944 Germany undertook to supply modern machine guns, mortars and other weapons in greater quantities, but their increasingly desperate home situation meant that they failed to deliver. In its early years, the Hungarian Army used the Skoda 17M and 18M mortars inherited from the Austro-Hungarian Army, but in 1936 the State Weapons Factory at Diósgyör started to produce the Model 1936 81.4 mm mortar, which, like so many others, was based closely on the contemporary Stokes-Brandt design.

above The Austrian Schwarzlose was a typical World War I machine gun: water-cooled, belt fed, reliable and extremely heavy.

right: A Schwarzlose in Hungarian service, in this case in the light anti-aircraft role.

above Hungarian forces also locally manufactured versions of the Kar 98 such as this one, known as the G98/40.

STEYR-MANNLICHER MODEL 1895 RIFLE

above The Steyr-Mannlicher was an effective bolt-action rifle.

Type: straight-pull bolt action
Origin: Steyr-Mannlicher, made under license by Fegyvergyar, Budapest
Caliber: 8 mm
Weight (empty): 8 lb 5 oz (3.77 kg)
Length, overall: 50.4 in (1.28 m)
Barrel length: 30.2 in (767 mm); four-groove rifling; right-hand twist
Ammunition: 8 x 50R Austrian Mannlicher
Magazine: 5-round box
Muzzle velocity: 2,030 ft/sec (619 m/s)

The *Steyr-Mannlicher* Model 1895, generally known as the M95 "straight-pull" rifle, was designed by Ferdinand Ritter Von Mannlicher, and was manufactured in Austro-Hungarian state arms factories in Steyr (Austria) and Budapest (Hungary). It was produced both as a long rifle (see specifications above) and as a short rifle/carbine, with a 19.7 inch (500 mm) barrel. Over 3 million were produced between 1895 and 1918 as the standard infantry and cavalry weapon of Austro-Hungarian Army, but, following the fall of the Empire it continued in production for the newly-created Hungarian Army.

Fegyvergyar then developed the short rifle version to take the more powerful Hungarian-Mannlicher 8 x 56R M31 cartridge, but which also incorporated a fully-turning bolt and a two-piece stock which was bolted to the receiver, but retained the Mannlicher, clip-loaded, fixed, five-round magazine. This weapon entered service as the M1935 Short Rifle.

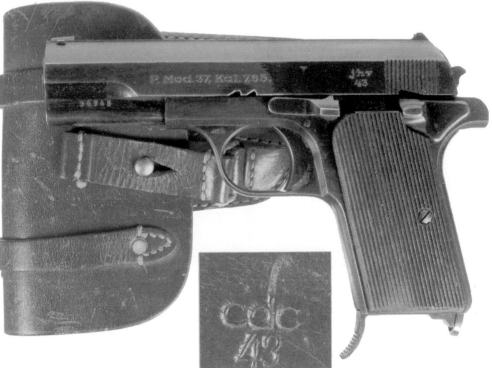

right The FEG 37M was a simple 7.65 mm automatic pistol produced in Hungary for both Hungarian and German forces.

REPUBBLICA SOCIALE ITALIANA (ITALIAN SOCIAL REPUBLIC, RSI)

The RSI was created on September 18, 1943 in the Italian territory remaining under German control. Head-of-state was Benito Mussolini, who had been rescued by Otto Skorzeny and his paratroopers. The nucleus of the RSI army was formed from 13,000 volunteers among the 600,000 Italian servicemen rounded-up by the Germans, and by March 1944 it had a strength of some 60,000 men. Most of these carried out anti-partisan duties, but a number of infantry divisions were formed which were trained and equipped in Germany and then returned to their home country where they fought, often with considerable bravery, against the advancing Allies until the Axis surrender. The minister of defense and, in effect, commander-in-chief of the RSI armed forces was Marshal Rodolfo Graziani and it fell to him to agree to their surrender on 30 April 1945. The RSI eventually fielded four infantry divisions, which were trained, armed and organized on German lines.

UNIFORM

In the rush and danger of its early days, the RSI army carried on wearing the uniforms of the old Italian Army, but simply removed any badges or insignia with royal connections, such as the crown on rank insignia, while the five-pointed star was replaced by a badge consisting a circle of laurel leaves upon which rested a Roman short sword set at a few degrees off the vertical. A whole series of new badges was devised in September 1944, but with defeat in sight this seems to have been a pointless exercise. The uniforms themselves became ever more mixed, with some units wearing standard German clothing and equipment, while others adopted some eccentric combinations of Italian and German items.

PARAMILITARY FORCES

The previous MVSN and its armed component, the CCNN, were considered "unreliable" so they was disbanded in November 1943, the MVSN being replaced by a new organisation, the *Guardia Nazionale Republicana* (GNR). This expanded and as the situation deteriorated it was decided to form a paramilitary organisation, the *Brigata Nere* (Black Brigades), which were, in effect, a replacement for the old CCNN. These seemed to fight just about everyone else, including Allied armies, partisans, political opponents, and even other members of the Black Brigades whose support seemed less than total. There were approximately fifty such units, although their title of "brigade" was very misleading and at best they were about 400 strong, but more often about 200. The *Brigata Nere* wore an amazing mixture of what could only loosely be termed uniform, but the common features were a black shirt or jacket and a black beret bearing the badge of a skull, usually shown gripping a dagger in its teeth.

above RSI forces made do with whatever weapons they could get, mainly Italian Army issue such as the Carcano Short Rifle.

ROMANIA

above Romanian troops march through a village typical of eastern Europe and the Soviet Union.

The Romanians enjoyed a period of relative calm between 1918 and 1938 when their long-held dreams of *România Mare* (Greater Romania) seemed to have been realised, but the tide of right-wing fascism could not be held back and in 1938 King Carol dismissed the parliament and established what amounted to a dictatorship. As a result of the Molotov-Ribbentrop pact, signed in 1939, Romania lost Bessarabia and parts of Bukovina, while, at the same time, German troops entered the country under the pretext of protecting their supplies of oil and gasoline. This was followed by irresistable pressure from Germany to hand more disputed territory to Bulgaria and Hungary. In November 1940 the effective head of government, Ion Antonescu, formally signed the Axis Pact.

At the end of the 1930s the Romanian Army was a huge but effectively second-grade force. It had a paper strength of 28 infantry divisions and eight infantry brigades, two armored divisons and one brigade, and nine cavalry brigades. Equipment was poor and outdated, as was the training. The Germans set-about improving both, sending in some 20,000 instructors to put things right. This massive program had not been completed by the time of Operation Barbarossa, but three divisions were made part of 11th German Army and advanced into southern USSR.

The Romanians did their best and eventually reached the Crimea, but suffered huge losses, estimated to be in the region of 130,000 men. Most of their transport had been lost along the way and most units were marching on foot, with virtually all logistic support being provided by horse-drawn carts and wagons. Despite great suffering, the remaining troops survived the winter and reonfircements were poured in to maintain the numbers. The Romanians were attacked by an overwhelming force of Soviet troops in November 1942 and were swept back, losing a further 189,000 lives in the process.

The Romanians, and their German allies, were pushed slowly but surely backwards and in August 1944 King Michael, who had resumed power from Antonescu, surrendered to the Soviet Union and then declared war on Germany. The Romanians paid dearly for their alliance with Germany: they provided the largest single allied component of the German forces in the East, but lost almost a quarter-of-a-million men in the process.

379

above The Romanian steel helmet had a distinctive flared appearance, clearly shown here. These soldiers have Czech rifles and are lying behind a pair of flamethrowers.

ORGANIZATION

Romanian fighting strength was concentrated in the infantry divisions, which were composed of three infantry regiments, a field artillery regiment, a horsed reconnaissance battalion, and the usual logistic units. There were three infantry battalions in an infantry regiment. Very few trucks were available, so the primary means of transport were, as they had been for centuries, feet or horses, although some troops had bicycles. By 1942, the infantry regiments had been reduced to two battalions and a few more trucks were available, but the early months of the war had shown up a major deficit in anti-tank capability, which the Germans tried to make good, providing six 75 mm anti-tank guns to each division.

UNIFORMS

The standard color of Romanian infantry clothing was khaki, which was adopted in the early 1930s and retained throughout the war. Officers' formal dress comprised a jacket very similar in style, cut and color to the English Service Dress, with open collar, shirt and tie, and rank badges on the shoulder straps. This was worn with a Sam Browne belt. Collar patches indicated the arm-of-service, except for generals for whom there was one standard gold-embroidered red cloth patch. Except in the field, normal dress included khaki breeches and high, black leather boots.

Soldiers wore a simpler outfit, originally with an open collar and shirt/tie, but in about 1942 this was changed to a stand-and-fall collar. Full length trousers were worn, with both boots and anklets made of brown leather. A belt carried two ammunition pouches, all of brown leather.

Formal headgear for officers was a service cap, with black leather peak and a black leather chin-strap edged with narrow band of gold lace. The steel helmet was the Dutch-pattern Model 1928, made under licence in Romania, with the Romanian coat-of-arms stamped at the front. Headdress when the helmet was not being worn was a cloth cap, similar to the German *Feldmütze,* but with a more pronounced, pointed crown and a soft peak. Ankle boots were of brown leather and the lower legs were bound with long, woollen puttees. The Romanian infantry, like other German allies, were very ill-prepared for the Russian winter, and apart from some hasty issues of fleece-lined caps had to make do – and suffer – with what they had.

WEAPONS

The Romanian Army did not produce its own weapons at this stage, and relied on foreign imports. Three of the widest used infantry weapons came from neighboring Czechoslovakia and, fortuitously as it turned out, were the same caliber as the weapons used by the German Army, which eased logistic probloems when they were fighting side-by-side.

CZ MODEL 1924 SHORT RIFLE

Type: bolt-action rifle
Origin: CZ, Brno, Czechoslovakia.
Caliber: 7.92 mm
Weight (empty): 9 lb 2 oz (4.14 kg)
Length, overall: 43.3 in (1.1 m)
Barrel length: 23.2 in (589 mm); four-groove rifling; right-hand twist
Ammunition: 7.92 x 57 mm Mauser
Magazine: 5-round integral box
Muzzle velocity: 2,576 ft/sec (785 m/s)

This was the standard Mauser Model 1898, but with a shorter barrel, thus making it handier and lighter. There were a number of other minor improvements, including a better-shaped butt, and, as always with the CZ factory, a better standard of finish. It was, thus, an unexpected, but welcome advantage that the Romanian infantry fired the same small-arms ammunition as their German allies.

above The CZ Model 1924 saw widespread service in many armies, including the Romanian.

ZB vz/30 LIGHT MACHINE GUN

Type: squad light machine gun
Origin: CZ, Brno, Czechoslovakia
Caliber: 7.92 mm
Weight (empty): 21 lb 5 oz (9.67 kg)
Length, overall: 45.8 in (1.16 m)
Barrel length: 26.5 in (673 mm); four-groove rifling; right-hand twist
Ammunition: 7.92 x 57 mm Mauser
Magazine: 30-round box
Muzzle velocity: 2,500 ft/sec (762 m/s)
Cyclic rate: 600 rounds per minute

In the 1930s the Romanian Army adopted the outstanding Czech ZB vz/30, which was being purchased by many armies at that time, either in its original 7.92 mm form or modified for 0.303 in as in the British Bren. The original design was the ZB vz/26, but several modifications and improvements, mostly related to easing production, led to this version.

right The ZB light machine gun was an outstanding weapon and was also the basis of the British Bren.

ZB vz/37 MEDIUM MACHINE GUN

Type: medium machine gun
Origin: CZ, Brno, Czechoslovakia
Caliber: 7.92 mm
Weight (empty): 41 lb 0 oz (18.6 kg)
Length, overall: 43.5 in (1.105 m)
Barrel length: 26.7 in (678 mm); four-groove rifling; right-hand twist
Ammunition: 7.92 x 57 mm Mauser
Magazine: 100-round metal link belt
Muzzle velocity: 2,600 ft/sec (792 m/s)
Cyclic rate: 500 or 700 rounds per minute

For its battalion-level direct fire support, the Romanian infantry used the very modern CZ ZB vz/37, an air-cooled, piston-operated, belt-fed machine gun. As with all weapons designed by Vaclac Holek, it was incredibly reliable, extremely accurate and easy-to-use, and like the vz/26, was widely exported. It was, in fact, very nearly adopted by the British to replace the venerable Vickers machine gun, the only reason this did not happen being that it could not be adapted to take the British rimmed 0.303 in round; it was, however, produced by the British as the BESA for use as a tank machine gun. In Romanian use it was mounted on a ZB-designed tripod, which enabled the weapon to be fired in both ground support and anti-aircraft roles.

Index

Acknowledgments

Editing and Project Management: Graham Smith
Design: Casebourne Rose Design
Cover: Phil Clucas
Original photography: Vincent Abbott, J.P. Bell
Historical images: Andrew Webb at the Robert Hunt Library

The publisher is grateful to the following individuals and organizations who helped with the supply and photography of original artefacts and equipment:

Ermanno Albertelli, Tuttostoria
Rudy D'Angelo
Maj Benson and staff of the SASC Weapons Collection
Roy Butler, Wallis and Wallis
John P. Conway, Manions Auction House
Eric @ Photofix
Lin Ezell, USMC Museum

Barbara Geresbeck, Hermann-Historica
Philippe Gillain, December 1944 Museum
Grant's Militaria
Patrick F. Hogan, Rock Island Auction Company
Barry Jenkins
Brian Keene
Lionel Leventhal
Tom McLeod, Museum of the Pacific
Paolo Marzetti
Museo Storico Italiano della Guerra
Charles E. Snyder, www.snyderstreasures.com
Tony Oliver
Guido Rosignoli
Ernst-Ludwig Wagner, Hermann-Historica
Andy Stevens, Pastimes
Terri Stewart, Stewart's Military Antiques
Robert Tredwen, Military Antiques
Jamie Wilson